Assembling Policy

Infrastructures Series
edited by Geoffrey Bowker and Paul N. Edwards

Paul N. Edwards, *A Vast Machine: Computer Models, Climate Data, and the Politics of Global Warming*

Lawrence M. Busch, *Standards: Recipes for Reality*

Lisa Gitelman, ed., *"Raw Data" Is an Oxymoron*

Finn Brunton, *Spam: A Shadow History of the Internet*

Nil Disco and Eda Kranakis, eds., *Cosmopolitan Commons: Sharing Resources and Risks across Borders*

Casper Bruun Jensen and Brit Ross Winthereik, *Monitoring Movements in Development Aid: Recursive Partnerships and Infrastructures*

James Leach and Lee Wilson, eds., *Subversion, Conversion, Development: Cross-Cultural Knowledge Exchange and the Politics of Design*

Olga Kuchinskaya, *The Politics of Invisibility: Public Knowledge about Radiation Health Effects after Chernobyl*

Ashley Carse, *Beyond the Big Ditch: Politics, Ecology, and Infrastructure at the Panama Canal*

Alexander Klose, *The Container Principle: How a Box Changes the Way We Think*

Eric T. Meyer and Ralph Schroeder, *Knowledge Machines: Digital Transformations of the Sciences and Humanities*

Sebastián Ureta, *Assembling Policy: Transantiago, Human Devices, and the Dream of a World-Class Society*

Assembling Policy

Transantiago, Human Devices, and the Dream of a World-Class Society

Sebastián Ureta

The MIT Press
Cambridge, Massachusetts
London, England

This book was set in Stone by the MIT Press. Printed and bound in the United States of America.

Library of Congress Cataloging-in-Publication Data is available.

ISBN: 978-0-262-02987-2

10 9 8 7 6 5 4 3 2 1

Para Chivi y Lucía

Contents

List of Figures   ix
Acknowledgments   xi
Abbreviations   xv

Introduction   1
1 **Crisis   23**
2 **Infrastructuration I: Active Citizens   47**
3 **Infrastructuration II: Modeling Consumers   67**
4 **Disruption   93**
5 **Reactions   113**
6 **Normalization   137**
   Conclusions   159

Appendix: Methods   171
Notes   175
References   185
Index   199

List of Figures

1.1. Evaluation of public services by consumers   34

2.1. Presentation of Public Participation Strategy, final slide   58

2.2. Winning proposal for the PTUS brand (first contest)   59

2.3. Winning proposal for the PTUS brand (second contest)   62

3.1. Origin-Destination Buses survey questionnaire   73

3.2. Model for the assignment of multimodal public transport networks   77

3.3. Parameters of walking and waiting times   78

3.4. Mathematical formulation of the business model of Transantiago   82

3.5. Visual representation of the business model of Transantiago   83

4.1. Diagram showing the space between seats in urban buses in the
     EU   102

4.2. Diagram showing the space between seats in urban buses in Chile   102

5.1–5.3. Posters attached to the kindergarten front on Environment
     Day   118–119

5.4–5.5. Posters attached to the fronts of houses in Villa Pehuén   122–123

5.6. Card reader at the entrance of a Transantiago bus   127

6.1. Percentage of people waiting for more than 10 minutes at bus stops   144

6.2. Overall evolution of travel and waiting times, morning peak time   146

6.3. Users queuing outside a Zona Paga in Plaza Italia   149

6.4. Design for the new Zona Paga at Manquehue Avenue   151

6.5. Entrance to the Zona Paga at Clínica Alemana   153

Acknowledgments

This book has many origins, but the one that comes most vividly to my mind is set in a lousy Internet café in downtown Mexico City on the night of February 10, 2007. Being on holiday my mood was relaxed, but it changed decidedly when, after cursorily checking my email, I had a look at one Chilean media website. For what I saw were pictures of incredibly crowded buses or masses of people descending the steps of an unnamed Metro de Santiago station. Having been carrying out fieldwork on the usage of means of transport by low-income inhabitants of the city for some months, I was certainly aware of the huge challenge that the start of Transantiago would entail, especially for everyday users. But I wasn't expecting it to materialize in such a bad way. I stayed there for several minutes more, going from website to website, finding everywhere variations of the same story. Transantiago was officially a mess, and in my head my current research project was already starting to change, becoming a story of Transantiago. I didn't know at the time which kind of story, but as I left the Internet café for the sidewalks of Reforma Avenue, I knew that I had to write it. Whatever it was.

I would like to thank the institutions that have housed and funded me while writing this story. The fieldwork on which this book is based started in 2006 when I was an assistant professor at the Instituto de Sociología of Universidad Católica de Chile, in Santiago. I appreciate the support of its then director Eduardo Valenzuela for allowing me the time necessary to carry out such a task. That fieldwork was funded by a FONDECYT grant from CONICYT, Chile's National Commission for Science and Technology (grant number 11060348). While carrying out this research I obtained an International Visiting Fellowship from the British Academy that allowed me to spend three very fruitful months at the Department of Sociology, University of Lancaster (United Kingdom), in the winter of 2008, a period in which the conceptual foundations of this book were laid. I appreciate the kindness of Professor John Urry for letting me act as a visiting scholar in the department. After finishing fieldwork in early 2009, I had the privilege of spending the next two years working full time on my data while acting as an Associate Researcher at the Center for Technology and Society of the Technical University of Berlin, whose director Hans-Liudger Dienel was welcoming from the very start of my enquiries and during my time at the center. Such a stay was generously funded by an International Incoming Fellowship given by the Marie Curie Actions of the European Commission (grant number PIIF-GA-2009–235895). The final write-up of the manuscript was carried out at the Jacob-und-Wilhelm-Grimm-Zentrum library of Humboldt University, an institution that opened the doors of its utterly beautiful premises to a researcher like myself who had no connection whatsoever with the university (long live open libraries!). Such a final period was possible because in parallel I acted as an associate researcher of the Innovation in Governance Research Group housed at the Sociology Department of the Technical University of Berlin under the direction of Jan-Peter Voss. I really appreciate Jan-Peter's invitation to spend a very nice year as a member of the group and the constant support and friendship of my colleagues there: Thomas Crowe, Nina Amelung, Arno Simons, and Carsten Mann. Finally the whole publication process of the manuscript was carried out while working at the Departamento de Sociología, Universidad Alberto Hurtado, Chile, which also gave me time to spend in the preparation of the final version of the manuscript. I also appreciate the support and comments of several of my colleagues in the department.

Several friends and colleagues were involved in different ways all along the process of researching and writing the book. First of all I would like to deeply thank my fellow Margeanos: Tomás Ariztía, José Ossandón, Ignacio Farias, Manuel Tironi, Matias Bargsted, and Ignacio Arnold, for all the years of friendship and lively intellectual debate. This book was definitely enriched by our endless emails of discussions and suggestions, including parallel reading and commenting on draft versions of the book's contents from its very start. I also appreciate the comments given on different versions of the full draft by Antoine Maillet and Jorge Castillo. Deep thanks to Endre Danyi, not only for his thoughtful comments on the full draft of the book but especially for all the discussions and support in Berlin, especially in our recurrent lunches in and around the Grimm Zentrum. Also thanks to Martín Tironi, Rodrigo Cordero, Cristian Monsalvez, and Eden Medina who at different points gave me support and hints about the book's further development.

I also appreciate the support of the Infrastructures series editors Paul Edwards and, especially, Geof Bowker, for believing in this project from my very first enquiries back in 2011. I'm also indebted to the MIT Press personnel involved in the process of turning a rather messy draft into a proper book: Marguerite Avery, Katie Helke, Sean Reilly, Susan Clark, and Matthew Abbate.

The fieldwork on which this book is based would not have been possible without the help of several research assistants and students who participated in different stages of it from its start in 2006. I'm especially indebted to Wilson Muñoz (who also took some of the pictures in chapter 5) but also to Miguel Ordenes, Juan José Richter, Pamela Ayala, Marcela Moraga, Juan Gabriel Harcha, and Antonia Devoto. I would like also to show my appreciation to Rosa María Bugueño for endless interview transcriptions and to Joanna Helen Dossetor for proofreading.

I would like to give thanks centrally to all the people who participated in this study as interviewees and/or by facilitating documents, both those involved in the planning and implementation of Transantiago and also the families participating in my ethnographic studies of public transport usage in Santiago. Without their generosity and openness this book would not have been possible.

Some sections of an earlier draft of the introduction appeared as a paper in *Policy Studies* under the title "Policy Assemblages: Proposing an Alternative Conceptual Framework to Study Public Action" (2014, volume 35, issue 3, pp. 303–318). A slightly different version of chapter 6 appeared as a paper in *Social Studies of Science* under the title "Normalizing Transantiago: On the Challenges (and Limits) of Repairing Infrastructures" (2014, volume 44, issue 3, pp. 368–392). I thank Taylor and Francis and SAGE Publications respectively for allowing republication of excerpts from those papers.

Finally I would like to thank my family for all their support throughout the years. Especially my mother Rosario Icaza has occupied an integral part in the whole process of becoming a researcher, starting from the day in which she didn't complain when I told her that I was planning to study a quite funky subject: *sociology*.

During the whole period of researching and writing up this book I was lucky to be accompanied by my partner, Sylvia Dümmer. Her love, humor, and high spirits were central to its success, the perfect counterbalance to my usual pessimism. These last two years of the process were enlightened by the arrival of our daughter Lucía, who brought us endless joy and offered me the opportunity to think over the book's contents during our countless sleepless nights together. The book is dedicated to both of them, for being the way they are.

Abbreviations

AFT	Administrador Financiero de Transantiago
APC	Automatic passenger counter
CdT	Coordinación de Transantiago
CdU	Comité de Usuarios de Transantiago
CGTS	Coordinación General de Transporte de Santiago
DICTUC	Dirección de Investigaciones Científicas y Tecnológicas de la Pontificia Universidad Católica de Chile
DTS	Directorio de Transporte de Santiago
EOD	Encuesta Origen-Destino
MINVU	Ministerio de Vivienda y Urbanismo
MOP	Ministerio de Obras Públicas
MOPTT	Ministerio de Obras Públicas, Transportes y Telecomunicaciones (2000–2006)
MTT	Ministerio de Transportes y Telecomunicaciones
ODS	Origin-destination scripts
PTUS	Plan de Transporte Urbano de Santiago (2000–2010)
SECTRA	Secretaria de Planificación de Transporte
SOCHITRAN	Sociedad Chilena de Ingeniería de Transportes

Introduction

Without a doubt, as all the sectors should recognize, [Transantiago is] the worst public policy ever implemented in our country.

Andrés Chadwick, Chilean government spokesman, speaking on Transantiago's fifth anniversary, February 10, 2012

A Forgotten Book, Forgotten People

There is a forgotten book about Transantiago. It was never printed, not even properly assembled. I found it by chance lying on the hard drives of a graphic design company in downtown Santiago, distributed in a number of folders. Some of them contained images and texts, others designs for its cover and page layouts. Its name was present in several places: "Transantiago: Hacia una Ciudad Integrada" (Transantiago: Toward an integrated city). The book was commissioned in 2005 by Chile's Ministry of Transport and Telecommunications (MTT) to celebrate what was supposed to be the successful inauguration of Transantiago in February of 2007. It was planned to be printed as a coffee-table book, with main text describing Transantiago's history and characteristics, supported by high-definition pictures and different kinds of charts with transport data.

The book was also going to include boxes with quotes from multiple actors such as academics, intellectuals, and users. Among them there were going to be two so-called "citizen testimonies":

I'm worried about the air I'm breathing. I can't stop thinking that in every breath I take, besides oxygen, my body also receives mouthfuls of smog with I don't know how many pollutants. I dream about a cleaner city, a city kinder to the people, where environmental care is a value for everyone. Santiago is the city where I live and I don't want to spend the rest of my life in a place in which I have to use a mask to go out.

Giovanna Pérez, 20 years old, student

I've been working in the city center for years and I've always seen it full of micros [buses]. It is difficult to cross the street with so many micros, especially when you are in a hurry. And if by chance you have to cross the city center by micro, you have to endure huge traffic jams. I would like the streets to be emptier, with fewer micros and cars, then there would be less of this honking that is making me deaf.

Hernán Quintana, 44 years old, worker (Maipú)

Each of these testimonies describes a well-known issue in Santiago at the turn of the century: air pollution in the case of Pérez and traffic jams and noise in the city center in the case of Quintana. Their tone shares a sense of urgency, of a situation that causes them distress and cannot continue as it is.

Quite expectedly, in the main text Transantiago was presented as an answer to such pleas:

Transantiago, inaugurated on February 10, 2007, is a world-unique project that looks to gradually transform the public transport system of Santiago, modernizing and improving its quality through a service in which buses and Metro form an integrated network. ... The central objective of Transantiago is the modernization of the public transport system with a special emphasis on improving the quality of service to users, offering efficiency along with social and environmental sustainability [and] promoting the use of public transport. ... Thanks to Transantiago the vast majority of the citizens of Santiago will have access, for the first time in history, to a secure, trustable, and clean public transport system that will equally welcome men, women, children, the elderly, and the disabled.

This passage tells a story of success, of improvement. Transantiago is a "world-unique project" that looked to transform completely the public transport system of Santiago. Almost every single aspect of it was going to change: bus fleet, route network, management, payment and information systems, etc. The final objective, it was claimed, was not so much to modernize the network but to provide "for the first time in history" a high-quality service to users such as Pérez and Quintana, to offer a "secure, trustable, and clean" public transport system in which all different kinds of people would be welcomed.

In all, the book's contents summarized the main storyline behind the plan from its very first drafts in 2000 until, we could say, February 9, 2007. However, the situation discovered the next day when Transantiago started carrying passengers forced a radical change in this narrative. From its very first hours of functioning it was very clear that some things were seriously wrong with the new system. There were not enough buses to satisfy users' demands, so the ones functioning and the Metro were completely over-crowded; people had to walk long distances and wait for hours in order to be able to travel; huge areas at the periphery of the city had very scarce bus service, the payment card didn't work properly, there was no way to check the quantity and location of buses on the streets, the users didn't know how to plan their route on the new system, and so on. In all, this Transantiago turned out to be quite different from the one presented in the celebratory book project. Given this, the authorities decided to cancel the book's publication altogether, and the draft was laid to rest for good on the hard drives of the authors' computers, where I found it at the beginning of the fieldwork in which this book is based.

This story could be taken as just another curiosity in the planning of a large and complex infrastructural policy, a project of such scale that it has even been called "the most ambitious transport reform undertaken by a developing country" (Hidalgo and Grafiteaux 2007). In researching the case I found several other, more pressing issues to deal with, such as the techni-cal failures experienced by several of the system's key components or the political turmoil that followed, transforming Transantiago into one of the biggest public controversies in Chile since the return of democracy in 1990. After all, I'm dealing with "the worst public policy ever implemented in our country," as Andrés Chadwick, the Chilean government's spokesman, declared a couple of years later. Nevertheless, Pérez and Quintana remained with me for a long time. Who were they? How did their words end up in the draft of the book? What was the role assigned to them by the book's authors? Did they feel disappointed, even cheated, when the Transantiago they faced on the street ended up being quite different from the one pre-sented in the book they had collaborated with? Or did they feel relief that the book was never published and they didn't end up appearing as sponsors of such a mess?

I certainly have no way to answer such questions; Pérez and Quintana are forever out of reach. However, they led me to a related set of queries that I felt more capable of answering. These are questions about the location of humans in the development of Transantiago. Or, more generally, about the devices through which humans, from individuals to populations, are brought into the planning and functioning of large and complex infrastruc-tural policies, especially ones involving important technoscientific knowl-edge and devices.

The relevance of this task is, I think, manifold. As the practitioners of science and technology studies (STS) have emphasized since its very beginnings, humans are always at the center of technoscientific practices like the production of complex infrastructural policies such as Transantiago. Even more, we could talk about technoscience and society as co-produced (Jasanoff 2004a), or the fact that certain products of technoscience and particular kinds of social order cannot be understood separately, but must be seen as emerging from the same operations. The technical is always "politics by other means" (Latour 1983); political orders are always technoscientific orders, especially in our society. The production of infrastructural policies never means only dealing with material or technical issues, but also enacting particular forms of political power. Given the contemporary centrality of large and complex infrastructures, the enquiry about the place of humans in them should be seen as one of the most pressing political questions of our time.

Besides its political relevance, the question of the location of humans in technoscience is also ethical. The ways humans are brought into infrastructures spills outside them, directing and imposing limits to the agency of individuals. This point is nicely summarized when Hacking affirms that "making up people changes the space of possibilities for personhood. ... What could it mean in general to say that possible ways to be a person can from time to time come into being or disappear?" (Hacking 2002, 107). As a central part of their political power, infrastructural policies transform the field of available options of personhood. These transformations can be meaningless and even go unnoticed, but they can also have important effects, originating or proscribing, motivating or punishing, differentiating or unifying ways to be human in contemporary societies.

Human Devices

"Where are we to situate the human?" asked Latour (1993, 136) in his well-known essay *We Have Never Been Modern*. A review of the existing conceptualizations of humans in STS shows that such a question has received several answers. We can start by noting the presence of the figure of the "system builder" (Hughes 1983), from engineer to policymaker, representing the active part in the assembling of new infrastructures. As a counterpart we find the figure of the "user" or "consumer," usually understood as co-constructed along with particular technologies (Oudshoorn and Pinch 2003). Along with the user there is the figure of the "(lay) citizen," commonly presented in a struggle with experts about their standing with regard to knowledge and technical power (Jasanoff 2004b; Wynne 1995). There are also conceptualizations such as "communities" (Knorr-Cetina 1982) or "publics" (Shapin 1992), developed mainly to study humans as forming collectives always entangled in multiple relations with technoscience. In parallel we find terms such as "human kinds" (Hacking 2007), referring mostly to the different types and standards by which humans are classified and governed. Each one of these conceptualizations is quite useful for describing and analyzing particular performances of humans, individual or collective.

However, they also refer to versions of the human with quite specific characteristics and agencies. In most cases the human/s thus brought into being are relatively solid, well-defined entities, with certain affordances and no others. For example, users/consumers are usually presented as focused on satisfying a certain individual desire or need through the use of technology, while citizens are presented in a constant struggle with experts to gain more space for the collective in the definition of technoscience. This is not merely a difference of emphasis but shows how these terms "pull in different directions" (Mol 2009, 270), so that they could hardly superpose or replace one another. Concepts such as communities, publics, or kinds have the advantage of allowing much more space for diversity but with the limitation of dealing poorly with the individual, with humans as single agencies. None of the available conceptualizations appears encompassing enough to cover the multiple ways in which human agencies are brought into technoscience. On the contrary, each concept carries a relatively well-defined set of attributes and excludes others.

Given this, if you wanted to deal with the place of humans in technoscience, you would have to choose to study them as *either* consumers *or* citizens, *either* individuals *or* a collective. This would be fine if humans could be dealt with in a singular and consistent way all through the process of designing and managing complex infrastructural policies such as Transantiago. However, as we will see in this book, this is seldom the situation. Much more commonly humans are enacted in *noncoherent* ways (Law et al. 2013), as entities that usually become consumers, citizens, part of a community or a public as they move along the multiple locations in which the infrastructure is enacted, even becoming several of these things *at the same time*.

An alternative to such a conceptual dead end is not to develop a well-rounded, unifying concept that will claim to *truly* include all the relevant aspects of the location of humans in technoscience. In this respect I agree with Hacking's assertion that "there is not and never will be any universally applicable theory of making up people" (Hacking 2004, 281). Besides being an authoritarian endeavor, such a concept will miss what is most important about humans in technoscience, how they exist not as solid entities but "in the delegation itself, in the pass, in the sending, in the continuous exchange of forms" (Latour 1993, 138). Each time we identify something as "human" we are dealing with an entity that is slightly or manifestly different from the ones before and after. For this reason the aim of this book is not to develop an ultimate overarching concept of the place of humans in technoscience, but a much humbler conceptual heuristic that could help us to connect the multiple ways and sites in which humans are enacted into being.

In this book I have opted to develop such an approach through the concept of *human devices*. These are going to be understood broadly as the highly heterogeneous sociotechnical devices that perform existing and/or projected humans for technoscience: A chart representing the critical opinion of the population toward genomics. A television news clip showing people protesting the construction of a highway. An engineering model that measures electricity consumption per inhabitant. A woman who has to behave in certain ways to use public transport buses. A focus group quote signaling how "Pedro, 54 years, middle class" demands a reshaping of science education in primary schools. All of them are going to be seen as human devices because they perform versions of humans that relate in particular ways to technoscience. The same applies when humans are referred to as "users," "consumers," "citizens," "publics," or "kinds." Each is a different variant of a human device because they all enact particular versions of the human.

To refer to such entities as "devices" is not casual. Following the use of the term by Muniesa, Millo, and Callon (2007), "objects can be considered as objects with agency: whether they might just help (in a minimalist, instrumental fashion) or force (in a maximalist, determinist version), devices do things. They articulate actions; they act or make others act" (2).

This claim constitutes one of the founding principles of actor-network theory, and has become relatively mainstream in contemporary STS. Devices are never inert, just tools to be used to achieve certain ends. On the contrary, they always carry a degree of agency in themselves, the capacity to alter the current state of affairs in one way or another. Therefore human devices are not merely a way to "represent" human individuals and groups existing somewhere else, but they are actively involved with (and affect in unexpected ways) the individuals or populations they claim to represent.

In contrast with common uses of the term "technology," these devices are not to be understood as stable or well-defined material objects but as concatenations of "materials and textuality spread across diverse and (in some parts) nonlocalizable networks and flows of discourse and practice" (Lee and Brown 1994, 786). This approach means, first, that any single human device is formed by a large variety of elements, both material and semiotic, widely spread in different locations and times. Human devices, even the simplest ones, are always a collective formed by diverse entities such as data, material artifacts, human bodies, images, etc. Second, human devices are not "created" or "constructed" once and for all and then used to represent humans but are always performative. In order to exist they have to be continually brought into being, and each performance produces a device that is, slightly or significantly, different from the ones coming before. Instead of a single device that moves around as a solid entity we always have continual processes that perform new entities with every mobilization.[1] Third, and derived from the above, a human device is not only a version of a human being made by other actors but also a matter of the human's own performance. Every time someone relates to technoscience in any way (using a technical device, giving opinions to a survey, participating in an experiment, etc.), she performs a particular human device; we could even say that she temporarily *becomes* a human device. Then human devices are as much designed as they are embodied, lived.

Therefore human devices are active, heterogeneous, and performative, both external and embodied. When seen through the lenses of STS they appear as the precarious products of practices in which several entities participate actively, from highly sophisticated technical knowledge to humans who have to behave in certain ways to use technical devices. They are ubiquitously performed in a wide range of incarnations every time a human being is connected to technoscientific practices. Beyond this they have no particular components, they claim or force no particular agency or characteristics. Human devices are intentionally fuzzy; they are used as a heuristic device connecting disparate concepts rather than having a specific content in themselves. Human devices are conceived as some kind of conceptual bridge connecting multiple territories, forcing them to talk, to face their mutual incoherences. As Mol has recognized, this is the only way in which human devices can be studied, "by investigating their contrasting identities as these are performed in a variety of sites and situations" (Mol 2002, 38).

Like any other product of technoscientific practices, human devices are intimately enmeshed in relations of co-production with multiple social orderings. Even more, human devices are *the* particular locations where human societies and individuals are (re)produced technoscientifically, or in accordance with technoscientific practices, devices, and ways of knowing. Given the centrality of technoscience in contemporary societies, human devices should be seen then as material forms of political power in themselves, establishing hierarchies and differences, exclusions and integrations, among the human beings who enter into contact with them.

In this book I am going to understand the politics of human devices as existing in the continual tension between particular ways of governing human beings and the overflowings that they undeniably cause. On the one hand, and following Foucault and others, I will see human devices as the most basic building blocks of contemporary governmentalities. Starting in the eighteenth century, governmentality has complemented power in the sense of sovereignty over a territory with its alternative understanding of power as the *conduct of conduct*, or a sum of techniques, devices, practices, rules, reflections, tactics, and calculations that allow governing the behavior of humans in certain preestablished ways (Foucault 2006). Under governmentality, "authorities came to understand the task of ruling politically as requiring them to act upon the details of the conduct of the individuals and populations who were their subjects, individually and collectively, in order to increase their good order, their security, their tranquility, their prosperity, health and happiness" (Rose 1999, 6). What is central is that under governmentality political power should not be seen as located in institutions such as the state or the market, but as always embedded into very concrete human devices that look to "render aspects of life calculable, knowable and amenable to intervention; that is, able to be managed" (Baistow 2000, 97).

Following the work of Akrich (1992), in this book I will refer to this governmental use of human devices in technoscience as *scripts*. Scripts can be defined as the result of the process through which some actors in power "define actors with specific tastes, competences, motives, aspirations, political prejudices and the rest ... [defining] a framework of action together with the actors and the spaces in which they are supposed to act" (208). These scripts vary in complexity and detail, from simple sketches to highly sophisticated entities including motivations and affordances. Through their concrete use in technoscience, scripts appear as central technologies of power because they "seek to translate thought into the domain of reality, and to establish 'in the world of persons and things' spaces and devices for acting upon those entities of which they dream and scheme" (Miller and Rose 1990, 8). Then under governmentality scripts should be seen as central components in the deployments of schemes to govern society, as "bound up with the constitution of the human and the social" (Barry 2001, 9).

When functioning as expected, scripts end up properly producing *subjects,* or human devices emerging when human beings embody scripts in, more or less, exactly the ways a certain governmentality expected them to. Foucault saw subjects as operating in two interrelated modes, as "subject to someone else by control and dependence, and tied to [their] own identity by a conscience or self-knowledge" (Foucault 1982, 212). Then subjects as human devices always emerge mixing in different degrees external coercion (Foucault's techniques of domination or discipline) and internal self-government (Foucault's techniques of the self). The emergence of such subjects is capital not only because they establish a continuity between different kinds of human devices but also because, by doing this, they give stability to a certain kind of power. Especially in the form of self-government, the emergence of subjects is at the very center of most kinds of political power in contemporary societies, from the state to the market.

However, such fluid movement between scripts and particular subjects is seldom the norm. As Foucault himself recognized, "there are no relations of power without resistances" (1980, 142). Even in the case of quite sophisticated and powerful scripts there is always space for unexpected outcomes, whether as a result of conscious resistance by the individuals or organizations being affected or simply because of unexpected nonhuman agencies. In the STS literature these reactions have been described using several concepts, such as anti-programs (Latour 1991), counterperformativity (MacKenzie 2006), or, the term I am going to use, overflowings (Callon 1998a). Their common assumption is that a certain number of unforeseen reactions have to be seen as unavoidable in any governing attempt, because there is no way in which the actors in power could deal with all the multiple agencies emerging from the attempts to govern human beings in all their complexity and specificity.[2] As Callon (2007, 347) affirms, "humans in their somatic envelope, made of neurons, genes, proteins, and stem cells, are constantly overflowing. A total, unambiguous configuration is impossible. There is always a remainder, something that hasn't been taken into account."

A key point of the politics of human devices is that overflowing does not merely mean the emergence of alternative or partial ways of being a subject, but produces an altogether different kind of human device that I will call *strange things*.[3] This concept relates directly to one of social science's earliest and more enduring performances of the human: the stranger. Starting from the work of Simmel (1908), the stranger has been continually seen as the main embodiment of otherness (Bauman 1990). Strange things share with the figure of the stranger this liminal character, this standing both inside and outside determinate orderings that render them "strange" to other actors more clearly located within or outside such limits. However, they differ from the figure of the stranger in that they are not an identity, burden, or stigma that some human being carries around (semi-) permanently.

Strange things are human devices emerging as a result of particular performances. These performances are fleeting and cannot be repeated in exactly the same way; there is always room for change and transformation. For this reason, strange things are not stable or solid but keep changing, emerging and disappearing with the passage of time. They can be reperformed several times and become semistable entities. But they can also appear just once and never reappear, being afterward seen as merely an inconsequential turbulence. In this sense all existing entities perform strange things sometimes. Even the more dedicated followers of order breach it from time to time. So during the same day an entity could perform "normal" subjects and strange things without major problems. Entities *perform* strange things; they *are not* strange things in themselves. This is so because strange things do not get performed into being solely by the agency of their components, but only when this agency challenges a certain ordering.[4]

Leaving aside the negativity of terms such as overflowing, it is essential to keep in mind that strange things are not antithetical in themselves, just from a particular point of view (usually that of the actors in power). Strange things are not only about "negative" resistance, but also about creative incorporations. Such devices "may [themselves] have their own logic and inventiveness; their own spaces and temporalities; their own forms of knowledge and technique; their own ways of restricting as well as opening up the terrain of politics" (Barry 2001, 6). Besides questioning existing governmentalities and their related scripts, strange things should be seen as an opportunity to territorialize new orderings, even to produce new governmentalities (which will in time, inevitably, produce new overflowings).

The fact that overflowings and their subsequent strange things are almost universal does not mean that they are passively accepted. On the contrary they are usually actively, even violently, resisted by the actors in charge of governmentalities, starting what Hacking (1995) calls a "looping effect" or the constant readaptation between a governmentality which inscripts human beings and the strange things that constantly overflow such inscriptions. To a greater or lesser degree such looping effects are unstoppable, ranging from occurring mostly under the radar to being noted as a source of instability, even menacing the existence of a certain ordering as such. The politics of human devices lies precisely in these tensions, in the continual loops between scripts/subjects and strange things, between multiple and evolving governmentalities and their constant overflowings.

Policy Assemblages

Through the case of Transantiago, in this book I will study a particular version of the politics of human devices, the one that usually receives the name of "policy." However, in dealing with it I will keep a distance from the two most usual conceptual paradigms associated with its study, respectively known as "instrumental rationality"[5] and the "argumentative/deliberative" approach.[6] Instead, and following recent encounters between policy studies and STS, I will see policies as always existing in the form of assemblages.

Following Deleuze and Guattari (1988), an assemblage could be seen as "a collection of heterogeneous elements. These elements could be diverse things brought together in particular relations. ... But the elements that make up an assemblage also include the qualities present ... and the affects and effectivity of the assemblage: that is, not just what it is, but what it can do" (Wise 2005, 77). Therefore, assemblages are never fully stable and well-bounded entities; they don't have an *essence*, but exist in a state of continual transformation and emergence. They exist "as a process of putting together, of arranging and organising the compound of analytical encounters and relations" (Dewsbury 2011, 150). In this sense the concept "offers the possibility of grasping how something … heterogeneous … hold[s] together without actually ceasing to be heterogeneous" (Allen 2011, 154).

What is key for the notion of assemblage is that the act of assembling a certain entity always goes hand in hand with disassembling other/s, or, using the terms developed by Deleuze and Guatari, the territorialization of a certain entity always goes hand in hand with the deterritorialization of other/s. Then any existing assemblage "contains lines of segmentarity according to which it is stratified, territorialized, organized, signified, attributed, etc., as well as lines of deterritorialization down which it constantly flees" (Deleuze and Guattari 1988, 9). Existing assemblages always include elements involved in this interplay of territorialization and deterritorialization, "components working to stabilize its identity as well as components forcing it to change or even transforming it into a different assemblage" (DeLanda 2006, 12). Assemblages are never inert or solid, but always involved in a continual process of demarcating *and* diffusing their components, a dynamism through which they are able to sustain the passage of time and the ever-shifting relations with other assemblages.

Seeing policies as assemblages implies treating them not as solid or stable entities but as temporary concatenations of heterogeneous entities, always on the verge of becoming something completely different. Then *policy assemblages* can be seen as "the collection of heterogeneous, often incommensurate elements that come together for a period of time, sometimes quite fleeting, to produce a policy construct" (Greenhalgh 2008, 12–13). Such a policy construct will be understood, in a quite ample way, as any scheme designed with the specific aim of transforming the real to make a new "mode of ordering" (Law 1994)[7] in accordance with a certain preestablished plan or idea. Modes of ordering are heterogeneous and variable but always include the search for strategic effects, the aim to transform an existing situation in a certain predetermined way through the establishment of particular sets of relations between new and existing entities. In some cases such a change is carried out in the name of the state or the nation (Mitchell 2002; Carroll 2006); in others it is enacted beyond such categories (Rose and Miller 1992). What unifies these endeavors in contemporary society, as the concept of governmentality reminds us, is that they always aim to govern certain human beings in some way. Then the enactment of human devices is compulsory to any policy assemblage, becoming the main way through which new orderings of the human are materialized (and resisted).

Policy assemblages are "not simply external, generalised or constraining forces, nor are they confined to texts. Rather, they are productive, performative and continually contested" (Shore and Wright 2011, 1). Instead of a linear process, they are seen as changing continually. "New issues emerge; the interaction may produce changes in the valuation of alternative outcomes, and the most acceptable outcome may not have been the intention of any of the participants" (Colebatch 2006, 311). Along with this, policy assemblages always exist between order and disorder, they are both constructive *and* destructive. Contrary to the overemphasis in the literature on policies as forms of order and planning, an assemblage perspective highlights how policy assemblages need also to enact effective forms of disorder, even chaos. The materialization of any ordering proposed by such assemblages always goes hand in hand with the erasure, even the violent destruction, of other/s. Then policy assemblages are seen as distributed and nonlocalizable entities, as performative events rather than well-defined instruments and/or processes. They are alive and moving, continually evolving as new elements are added, removed, and/or transformed.

Summarizing, in this book human devices will be seen mostly as a heuristic to designate those devices and concepts through which human beings are brought into policy assemblages. They are quite fuzzy and variable in terms of sizes and levels of organization, from single and fleeting entities to large and stable orderings. In terms of their agency and relation to certain governmentalities, they range from scripts that look to produce disciplined self-governing subjects to strange things that violently challenge, even destroy, such orderings. What unifies them is that they all attempt, using very different means and producing contrasting results, to perform human beings in relation to particular policy assemblages; they perform heterogeneous entanglements always involved in the task of territorializing and deterritorializing both technoscientific entities and political power.

The Four Configurations of Transantiago

In this book I am going to study a particular period in the history of Transantiago, ranging mostly from its initial conception in the form of policy proposals made in 2000 until the implementation of measures trying to

"normalize" the system in 2009. In this period I will distinguish four different configurations of this policy assemblage, or particular orderings emerging along the way. Before dealing with them in detail I have to make two
points. First, these configurations should not be taken as fixed stages in a
linear process. They frequently overlap and mix, extending over different
locations at the same time. Second, they should not be taken as a definitive list that could be easily mobilized to analyze other cases. Transantiago's
configurations emerged out of the very specific concatenations and entities
participating in the genealogy of that plan. For this reason its very existence
and characteristics are intimately united with the particular characteristics of
the process. Whether they could emerge in similar terms in other cases is a
matter for empirical testing, not a given. Much more probably, in other locations and times different configurations and human devices may emerge.

The first configuration of Transantiago to be dealt with is that of *crisis*.
As Koselleck (2006) has noted, the classical definition of crisis never meant
only a moment of rupture and confusion, "but also 'decision' in the sense
of reaching a crucial point that would tip the scales" (358). Then "crisis"
as a conceptual device goes along quite nicely with the deterritorialization/
reterritorialization character of assemblages. A crisis configuration is both
"a progression of disorders, instabilities and hazards" (Morin 1993, 14) and
"a moment of decisive intervention, a moment of thorough-going transformation" (Hay 1999, 323). A crisis always deterritorializes a certain entity
while opening the ground for the reterritorialization of another: "because
of its uncertainties and randomness, because of the mobility of the forces
and forms within it, because of the multiplication of the alternatives, [a
crisis] creates favorable situations for the development of audacious and
innovative strategies" (Morin 1993, 18). For this reason such a concept has
become "a structural signature of modernity" (Koselleck 2006, 372), given
that "once crisis has been identified as an inevitable and necessary phase of
history, it can be overcome through proper prognosis and planning" (377).[8]

In the case of policy assemblages, the crisis configuration is usually
enacted through the interrelations among several components. First of all
a crisis must include an issue. In a broad sense, issues will be understood as
quite open, undefined situations that put into question existing systems of
control and government. As recognized by Dewey (1927; cf. Marres 2007),
issues do not exist in themselves but always related to a certain public
that feels affected by them. However, the organization of this public is not

enough to transform an issue into a crisis. Besides them the issue needs to be associated with two other entities. On the one hand, a crisis configuration needs to include scripts in the form of exemplars of individuals and groups who are experiencing a certain displeasure because of the issue. Such exemplars are endowed with the task of connecting the issue at hand with a "social" realm and, by doing so, transforming its resolution into a "social problem." On the other hand, a crisis must also include the figure of the state,[9] usually presented as a proper "actor" summing up all the "actions necessary to defend and protect this harmed 'public'" (Gomart and Hajer 2003, 57). Then the state is always enacted as the active part, the one that is going to intervene (either directly or through intermediaries) to solve the issue affecting these people. Then a crisis configuration as a particularly modern disposition never simply deterritorializes but also reterritorializes; it is always *productive*, in the sense that it calls for (even forces) intervention, transformation.

The second configuration of Transantiago to be studied is called *infrastructuration*. In a well-known article Star and Ruhleder (1996) define infrastructure as a relational entity that emerges when a variable number of devices is organized as a larger collective, usually including entities such as "material technologies with organizations, institutional rules, and cultural values" (Moss 2000, 65). Beyond these single components, "infrastructures are ... accomplishments of scale, growing as locally constructed, centrally controlled systems are linked or assembled into networks and internetworks governed by distributed control and coordination processes" (Jackson et al. 2007). Then infrastructuration is going to be understood as all the multiple practices necessary to turn into a proper infrastructure a new ordering posed as the ultimate solution to the crisis.

Infrastructuration is usually not so much about building new sociotechnical systems as about the development of "material or social technologies (*e.g.* standards and protocols) that permit the linking of heterogeneous systems into networks" (Jackson et al. 2007). Such a process always includes deterritorializing practices that look to transform and/or dismiss the existing orderings in order to implement the new ones, a process that is never strange to resistances and unexpected bifurcations. Besides this, as an important body of research has shown (Bijker, Hughes, and Pinch 1989; Coutard 1999; Hughes 1983; Myantz and Hughes 1988; Summerton 1994), infrastructuration never simply happens in one moment of time. On the contrary it is a continual process, because infrastructures are constantly emerging "in practice, connected to activities and structures" (Star and Ruhleder 1996, 112), implying in such an emergence a continual change and redefinition as new elements are included, redefined, and/or discarded.

One of the key components of infrastructuration is the performance of the human individuals and populations who are going (supposedly) to deal with the future functional infrastructure. After all, for an infrastructure to be assembled, "people's discursive and work practices [need to] get hustled into standard form as well. Working infrastructures standardize both people and machines" (Star and Bowker 2006, 154). In this task scripts occupy a central place, working as the entities through which the actors involved look to prefigure the human being/s who are expected to interact with the different components of the infrastructure once operational. In doing this, scripts operate as devices developed "for smoothing over the complexity outside their departments and rendering manageable" (Low et al., quoted by Mackay et al. 2000, 754). Commonly policy assemblages (especially large ones such as Transantiago) are populated by a multiplicity of scripts, some of them with radically different agencies that will openly try to deterritorialize each other, as we will see.

The third configuration to be explored is called *disruption*. A disruption emerges when the continuities of certain processes are suddenly altered. As Becker has noted, "stories of disruption are, by definition, stories of difference" (Becker 1997, 13). Then from one moment to the next things start to operate differently, to be perceived as different, and "some of the assumptions upon which the responses of the participants had been predicated become untenable, and the participants find themselves lodged in an interaction for which the situation has been wrongly defined and is now no longer defined" (Goffman 1990, 6). The ultimate consequence of such a configuration is that "the reality sponsored by the performers is threatened" (Goffman 1990, 134). Such threats, however, should not be seen as something necessarily negative. Like any other assemblage, disruptions are always both destructive and creative; they generate disorder and confusion but also open the door to the generation of new orderings, of new realities.

To a certain degree any policy assemblage is a disruption. After all, they were thought from the very beginning to change the status quo of certain issues, hopefully for the better. At first, such disruptions "underline the very (albeit useless) presence of the vast stretched-out system that usually remains so invisible" (Graham 2010, 18), as long demonstrated by the social studies of infrastructure. At the level of human devices such disruption is marked mainly by the fact that, using the term developed by Hayles (1999), human devices now have to be "incorporated" by the people who want to use the new infrastructure, or "encoded into bodily memory by repeated performances until [they become] habitual" (199). In contrast with scripts, an "incorporating practice ... cannot be separated from its embodied medium, for it exists as such only when it is instantiated [in practice]" (ibid.). Such a process usually goes hand in hand with a certain disorientation and/or stress on the part of the actors involved, derived from the recognition that things are different from what they used to be and that they need to alter the "virtual infrastructures of habit" (Bissell 2015) they had applied to deal with the issue up to this point. As could be expected, and as was very much the case with Transantiago, incorporations go hand in hand with the emergence of overflowings, as human beings challenge and transform the designed scripts in multiple ways through the performance of multiple strange things.

Finally, a fourth configuration of Transantiago to be dealt with is *normalization*. Starting from the work of Canguilhem (1978), the concept of the normal has been seen, using the words of Foucault (1979), as "one of the great instruments of power at the end of the classical age" (184). The power of such a concept is derived from the double sense of the term normal: "(1) normal is that which is such that it ought to be; (2) normal ... is that which is met with in the majority of cases of a determinate kind, or that constitute either the average or standard of a measurable characteristic" (Canguilhem 1978, 69). Therefore the normal, as a concept, is always descriptive *and* prescriptive: "[O]ne can, then, use the word 'normal' to say how things are, but also to say how they ought to be" (Hacking 1990, 163). The normal always lies in this tension; it describes a supposedly average reality while at the same time it performs a desirable state toward which the existing reality should evolve.

Normalization as configuration refers then to the practices through which a particular assemblage is forced to reach a predefined normal state. It usually consists of a double process: "first of all in positing a model, an optimal model that is constructed in terms of a certain result[;] and the operation of disciplinary normalization consists of trying to get people, movements, and actions to conform to this model" (Foucault 2007, 85).

Such processes usually take the form of repair practices, understood as "the techniques actors use to maintain the practices, institutions, and technologies that form a system" (Sims and Henke 2012, 326). Repair practices, then, are never solely directed at keeping a certain infrastructure working but also, and centrally, at maintaining a certain ordering scheme, and hence must be considered as political to the utmost (Henke 2007).

Regarding human devices, especially strange things, normalization becomes "people repair" (Henke 2000, 65). Such a particular kind of repair usually starts with positing "normal subject/s," usually based on the scripts made during infrastructuration. When compared with the human devices being incorporated by human beings, with all their overflowings, they usually highlight certain *abnormalities* or components "incapable of conforming to the norm" (Foucault 2007, 85), in this case strange things. After this, certain disciplinary devices (Ureta 2013) are introduced to align such abnormalities to the plan, ranging from directly (even physically) aligning them with the model to setting new regulations and standards through which they are governed or called to self-govern in certain *normal* ways. As might be expected, such practices are always only partially successful, usually causing new overflowings that start new normalization processes, constituting a constant loop that runs all along the existence of a policy assemblage.

In this regard, the main objective of this book will be to make a genealogy[10] of the human devices emerging during the design and daily operation of Transantiago from 2000 to 2009, from the initial scripts made in the set-up of the crisis configuration to the strange things whose repair was attempted during normalization. In doing this it will also be making a story of political power in contemporary Chile, but not in the usual form of a State that is more or less effective in turning human beings into subjects with the help of technoscience. Beyond this, what the concept of human devices wishes to highlight is how the very notions of what it means to be human and how they should be organized politically are a contested and always changing field in which multiple kinds of entities participate, certainly some technoscientific ones but also several others, not least the human beings themselves that are intended to be governed. Everyone has a voice, even the ones who traditionally appear almost completely powerless, and they put it constantly in play along the way, as we will see.

Structure

Using the conceptual scheme outlined above, the book begins by analyzing the crisis configuration at the origins of Transantiago through an analysis of the "Plan de Transporte Urbano de Santiago" (Urban transport plan for Santiago, PTUS in Spanish), a policy proposal published in 2000. Recasting an argument made by transport experts since the mid-1960s, the PTUS first deterritorializes the existing public transport system by claiming it is subject to a terminal crisis. In order to ground this claim, human devices are introduced in the form of, first, data on residential and mobility patterns showing growing demand for public transport in the city and, second, public transport users experiencing distress due to the bad quality of transport and demanding decisive intervention by the state. Later, and in accordance with the territorializing aspect of any policy assemblage, the document proposes a way out of such a crisis in the form of a radical transformation of the public transport system. Such a move would not have been possible without the inclusion of human devices in two main ways: first as consumers who will fully fund the functioning of the system through their fares (so the state does not have to subsidize it) and then as citizens who will participate actively in the good functioning of the plan. In all, the plan proposes a particular kind of governmentality based on scripts of users who, after some careful initial planning, would be very active in governing themselves while using public transport under the constant supervision and guidance of an active state. In doing so, human devices would not only contribute to making a functional public transport system but also to building a *world-class society* in which several key social issues of urban life in Chile had been finally solved.

Chapter 2 explores the first year after the official approval of the PTUS in March of 2002, when the proper infrastructuration of Transantiago actually started. At its center the chapter deals with the struggles to materialize one key human device included in the PTUS: the active citizen. The mobilization of this script in the different components of the new system occupied a very prominent part in the work of the actors involved during this period, who saw it as a way to enhance at the same time the ailing democratic credentials of Chilean policymaking. Such a push was materialized in a series of activities like contests to design components of the plan or the formation of a committee of users. The effectiveness of such measures in fully materializing this active citizen was curtailed, first, by the multiple and contradictory scripts embedded in each scheme, making it quite difficult to know what an active citizen really was. In parallel, such devices were openly resisted by other members of the government involved in the process, causing a severe controversy that was only settled with the removal of most of the devices used to perform the active citizen, along with their proponents.

Chapter 3 explores how the void left by the removal of the active citizen was filled by the other major kind of entity included in the PTUS: human devices enacting future users as *fare and time optimizers*, especially through the development of models. First, an engineering *design* model was developed to produce a new bus network structure. This model performed the user as a rational consumer of public transport who values speed and low prices above all. Second, an economic *financial* model was developed to establish the mechanism through which the system would cover its operating costs. This model performed the user as a low-income person who cannot afford an increase in the fares but nevertheless is going to fund the whole functioning of the system. After deterritorializing competing human devices (mainly in the form of the user as a carrier of habits), these *fare and time optimizers* were further mobilized in the design of some of the key components of the system.

Chapter 4 deals with the massive disruptions caused by the official start of operations of Transantiago. It first presents the inauguration of Transantiago on February 10, 2007, as the biggest disruption that public transport in the city has ever experienced. Then it explores how such disruption was manifested at the level of the inhabitants of the city, who now had to start behaving as in-scripted users of Transantiago in order to travel throughout the city. Using the seats of the new buses as an example, the chapter shows how certain scripts developed during the infrastructuration forced users to travel in very uncomfortable circumstances, disrupting long-held habits of comfort. Such an outcome was not only amply despised by users themselves but also was mobilized by the media, especially television, enacting the figure of the *sufferer* as the ultimate human device of Transantiago, transforming the disruption into an urgent political issue.

Chapter 5 explores how this disruption also caused massive overflowings, especially on the part of users who started incorporating Transantiago in *strange* ways. In order to explore these incorporations, two key examples are analyzed in depth: first, a protest organized by a group of neighbors living in southeastern Santiago to remove an informal parking lot of Transantiago buses that defied government actors' expectations about social mobilization; second, the subversion of the devices designed to control fare payment that defied expectations about consumer behavior. Both practices ended up performing strange things, or human devices that had no antecedent script and openly defied the kind of ordering proposed by Transantiago. Such strange things, flourishing massively in the first weeks and months, threatened to enact a new crisis configuration in which the disrupted ordering would be challenged fundamentally, one that looked to transform not only Transantiago but also Chilean State governmentalities.

Chapter 6 shows how, after some weeks of hesitation, the actors from the government ultimately challenged such a crisis, opting instead for an alternative configuration of the assemblage: *normalization*. Under such a configuration the problems experienced by Transantiago and its related strange things were deemed abnormal, and disciplinary devices were introduced in order to align them with the original scheme. In order to explore this operation in depth, two particular normalizing practices are analyzed: attempts to challenge the media assertion of sufferers as the main users of Transantiago through the use of commensurations as a matter of repair by numbers, and the introduction of an unexpected type of infrastructure to deal with strange things as repair by buffering. This strategy, the chapter concludes, was successful in challenging the crisis configuration, but at the cost of transforming Transantiago into a permanent failing system, a working sociotechnical system that is almost permanently a matter of controversy and critique.

The conclusion explores possible alternatives to such an outcome. It starts by discarding the usual answer provided by the literature on cases such as Transantiago: the claim that such a situation could be averted by increasing the degree of democratization in policymaking. Democratization, in itself, solves nothing. After all, even active citizens are products of a particular kind of government; they are subjects of power and need to be mobilized like any other kind of subject. What is needed, it is argued, is to take seriously the claim that policies are assemblages. Such a recognition would position policy assemblages as orderings that always territorialize and deterritorialize entities, platforms of struggle and accord among multiple human devices and their proponents. Along with this it would be very much open to surprise mainly through heterogeneous testing and keeping the assemblage porous, incorporating strange things appearing all through the development of particular projects. Given this multiplicity, such assemblages should devote important efforts to both coordinating the multiple versions of the human available and taking into account their own politics on the whole process. Although quite challenging, the understanding of policies as assemblages could contribute to advancing toward higher levels of plurality, reflexivity, and responsibility in the enactment of both infrastructural policies and political power.

1 Crisis

The Four Sages

In March of 2000, a couple of months after Ricardo Lagos was elected president of Chile (2000–2006) representing the center-left coalition La Concertación,[1] Clemente Aguilar,[2] a high authority in the Ministry of Public Works, Transport and Telecommunications (MOPTT), invited four people to a lunch at the ministry. What unified the guests was that all of them had a certain degree of insider knowledge about the way public transport functioned in Santiago at the time, either from past appointments as authorities in the area, as consultants, or as former public transport entrepreneurs.

One of the participants, Ramón Acevedo, recalled the lunch in the following terms:

In 2000, at the beginning of Lagos's government ... [Aguilar] invited us for lunch ... and his concern in this first talk was that already at this stage, the end of March, only days after the start of the government, the micreros were asking for meetings saying that they wanted to change the engine [of buses], which was at the back, to the front, that they didn't want automatic transmission, that a manual transmission was better, they started to ask for things so they could reduce the fare, and these petitions were always accompanied with threats. At the very end he called to ask us how he could deal with this threat from the micreros ... and then Pablo Azócar and I abruptly challenged him and said: "Here the issue is not to go after the transmission or to move the bus engine to the front or back, the exhaust pipe up or down ... seeing little issue by little issue, you are not going to modernize this thing, it's not going to change, you are not going to solve the transport problem of Santiago and Santiago's needs." Then we changed [the subject] and from this lunch to the lunch next week I wrote down one draft and Pablo Azócar wrote another, but the thing is that we coincided a lot, [saying] that the issue of public transport in Santiago needed a different vision, I mean, a structural thing, not little issue by little issue. Then besides that, public transport is part of transport in general ... and he said, "OK, work on this, propose to me what to do."

At the time the "micreros," as the thousands of micro-entrepreneurs running the surface bus-based public transport system of Santiago were popularly known, were one of the most prominent, and resisted, actors in the system. Each time the issue of public transport was mentioned, both in the media and in academic publications, the micrero was seen as the figure embodying all that was wrong about the system.

At a quotidian level, users experienced the power of micreros in the form of bus drivers who were usually rude and violent, deciding who could enter their buses and risking everyone's lives by driving recklessly in order to pick up more passengers, transforming themselves into the epitome of urban aggression (Tomic and Trumpen 2005). At the government level, such power was manifested when the micreros, this time organized in cartels, largely successful resisted substantive regulation of the sector during the 1990s, especially through the use of strikes that paralyzed the city almost completely (Diaz, Gómez-Lobo, and Velasco 2004). For this reason when their representatives started calling for meetings soon after Lagos's inauguration, the actors at MOPTT knew what was coming and started asking people with experience in the area how they could deal with them.

However, what both Acevedo and Azócar had in mind in dealing with the micreros went far beyond merely developing new strategies to answer and/or mitigate their requests. They had both occupied high positions in the MTT during Patricio Aylwin's administration (1990–1994), implementing the first major regulations in the public transport area after the radical neoliberal program of deregulation carried out during the dictatorship of Augusto Pinochet (1973–1990). They also shared a degree of frustration over the small accomplishments in the area during the Eduardo Frei Ruiz-Tagle administration (1994–2000). For this reason, and taking advantage of the initial resistance by the government to bending to the micreros' threats, they pressed to move the matter beyond dealing with single issues toward a more ambitious reform program that would not only tame micreros but fully abolish them.

After discussing the matter in a second lunch, Aguilar ended up agreeing to further study the matter and gave them three months to produce a detailed proposal for the reform of the system. The process of producing such a draft was intense. Given their aim of developing a scheme dealing with the city as a whole, they started by "seeing where this city was going," in the words of Azócar. At first, the endeavor centered on dealing with the technical literature developed mostly by transport experts since the early 1980s, both at academic and government levels. Along with this, they carried out several activities to involve a wider sample of relevant publics, such as workshops with experts from several fields, focus groups with users, interviews with different stakeholders and academics, etc. Then such information was systematized into several plans for the transformations of the different aspects of mobility in the city, from pedestrians to massive public transport.

At the end of the process these "four sages," as they were nicknamed at the MOPTT given the amount of information they had accumulated, produced a one-hundred-page document summarizing their ideas entitled "Plan de Transporte Urbano de Santiago 2000–2010" (Urban transport plan for Santiago 2000–2010) commonly known as PTUS (MOPTT 2000). This document was later transformed into a summarized version (SECTRA 2000) and distributed among government, academics, stakeholders, and the media.

Like any other policy assemblage, the PTUS exists in the tension of deterritorializing and territorializing orderings. In this case, as could be expected, such deterritorialization was focused on enacting the current public transport in a terminal crisis, territorializing as its only possible solution a new system based on a completely new scheme. As we will see in the rest of the chapter, human devices occupied key positions in both these efforts.

Deterritorializing Micros

The PTUS starts with the following sentence:

The deterioration of the quality of life in the city of Santiago, caused by an increase in vehicular congestion and environmental pollution, along with the low level of service offered by public transport, is a cause of concern for the government and all its inhabitants. (1)

Here we can see a first hint of the existence of a certain crisis materialized in the "deterioration" of the quality of life in Santiago. The causes of such a situation are clear: the characteristics of the transport system, both private and public. As in any other crisis configuration, the state and the inhabitants of the city are performed as "concerned" over such a situation.

Among the problems of the city's current transport system there is one that is especially critical, as identified a couple of pages later:

The problems of public transport in Santiago are widely known, as well as their negative consequences for the quality of life of the city's inhabitants. The informality in the supply of services and in the entrepreneurial organization of their operators, the inefficiency and scant rationality in the exploitation of the sum of means of transport derived from their lack of integration, the lack of correspondence between the supply and demand of service, the high externalities produced in terms of air and acoustic pollution, the aggressiveness of the system toward its users are elements, among others, that characterize this activity. (3)

The opening phrase is quite revealing of the intention of the paragraph. There are problems, in the plural, with public transport in the city that have consequences for the quality of life the inhabitants of the city. These problems are "widely known," so they were not only an idea of the authors, giving more stability to the claim. After this the main problems of the system are named: informality, inefficiency, lack of integration, pollution, etc.

Following this, the aim of the proposal is stated:

Most of the proposed solutions go in the direction of heightening the quality of life of the city, both at a global level and in the neighborhoods; of recovering for its inhabitants many spaces and years lost, in which flawed economic views and a lack of relevance of public issues caused situations that for a great majority cannot be maintained and which it is a civic duty to change. (3)

The ultimate justification for the policy, then, is not to improve public transport (or mobility in general) but to deal with a crisis in the quality of life in Santiago, reaching almost every aspect of the urban environment ("both at the global level and in the neighborhoods") and whose consequences cannot be more dramatic ("many spaces and years lost"), not only for users of the system but for the whole population of the city.

Such a move was not a novelty. A review of the history of urban planning in Chile (Gross 1991; Pérez and Rosas 2002) shows how arguments about the existence of a "crisis" have almost always accompanied any attempt to reform urban infrastructures. At first during the 1930s, with the emergence of "urbanistas" (usually architects and engineers with a strong influence from European urban planning) as the first proper experts in urban matters, such a crisis was framed as a matter of a city that was organized in a completely chaotic way (Cáceres 1995; Pérez and Rosas 2002). Regarding public transport such a situation was translated into an argument about the poor quality and inefficiency of the means available (Errázuriz 2010), usually paired with arguments about the need to build "modern" infrastructures, especially in the form of underground metro systems. As a response new policy assemblages were progressively assembled, from zoning schemes to the country's first urban highways. Among them the most relevant referent for the PTUS was the Metro de Santiago, for which construction started in 1969 after decades of planning (Pavez 2006). Its original plan included not only underground metro lines but also a complete reorganization of the surface bus-based transport system not very different from the one proposed in the PTUS.[3]

These infrastructural schemes were relevant not only in terms of alleviating certain transport problems, but also in relation to a particular kind of political power. Such power was based, on the one hand, on a state presented as strongly intervening to transform reality with the help of actors with technical expertise, mainly engineers. Then we could say that the Chilean "rule of experts" (Mitchell 2002) and its associated strong state were co-constructed with these public works, stabilizing a certain kind of "infrastructural power" (Mann 1984). On the other hand, such power was based on the emergence of a particular kind of human devices in the form of quantified populations. Especially through the application of the first origin-destination surveys[4] in 1965 (MOP 1966), as part of the studies for the Metro project, each single city inhabitant with her idiosyncratic demands and patterns of behavior was merged into fully quantified datasets, out of which emerged populations whose motivations and daily practices could be known in detail. With the use of prospective technologies such as modeling, these populations then became a matter for control and intervention, the perfect basis for sophisticated state governmentalities aiming to materialize increasingly utopian reform projects.

The military coup d'état of September 11, 1973, that ousted socialist president Salvador Allende meant an important reconfiguration of this kind of power. The challenge began with the arrival of a new kind of experts in the public sphere: economists working with a body of neoliberal concepts and technical devices mobilized from members of the University of Chicago Economics Department (Valdés 1995). The proponents of this approach, known as the "Chicago Boys," started affirming that beyond the political instability associated with the attempts of Allende's government to transform Chile into a socialist society, the predicaments of Chilean society were caused by the saturation of a particular form of politics in the country, based on a state that is presented as intervening excessively in society. For this reason the economy, instead of reaching a natural equilibrium in which both buyers and sellers benefit, tends to unnaturally favor certain groups over others.

The acceptance of this reform program by the military authorities, around 1975,[5] gave neoliberal economists open ground on which to massively install their technical devices to reform the economy and society. In this reform, the ultimate human devices to be governed changed from the quantified populations to the figure of the consumer, understood as a rational actor who autonomously satisfies her needs in the market, leaving the state only the role of assuring that these markets function properly. Guided by these principles, a new governmentality was launched looking to increase private actors' involvement with public issues, mainly consisting of an extensive program of privatization and deregulation reaching almost any issue of public significance, from basic education to the pensions system.

In the public transport area, the neoliberal program was translated into a complete redefinition of the causes of the crisis in public transport. In open contrast with the previous period, such a crisis was seen as caused not by the lack of regulation but by regulation as such (Gross 1991). If the noxious state intervention was removed, then the market of public transport would naturally reach an equilibrium in which everyone would benefit. Such a mandate importantly challenged the infrastructural power of the Chilean state, but did not erase it.[6] Instead of directly providing the needed infrastructures, the state became the actor in charge of setting the conditions for the free market to flourish. The first step was to privatize the state's public transport company, finishing its involvement in direct provision of surface public transport. Secondly, an extensive deregulation of the operation of the system was introduced, including the progressive removal of most former standards regarding the characteristics of the service. In all, these reforms materialized "one of the most consequent and profound cases of application of neoliberal policies in the urban services sector" (Figueroa 1990, 23). One of the most visible overflowings of such liberalization, from the standpoints of the actors involved, was the emergence of micreros as the most powerful actor of the system, having almost complete freedom to set many elements of the system (routes, frequency, fares, etc.).

The return of democracy in 1990 was marked by a new shift in state governmentality and its preferred kinds of human devices. Given the consensus among the members of Aylwin's government[7] about the impossibility of returning to the model characteristic of Chilean public action until the coup of 1973 (for an analysis of the reasons for such consensus, see Silva 2008, 176–178), they opted to develop a hybrid model, later labeled as "growth with equity," that tried to combine the virtues of both social democracy and neoliberalism. This first implied the maintenance of certain key elements of the neoliberal model developed during the dictatorship, mainly in terms of certain limits to public action (Taylor 2006, 113). Balancing this there was "an emphasis on an active state, on the priority of social policy and equity, that constituted a strong social compromise that was clearly differentiated from the existing neoliberal policy" (Boeninger 1997, 359). Under this guideline the new approach to planning had the main aim, while moving within the limits imposed by the neoliberal framework, of correcting some of the problems and scarcities in the country, either through direct state action or, preferably, by developing regulations that would incentivize or force private actors to correct the situation themselves.

In doing so the actors in power looked to perform a new kind of human device in the figure of the "citizen-consumer," a hybrid entity that would materialize the tenets of "growth with equity" governmentality. On the one hand, the "citizen" component was mostly equated with a principle of delegative democracy, seeing its involvement in politics as materialized mostly through its participation in regular elections and opinion polls, both instances enacting "respondents as choice-makers. This sense of being able to choose is a fundamental property of both electoral democracy and the market" (Paley 2001, 143–144). On the other hand, the "consumer" component was materialized through the introduction of instances of self-government in the application of policies. Especially in areas of direct public involvement such as health and education, these procedures looked to perform a particular kind of individuals who would become "responsible, through their own individual choices, for themselves" (Schild 2000, 276). In all, citizen-consumers were expected to act autonomously and responsibly, but in a collaborative way, to satisfy their demands and needs in the particular ways and spaces that the state had opened to them and, by doing this, to legitimize state policies as well. However, and as would happen in any other state governmentality, the materialization of this project has faced overflowings from the very beginning, producing multiple kinds of strange things that have accompanied the imperfect development of Chilean society since 1990.

In the transport planning area, the return of democracy meant an important renovation of the technical personnel in the government transport offices, many of whom were transport engineers, a highly prestigious new breed of transport experts who flourished in universities and in the government's technical departments during the dictatorship. Mixing engineering with economics, they restated the crisis as a matter of a public transport system that has been evolving for the worse due to the deregulatory excesses of the dictatorship. From there they pursued, in the words of a key actor of the period, "a change of policy consisting in a retaking of the regulating and normative role of the state in relation to a market that contemplates preponderant participation of the private sector as the provider of collective transport services" (Hohmann 1993, 18). This quote illustrates the new approach championed by the transport engineers arriving in government positions, very much in the line of "growth with equity." While still considering public transport as a market run by private actors, it also presents the state as directly intervening in it in order to secure better standards of service. So the emphasis on state action would not be mostly on the direct provision of infrastructures but on the *optimization* of the existing network, especially through new functional standards that would allow a higher degree of regulation and the proper integration of the technical devices of the system, as a large study carried out by the government in late 1980s concluded (SECTRA 1990).

The limited success of these measures to rule the micreros during the Aylwin administration[8] strengthened claims about the need to radically transform the public transport system of the city, to bring it more in line with transport planning before 1973. This emphasis was materialized in a series of policy drafts (such as MTT 1996) proposing schemes in which the infrastructural power of the state was restated to a certain extent through the public provision of some infrastructure while the daily operation of the system would still be in the hands of private actors, although now operating in a highly regulated way. Most of these measures were never applied, though, and by the year 2000 several actors of the area shared with Azócar and Acevedo a degree of frustration about the incapacity of the state to truly reform public transport in the city, mainly in the form of deterritorializing micreros once and for all and producing the modern infrastructure that Chilean urban planning had sought since the 1930s.

Angry Consumers

However, providing arguments about the need to deterritorialize micreros or the "irrationalities" of the current public transport market was not enough. In order for the PTUS to truly enact a crisis configuration, considerably enhancing its chances of becoming insfrastructured, several other entities had to be brought into the proposal, central among them human devices.

As described in the introduction, the main function of human devices in a crisis configuration is to work as exemplars connecting the claims made with a particular human population supposedly existing in "reality" and, by doing so, to give *social relevance* to the proposal, a practice quite common in such documents (for examples see Marante et al. 2003; Shove and Rip 2000; Wilkie and Michael 2009). Any proposal involving the radical transformation of the public transport system of Santiago would hardly gain approval based only on internal arguments about the need to optimize bus routes or to tame unruly actors such as micreros. In the end, and as in any other governmentality, "the regulation of things ... is uninteresting except in so far as that regulation bears upon the regulation of human conduct" (Mitchell 1995, 561).

This was also understood in most proposals of the past, in which the need to enact either a state that directly intervenes or a market that rationally organizes private actors was always joined by claims about populations who were going to benefit from this intervention. Thus if the PTUS wanted to be successful it needed to convincingly show how the inhabitants of the city were experiencing problems because of the current public transport system and were actively demanding its reform. It had to show, in other words, that the inhabitants were embodying the crisis of public transport and would be the ultimate beneficiaries of any change: that they would be governed in a *better* way as a result of the intervention; that their comfort, efficiency, and ultimately their happiness would be increased as a direct consequence of the new ordering.

Such a focus on the city's inhabitants was materialized at first with the production of a "diagnosis" about the population of the city and its mobility patterns. Following the trend toward quantification as a way to show that arguments were "technical" (Espeland and Stevens 2008), the strategy here was to include human devices in the form of data on the mobility and residential patterns of the population of the city. First the PTUS supplied data on household income (whose source was not identified) showing how much of the population of the city had low incomes and, for this reason, that their "budget available for transport is seriously limited and will continue this way in the near future" (10); for this reason they were going to keep using public transport. Next, data from the Internal Revenue Service was added to present these people as increasingly living in the same places and going to the same destinations for their daily activities, hence traveling in the same directions (12). There was thus an important group of the population who would keep using public transport in the foreseeable future and travel in the same directions, a situation that would "aggravate the transport problems, even in the absence of other problems that influence the conditions of circulation" (12–13).

In parallel, and in order to present the mobility patterns of the members of this community, the document introduced a kind of human device that was going to occupy a central place in the different configurations of the plan: origin-destination scripts (ODS). ODS were first produced in the country in 1965 through the first origin-destination survey carried out to quantify the transport demands of Santiago's population. Its main novelty, in comparison with previous kinds of quantifications, was its capacity to perform the inhabitants of the city as flows of people that move between predetermined points at certain hours of the day, without reference to any other aspect of the trip. As a consequence urban space becomes a sum of origins and destinations between which users try to establish the most rational routes, acting as perfect choice-makers. Such a notion transformed daily transport from a heterogeneous mess of patterns and habits into neatly quantifiable flows, opening the way for increasing levels of forecast and intervention. The city, with all its obdurate materialities, disappears; only the moving populations are relevant.

ODS were introduced into the PTUS by way of a comparison between the results of the 1977 and 1991 origin-destination surveys (cited from SECTRA 1991, chapter 4):

The mobility of population has augmented as a consequence of the increase in incomes. Only between 1977 and 1991, the rate of trip generation has grown from

1.14 to 2.12 trips per person per day. In the same period the participation of cars in total trips has grown from 11% to 23%. The temporal distribution of trips shows an important concentration. In the three peak hours (morning, midday and afternoon peaks), which represent 12.5% of the day, 35.2% of the motorized trips are made. Among them 16% are concentrated in the morning peak. (15)

With this last step the population of the city is constituted as a large group of mostly low-income individuals who cannot afford other means of transport than public transport and who travel increasingly in the same directions and during the same times of the day. Given such a situation, this section concludes that the current situation "will produce an explosive increase in travel times in the coming years, unless actions are taken to counter these tendencies" (15). Then the crisis becomes not only a "social" problem but an urgent one; it must be tackled right now or its "explosive" consequences in terms of mobility would be felt throughout the city.

A second set of human devices included in the PTUS performed the current users of the system as consumers of public transport who were openly dissatisfied with the service they were receiving. Such performance was not irrelevant. As seen in the previous section, since the massive adoption of neoliberalism in the mid-1970s, the consumer became the leading figure toward which public action was oriented. Replacing former conceptions, "individual freedom was redefined as representing the free access to open markets, while the 'pleasure of consumption' was presented as an instrument to express social differentiation and as a way to obtain personal rewards" (Silva 2008, 162). If the consumption of transport was not experienced as a "pleasure," one of the main mechanisms to differentiate and obtain gratifications in contemporary Chilean society appears not really to have been working for millions of daily public transport users.

In the original PTUS proposal this dissatisfied consumer started to be performed through the affirmation, derived from the material obtained in a focus group carried out with users, that "in the public image there may be no other service with as bad an evaluation as this one" (3). The feeling is so intense that the public transport system has become "one of the main factors that users identify as daily embittering their lives when they leave home" (3). Then the document identifies the reason for such critical opinions: a quality of service offered to users that "does not recognize them as clients" within a market of transport services.

Users often experience a hostile attitude on the part of drivers, and the quality of services and vehicles in some areas is far from acceptable minimum levels, all of which, from the point of view of the long-term survival of the business, is absolutely counterproductive. Today a public transport system that offers quality services is demanded by the vast majority of users ... and we are quite far from that goal. (14–15)

Therefore the system, especially the micreros, had to stop seeing users as merely bodies to transport from one place to another in the city (similar to freight), but had to see them as consumers, or clients, who demand "quality services."

Later, a complementary version of the dissatisfied consumer of public transport was produced in the form of a graph introduced on page 11 of the executive summary of the PTUS published by the Secretariat of Transport (SECTRA) in November of 2000 (SECTRA 2000), reproduced here as figure 1.1. What this device is telling us is quite straightforward: public transport receives the lowest evaluation among five "public services," with only 34.6% of all the people surveyed assigning it a grade of 6 or 7.[9]

After this first introduction, the graph and/or its data were later extensively used as the ultimate exemplar of the dissatisfied consumer of public transport in PowerPoint presentations, book chapters, research papers, etc., until well after the start of Transantiago in 2007.[10] With each successive

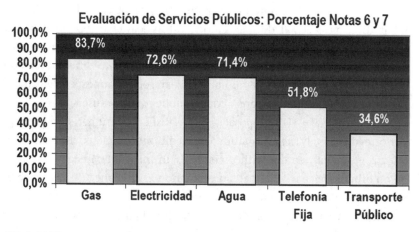

Adimark: Oct 2000

Figure 1.1
Evaluation of public services by consumers, PTUS executive summary (2000). Image reproduced with permission from SECTRA.

use, this angry consumer became more and more stable, more and more official, to the point of transforming itself into the most widely accepted *fact* about the users of the public transport system that existed before Transantiago, the final proof that all of them hated it and actively asked for its improvement. This was especially strong given the high validity ascribed to opinion polls in postdictatorial Chile as direct and valid reflections of the *real* opinions of the population and, for this reason, an indirect mechanism of public participation (Paley 2001; 2004).

Through the graph the PTUS was able to show that the need for a radical reform in the public transport system was not only a fantasy of some utopian academics or ambitious politicians, but also a demand coming directly from its consumers, from the very people who used the system in their everyday lives. The graph was not merely there, representing a group of "real" dissatisfied consumers of public transport, but it played an active part in the process through which this reality was performed and used to heighten the relevance of the proposal.

This last point will be clearer when we explore the genealogy of this particular device. A little inscription at the bottom of the image says "(Adimark: Oct. 2000)," connecting it with its original source: the published results of a survey called "Indice Nacional de Satisfacción de Consumidores" (National index of consumer satisfaction) for the second half of 2000, carried out by ProCalidad.[11] This survey, part of a regular series, looked to quantify and compare consumer satisfaction with a series of highly diverse goods and services from 22 different economic areas, among them public transport.

To construct figure 1.1 out of this original source was not straightforward or automatic. The dissatisfied consumer wasn't just there waiting to be mobilized for the project proposal. Before occupying such a position she needed to be performed into being, a practice that involved certain decisions and transformations on the part of the graph's unknown authors. The original graph on which figure 1.1 was based presented 18 different services, so a criterion must have been introduced to select the five services included. The caption of figure 1.1 gives us a hint about such criteria: "Evaluation of Public Services." To be mobilized on this graph, then, each component must have belonged to this category. But what is a "public service"? How were these services defined in order to be able to discriminate among the 18 services present in the original graph? Or, even more pressing, what do gas, electricity, tap water, landline telephony, and public transport have in common to make them belong to this category of public services? For example, the item "Municipalidades" (boroughs) was also included in the original graph and, more importantly, it had a lower valuation than public transport. Given that Municipalidades offer several services that are open to the public, they could easily have been considered "public services" and included in figure 1.1. But they were not, and it was by excluding them that public transport became the service with the lowest valuation by consumers.

This example does not mean to imply that a "better" selection would have produced a more trustable version of the consumer. The point is not to clean up the process, but just to show how the results cannot be seen as independent of the practices through which they are generated (Law and Urry 2004; Law 2009b). In fact, these practices, as Latour and Woolgar (1986) noted in their analysis of the production of scientific papers, were relegated "to the realm of the merely technical" (63). As a consequence the graph was taken as a completely valid embodiment of consumers' opinions about different public services, the ultimate confirmation of their ample dissatisfaction with the existing public transport system.

Along with the human devices effectively being performed, the diagnosis section is also telling for its absences, for the devices it failed to territorialize. After all, as recognized by Roitman (2013, 81), "once crisis is posited, some questions are asked, others are foreclosed." The emergence of a crisis configuration always goes hand in hand with the closure of alternative orderings and entities. In this case we can note one key human device that was not territorialized by the authors of the PTUS: a version of the users with something positive to say about the existing system. Even though the technical literature recognized some aspects of the system that were laudable (especially the great coverage of the bus route network and the relatively cheap fares), the user enacted in the PTUS is all negativity. In no place of the document can we find a human device positing a user that might be less angry or dissatisfied—probably not really happy but at least with long-established habits and/or enjoying a certain degree of comfort when using public transport. The users of the PTUS had no such elements; they uniformly despised the existing system and openly clamored for its replacement.

Given this state of affairs, it is not strange that the section concludes that "there is consensus that the state must more strongly carry out its duty as guarantor of the common well-being and assume a much more active role in the transport sector" (17). Crisis demands the state, demands radical intervention. With such intervention, not only would the problem be solved but also a new version of the state—caring, protective of its subjects—would be performed. Thus the PTUS enacts a state that no longer leaves everything in the hands of the markets but to which its capacity for "radical" intervention is restored, a version closer to the kind of infrastructural power existing before 1973.

Failing to do so involves great risks, as affirmed in the closing lines of the diagnosis section.

Seen from another point of view, if the transport problems of the city are not faced with an approach like the one developed in this proposal, the social costs and the costs in terms of quality of life for Santiago at the end of this decade are going to be of a hardly reversible magnitude. We think that the moment to start these intensive changes is now.

The existing public transport system cannot continue to exist as such, it must be radically deterritorialized. But, as always in this kind of policy assemblages, such deterritorialization went hand in hand with the territorialization of a new future ordering that promised to solve all of the problems of the former. Only with a believable alternative is the crisis complete, and this alternative was precisely the PTUS.

Active Citizens

After the diagnosis, the rest of the document was devoted to explaining the different measures to be developed as part of the PTUS. Given the acute crisis, it was argued that such a new policy configuration should be "larger and more radical and with a systemic and integral coverage, a policy more complex and comprehensive but also with better prospects of reaching the roots of the problem" (4). This emphasis was materialized in ten programs of action involving most aspects related to the mobility of the population of the city, even reaching to proper urban planning in terms of the location of new neighborhoods, schools, and workplaces.

The first of the ten, "Program for the modernization, ordering, and integration of public transport services," proposed a reconfiguration of the surface public transport network based on a completely new scheme: "routes organized in zones, in accordance with the demand structure, that flow through a network of structural corridors and trunk lines as well as feeder corridors, all of which are integrated physically and in terms of fare transfers between them and with the Metro in especially designed transfer stations" (23). The main points of such a program are summarized in table 1.1.

Leaving aside the new terminology and the higher level of detail, the PTUS shared several elements with proposals made before 1973 (especially MOPT 1969), in particular an important degree of radicality and (to a certain extent) monumentality. To these was added the neoliberal emphasis on the need to keep markets at the center of the system, limiting regular state intervention to the correction of externalities through optimization. In all, it managed to present a sophisticated mixture of the different versions of the Chilean state's infrastructural power, from the grandiosities of

Table 1.1

Comparison between PTUS and the existing public transport system of Santiago

	Existing System	PTUS
Bus routes	Almost deregulated, usually very long and intersecting heavily at main streets, high competition	The city divided into 10 main feeder areas connected by several trunk lines run by five companies, with no competition among them
Management	Hundreds of micro-entrepreneurs	15 areas of business operated by one independent company each, centrally managed by an independent entity
Payment	In cash, paid on each ride of a bus or Metro	Made through a contactless smart card; integrated flat fee between buses and Metro
Buses and drivers	Old and highly polluting fleet; drivers receive their income depending on tickets sold	New custom-designed buses; drivers receive a regular salary, eliminating the need to compete for more passengers
Metro	Operating independently	Fully integrated both financially and in terms of routes to the bus network
Infrastructure	Only basic infrastructure	Development of a considerable amount of infrastructure, from bus-only lanes to new bus stops
Information	No formal information system	Information would be continually produced and distributed both to users (travel information) and the general system (fleet management)

urbanistas to the restraints of the Chicago Boys. As a result, as promised in countless brochures later made for the plan, the public transport system of Santiago would be "modern, efficient, integrated, and with the highest standards of quality for its users" (MOPTT 2004, 3).

For the success of this plan, again, it was necessary for the PTUS to show not only that the so-called technical components were identified and available, from detailed calculations about the demand for the future system to up-to-date transport technologies; but also that the future users were willing to actively cooperate with the implementation and functioning of the new scheme, as was explicitly recognized:

It is fundamental for the success of a policy like the one proposed to have *actively participating users*. Such participation recognizes different levels and moments of the process. Of course, at the most global level it means that the citizenry must assume that each of them has a role of the greatest importance to perform in order for the proposal to be implemented. (102, emphasis in the original)

Such "actively participating users" were going to be active in several senses. First, future users of the plan were going to be active as consumers of public transport who agreed first and foremost to pay their fares for using the system. Such a demand started from the recognition that high levels of fare evasion were common in the existing system (estimated to involve a loss of 25% of total revenues). Given this, it was affirmed that "reducing fare evasion is crucial for the good functioning of the whole system" (36). Such evasion was a risk for two main reasons: "Along with unfair pressure over the fares, it generates a great deal of uncertainty that stops entrepreneurs from introducing the large-scale investments necessary to implement this policy" (36). This second effect of evasion was especially relevant for the PTUS authors.

Supported by a host of government and academic studies carried out since the 1980s, one of the central claims of the PTUS was that with the proposed reconfiguration, the private entrepreneurs replacing micreros in running the different services would be "in the position of assuming an important share of the investment necessary for this plan" (29), given the increased revenues derived from the optimization of the whole system. As the proposal affirmed,

In effect, the economies of scale allowed by the global volume of trips and the virtual operational monopoly will make this kind of concession a large and stable [source of] revenues. For this reason it is possible to ask them [concessionaires] to invest the funds necessary in technological changes to the vehicles … and possibly in some necessary components of the infrastructure. (29)

In later versions of the proposal such a conception was reduced to a simpler yet more attractive formulation: no public subsidies. A public transport system functioning under the scheme proposed by the PTUS would be able to importantly improve the quality of service while not requiring extra expenses on the part of the state. Such an outcome materialized the aim of combining different kinds of infrastructural power behind the PTUS in the figure of a state that intervenes to provide substantive improvement in the quality of life of the population while at the same time leaving it to the market to fund most of the necessary infrastructures. However, for this system to function properly it was critical to have users who paid the correct fare for their trips, avoiding any kind of evasion. Such a disciplined fare-paying user was the basis on which the economic autonomy of the plan would be built (and the source of many of its problems, as we will see in later chapters).

Paying their fares was not the only way in which future users were expected to be active. They were also presented in the document as acquiring and distributing information about the plan, expressing opinions, being vigilant about the good functioning of the different components of the system, etc. In particular, "in order for the proposed system to function smoothly, each person has to produce the changes and adaptations in his or her daily behavior that the system demands" (102–103). Thus it was clear from the beginning that users would have to consciously modify their habits related to the use of public transport in Santiago, from accepting a completely new way of paying their fares to changing their routes to their usual destinations. The complexities involved and/or possible resistances to changing long-held habits were not really thematized. In line with most transport planning, all these changes were seen as feasible under the implicit assumption "that habits are the part of us that can be adjusted, altered, oriented in one way or another, that they are the part of us that can be manipulated, perhaps even from the outside, to attain various goals" (Grosz 2013, 234). As long as the users received all the relevant information, they were going to understand the benefits of changing their daily habits in order to become "normal" users of the new system. Any notion that users might have problems incorporating such scripts, or might even reject them altogether, was completely absent from the document; with the rational ODS there was no space for such overflowings.

In all, the PTUS enacted users who were very active in the management of their own (and others) bodies. In a similar way to Foucault's concept of biopower, these human devices implied a transfer of power from the traditional externally exerted discipline, based on the direct control of bodies, to technologies of the self through which future users would "form and transform themselves, constitute and modify their very being, their thoughts, conduct, and bodies" (Smart 1985, 90) in accordance with a pregiven script to be developed during the infrastructuration of the plan.

However, the performance of the future user as active was not only related to the need to have self-governing users for the good functioning of the new technical system. In parallel, the PTUS performed a further kind of active user:

The truth is that the citizenry, as a community of individuals, is an absolutely absent actor in the task of giving definitions to [the transport] area. Experience indicates that the participation of citizens, through the institutions that represent them, constitutes a relevant element to capture, in order to understand and improve the diverse aspects that urban transport involves. Thus it is necessary to promote the participation of the community in all stages of the process of design and implementation of policies and projects of urban transport, in the decision-making spaces of the investment project, in the definition of the operative or managerial aspects, or even in the phase of control. ... The basic concept is that the citizens of Santiago are the ones who have the legitimate right to define the type of transport that they want to have, and not, as has been usual for decades, a reduced group of entrepreneurs who define the rules of the game. (20)

This paragraph postulates a revolution. As has been noted (Silva 2008; van der Ree 2007), public action in Chile has been characterized since the 1930s by an emphasis on top-down technical planning as the ultimate precondition of good government. Such an emphasis has been especially strong in the transport planning area. Since the beginning of the discipline in the 1960s, its practitioners have been involved in careful "boundary work" (Gieryn 1983), looking to demarcate for themselves a "technical" space of action distinct from the despised "politics." One of its key manifestations was the demand that only quantified entities could become proper components of transport planning; hence it only recognized moving masses (through ODS) and, later, consumers (through econometrics) as proper human devices. As a consequence the figure of the "citizen," understood as an actor who actively participates in the planning process, was almost completely absent from the area, as the quoted paragraph recognized.

Looking to deterritorialize such a state of affairs, the paragraph performed users who were going to be actively involved in the different processes of planning and running the system. This involvement did not simply mean the usual communication/education campaigns or single instances of public participation. Beyond this, the PTUS stated, "it is necessary to promote the participation of the community in all stages of the process of design and implementation of policies." In *all stages*. From the initial decision making to the control of the functioning system, citizens were going to be present not only as entities to be governed but as carriers of certain knowledge that allowed them to become equal participants in the planning process. If this program of public involvement were to be effectively applied, it would mean, in simple terms, one of the most significant transformations of planning in the country in the last 80 years, constituting an important step toward an effective democratization of policy assemblages in Chile. In doing so the PTUS would contribute not only to the improvement of transport planning, but also to reducing the democracy deficits that were widely perceived to characterize public action in Chile at the time.[12]

Thus in detailing the components of the PTUS, the four sages did not only propose an alternative public transport system for Santiago. They also proposed a new social ordering, in which both fare-paying users and active citizens would materialize, transforming into a reality two key components of the infrastructural power sought by the Concertación since its arrival in power in 1990: that an active state could be combined with a healthy market and that policymaking could be both technocratic and democratic, virtuously combining high degrees of technical expertise and lay knowledge.

A World-Class Society

Contrary to the expectations of the four sages, the initial reception of the PTUS by government authorities was, at best, mild. Even though it was publicly announced as a public policy at a press conference in September of 2000, nothing much happened besides the MOPTT commissioning certain specific studies from SECTRA and the plan being enthusiastically endorsed by technical actors such as transport engineers.[13] By the end of the year the future of the proposal looked bleak, its more probable destiny being to follow the same path toward oblivion that dozens of other policy proposals on the reform of public transport in Santiago had taken through the years.

In mid-2001, however, this situation suddenly changed, as Azócar recalled:

When Lagos arrived [in the presidency], he arrived with this idea of the [Chilean] bicentennial [commemoration], to make ten big projects, enormous, in ten cities of the country, I don't know, the Cerrillos park in Santiago, this other thing in Iquique; and this [PTUS] didn't exist for him. But what happened to Lagos was that, given the persistence of the Asian crisis, ... all the pyramids that he wanted to build fell down, and while the pyramids were falling the PTUS, from its very low position, started to go up: the pyramids fell and fell and the PTUS went up and up, and at last it was the only proposal that remained on the table of a Laguean scale, I mean, of the kind of grandiosities that Lagos wanted. ... So Lagos was left without big schemes and suddenly he found this ... this wasn't a priority, it wasn't his star project, not at all, he arrived at it by default, let's say.

As the first socialist president of Chile since Allende, Ricardo Lagos was urged from the beginning of his presidential campaign to show his credentials in terms of good management, especially to maintain the mixture of market-based policies and proto-welfare measures characteristic of the two previous Concertación governments. But at the same time, Lagos's own inclinations were to make his time in office one of the best in Chile's history, "thinking of the Chile of the future and fascinated with the idea of the bicentennial to be celebrated in 2010" (Silva 2008, 196).

In order to deal with this second aim, the Comisión Bicentenario (Bicentennial Commission) was established to propose several monumental infrastructural projects in different parts of the country to mark Chile's bicentennial as an independent country, to be commemorated in 2010. But the slower-than-expected recovery of the country from 1997's Asian financial crisis[14] made implementing most of these projects impossible due to their high costs. In these circumstances the PTUS, which until this moment had not really been considered, became relevant as one the few "pyramids" attractive enough and possible to be implemented.

In this ascendance the crisis narrative, and its related human devices, proved vital. First of all, and connected with the deterritorialization of the existing system, the issue and its proposed replacement were easily presented not only as deriving from the reformist agenda of some transport experts but as an utterly "social" problem affecting large numbers of the city's population. Second, the narrative had a widely despised villain in the form of the micreros. Third, the issue had been known for a long time, but most solutions that were applied had been unable to deal with it. So the proposed intervention was easily furnished with the epic narrative of a long-lasting crisis that no other government had been able to solve.

However, and given the steep reduction in the available funding, such a narrative would have been meaningless without an extra component derived from the territorialization of the PTUS: the promise that the whole policy could be carried out without the need for massive public spending. Such an outcome was related not only to the substantial economies of scale derived from the reorganization of the system but also to the in-scription of users of public transport who would finally start paying their full fare every time they used the system. Thus in the PTUS they had a monumental infrastructure solving a long-lasting "social" problem and that promised to cost quite little if implemented as projected—the perfect "growth with equity" project.

In consequence, from its original secondary position the PTUS suddenly became one of the most visible projects carried out during the Lagos administration. Beyond fixing public transport in the city, the PTUS was seen as an opportunity to materialize the successes of his government through the transformation of Santiago into a "world-class" city, leaving it ready for the celebrations of the bicentennial in 2010, as was repeated over and over again in presentations and brochures about the plan produced later. Presented this way, the PTUS became a "worlding project," to use the term developed by Ong (2011), or a project that "attempt[ed] to establish or break established horizons of urban standards in and beyond a particular city" (4), promising to give Santiago a particular location in an imagined global map as an exemplar of successful urban transformation.

Such a world-class Santiago would be composed not only of the up-to-date infrastructures of the new public transport system. This was clear in the section of the PTUS detailing the proposal's final objective:

It is intended that Santiago in 2010 becomes a city where people move with tranquility and in an expedited way between one place and another, in comfortable and safe conditions, through a fluid public transport network that integrates the different means available ... in a harmonious and intelligent way. ... Both at bus stops and during trips, people relate to each other in a friendly way, and so do drivers and the system's support personnel. ... Besides, many car drivers have opted to travel by public transport, in order to take advantage of its speed and cheapness ... passengers pay differentiated fares, in accordance with the service and distance, and students, old people, pregnant women, disabled people, and those who belong to the most vulnerable social sectors take advantage, as well, of the special facilities that the system of public transport gives them. ... In the Santiago of the first decade of the 2000s, the harmony between city and transport, absent for quite a long time, has been recovered. Everyday life is, at last, much nicer and easier. (22–23)

Besides having a modern transport infrastructure, world-class Santiago would be populated by a new kind of humans: multiple entities who were at once ODS, (finally) satisfied consumers who paid their fares, and citizens who self-governed and were actively involved in planning/running the system. Such new humans would also face a new kind of power. Replacing the micreros' "rule of terror," the state would now be in charge, optimizing incoherences while leaving the daily functioning in the hands of the market and professional companies. As a consequence it was promised that the general texture of everyday life in the city would be modified, transformed, finally enacting a new "world-class" society whose elements would seem to match much more nicely than in the imperfect existing versions.

From this we can see how a crisis configuration is never only a moment of rupture and confusion. As shown by the analyses of Koselleck (2006) and others, a crisis is always also a moment of transformation, of intervention. Thus the crisis of the public transport system of Santiago enacted in the PTUS was never meant only to signal the serious shortcomings of the system, albeit these were (probably) real ones. In parallel, such a configuration looked to open the way for territorializing new orderings claiming to be the ultimate solution to such a situation, continuing a line that goes back to the first proposals for modern transport systems made in the 1930s. But the effects were never solely expected to be limited to the transport or urban area; a "world-class" society would also emerge from this intervention, the perfect ribbon for the bicentennial celebrations of 2010. In this account we can see how a crisis configuration, quite paradoxically, combines the uttermost negativity of the current situation with "an eternal optimism that a domain or a society could be administered better or more effectively, that reality is, in some way or other, programmable" (Miller and Rose 1990, 4). It is always a promise of progress, of ultimate improvement, and for this reason it has become one of the landmarks of modernity.

Finally in March of 2002 the PTUS was relaunched as a proper policy of the Lagos administration, including a schedule among other things. After more than 70 years of discussion and evaluation, a proposal for a radical reform of the surface public transport network of Santiago could finally start to be transformed into a proper infrastructure.

2 Infrastructuration I: Active Citizens

How "Active" Is the Active Citizen?

On March 1, 2002, Pablo Azócar became director of the nascent Coordinación General de Transporte de Santiago (General Coordination of Transport, Santiago; CGTS in Spanish). The CGTS was established by the government as the organization directly in charge of the concrete implementation of the different measures in the PTUS regarding the reform of public transport.[1] As an operational office, the CGTS was going to work under the supervision of a Directorio de Transporte en Santiago (Directorate of Transport in Santiago; DTS) formed by the ministers and high authorities of a series of public entities related to transport like the MOPTT, the Secretariat for Transport (SECTRA), and others. Established to deal exclusively with the implementation of the PTUS, the DTS was going to operate on a regular basis as the highest decision-making authority in its infrastructuration.

The tasks ahead for the CGTS were staggering. First of all, the infrastructuration of the PTUS proposal involved the development of dozens of new technical devices, many of them nonexistent in the country until then, such as bendy (articulated) buses or an up-to-date transport information system. Even more challenging, all these devices had to work in a highly coordinated fashion to really constitute a proper public transport system. As described in the introduction, such a process was as much a matter of new technological design as the development of standards through which all these different devices would be able to act together. Then besides the new technologies, several existing infrastructures, especially the Metro, had to be radically transformed in order to work in a coordinated way with other components included in the PTUS. Such a process was further constrained by an important foreshortening of the deadline for the system to start operations. From the ten years established in the original proposal (2000 to 2010), in the process of approval it was demanded that the PTUS should be functional in four years, so that Lagos would be able to inaugurate it before the end of his administration in March 2006, clearly establishing the system as a central component of his administration's legacy.

A key part of any infrastructuration is developing the human devices to be used in the process. As discussed in the introduction, such devices usually take the form of "scripts," or blueprints of supposedly existing or expected human beings comprising a sum of characteristics and affordances, which can go from quite general assumptions about populations to highly detailed "personas." Once performed, such scripts are taken into the design of the different components and standards to be included in the system being infrastructured, occupying the central role of supposedly valid spokespersons for the human beings who are expected to use and/or relate to the assemblage once it is working. For this reason the making and using of scripts are central practices in any infrastructuration; it is through them that the populations to be ultimately governed by the policy assemblage (or which will resist such governing) are brought into the design process.

Given the highly distributed materialization of infrastructuration, especially of complex systems like the one proposed by the PTUS, scripts are always multiple. Not even the most centralized and/or tightly controlled infrastructuration performs just a single and well-defined script of the future users of a device. As we saw in chapter 1, the PTUS included several kinds of human devices in the form of ODS, consumers, and citizens. After the proposal was accepted and started to be infrastructured in 2002, each of these looked to be further mobilized in the assemblage, becoming different kinds of scripts of future subjects, with different degrees of success, as this and the next chapter discuss.

This chapter deals in particular with a kind of script that occupied a central place during the first year of infrastructuration (March 2002–March 2003): active citizens. The original PTUS proposal regarded the issue of public engagement as central for the materialization of the proposed policy assemblage. The future users of the system, it was argued, could not be simply flows of ODS or fare-paying consumers looking to satisfy certain individual demands in a transport market. Given its complexity and novelty, the system needed also to perform users as active citizens, subjects willing to participate actively in the development and daily running of the system.

Such emphasis was a direct influence of Azócar, who, as a sociologist with previous experience in participation processes,[2] regarded an active citizen as central to the ultimate success of the plan. As he affirmed,

I always said to my team, "Look, the designs from the universities that you give me are one thing, but this design from the university must be contrasted with the university of the street, which is the users. ... All the network designs that you give me have to be checked there, because from there comes the final adaptation." And this is for them, after all, this is not for me, this is not for the engineer who has the pleasure of saying that "the demand started here and then went there, and here and there it's distributed," no, no, no, this could be well sketched but at the end [the idea] is to give good service to the people, and they know better than anyone else.

In this quote Azócar performs active citizens as carriers of a certain knowledge that is necessary for the good implementation of the policy and cannot be obtained by merely applying transport planning technical devices. In particular his insistence on the need to "contrast" the knowledge produced by traditional universities with that coming from the "university of the street" shows a particular kind of understating of the relationship between experts and lay people, similar to what Callon (1999) calls the *public debate model*.

From this perspective, while scientific knowledge has universal value, "by construction it is, however, incomplete and deficient, for its exactitude and generality are undermined by its abstraction and deficiency" (Callon 1999, 85). For this reason, "it is advisable to open the forum for discussion and deliberation so as to create the conditions of its enrichment" (86), especially with the knowledge coming from the "university of the street" in this case. This performance of the active citizen represents a departure from the nonexistent or merely informative involvement of users in policy planning, but it shares with them a central element: the issue of demarcation, or the fact that both approaches "deny lay people any competence for participating in the production of the only knowledge of any value: that which warrants the term 'scientific'" (89). In other words, although central to the planning process, an individual carrying a degree from the university of the street still has much less weight than someone with a degree from a real university.

After being appointed as head of the CGTS, Azócar started right away to look for ways to enact such active citizens. Finding human devices capable of doing such a work was not easy, however. As mentioned in the past chapter, transport planning in Chile since its beginnings has been practically insulated from the use of any kind of human devices enacting active citizens, something it shares with transport planning elsewhere (Schiefelbusch 2005). Thus no prior experiences, guidebooks, or experts on citizen involvement specifically designed for transport planning schemes were available. Such expertise had to be found elsewhere and then adapted to this particular assemblage. The first step toward this aim was to constitute an interdisciplinary team at the CGTS, including the more usual expertise of transport engineers but also some social scientists with previous expertise in the matter. These actors brought with them multiple and contrasting human devices for enacting active users, mainly taken from their experience in implementing participatory schemes in other departments of the government and nongovernmental organizations.

Some of them enacted future users as carriers of emotions and habits that would need to "sign on" for the future system to function correctly. This was clear in the words of Matias Bonilla, an engineer occupying a key directive position in the organization.

We considered that if communications were not working and the people did not sign on emotionally to the plan ... the plan would be threatened with death, so we gave the highest relevance to communications and I got a lot of money for communications, I talked with the people at the Ministry of Finance ... and my point was that we needed to train practically the whole city, and if this [training] did not work it was going to be a hell of a mess, and this was not marketing but passengers' training.

Very much like the technologies of the self identified by Foucault (2008), the main objective from Bonilla's point of view was developing human devices through which "individuals [will] act upon themselves, rendering themselves subjects of government" (Nadesan 2008, 9). The future users were accordingly performed as active citizens who needed to be very much open to changing their behaviors in order to correctly use the new system, a task in which the government should act by "training" them. Behind such a development was, again, the notion of users who so despised the current system that they would be willing to change most of their habits of public transport use, no matter how long these had been held, to see it transformed.

Others took a different view of the "active" component of the active citizen, as was clear from comments by Beatriz López, a key actor in the nascent citizen participation unit. She had extensive experience in carrying out participation schemes in other offices of the government and was quite conscious of the challenges they entail:

What we thought at this moment was that we were going to make a revolution in Santiago because what we were going to do was to modify the whole urban life of Santiago's inhabitants … but this transformation of the city could not be made without incorporating the citizenry from the beginning, and we were talking about incorporating them for real, in all the stages of designing the plan. I mean, it was not a vision of an informative or consultative participation, but more like a process that we were going to construct among them all, and the experts were part of the process but the citizens that were going to be affected by this change must be leading actors in the process too.

Instead of having the role of only validating knowledge produced elsewhere or having to learn how to self-govern while using the new system, the active citizen for López was to be directly involved in the planning of the system. Using again the analytical framework developed by Callon, from her perspective the success of the infrastructuration process would depend ultimately not on the knowledge produced by technicians that was validated by members of the university of the street but on "a constantly renewed tension between the production of standardised and universal knowledge on one hand, and the production of knowledge that takes into account the complexity of singular local situations, on the other hand" (Callon 1999, 89).

Thus from the very beginning it was not clear what the "active" component of the active citizen meant even among the small group of actors gathered at the CGTS, what specific entity they wanted to territorialize in place of the traditional passive user of transport planning.[3] In this respect we can see at least two different governmentalities, and their related human devices, cohabiting within the CGTS. For one of them, favored by Bonilla, citizens should be active mostly in terms of self-governing in certain ways, leaving the design and management of the system to actors with technical credentials. For the other, favored by López, the infrastructuration of the PTUS could not be successful without giving the citizen a proper role in the production of knowledge. Instead of trying to find a way to balance or coordinate them, during this first year these two human devices were territorialized in parallel in relation to two main tasks: educating users about the characteristics of the new plan and promoting their active involvement in the design of one of its key components.

Educating the User

The first way in which the script of the active user was materialized was in relation to the need to "educate" the population of the city about the changes in their daily travel habits that the implementation of the PTUS would entail. In line with the first definition of active citizens, what was looked for here was to territorialize a human device in the form of a public transport user who carries an important degree of knowledge about the characteristics of the new system, knowledge that was going to be useful during her daily trips to make correct use of the system and, in doing so, optimize its overall performance. Also, and as in any other governmental-ity, the ultimate territorialization of such a script would also contribute to enhancing the kind of political power that the PTUS proposed, material-izing its promises about the creation of a world-class society.

The first task in fully materializing this self-governing user was to secure funding to implement a massive educational campaign about the charac-teristics of the future system and the way users should behave on it. The problem in running such a campaign was that the CGTS was only an opera-tional office whose allocated funds were limited to paying wages and carry-ing out a few particular studies. Anything that demanded funding beyond this, especially given the financial constraints under which the govern-ment was operating, necessarily needed the approval of the Ministry of Finance. In order to obtain this, Azócar had a meeting with the minister and, after lengthy discussions, managed to get approval for funds to run the campaign.

However, the Contraloría General de la República (Treasury Inspector's Office), the body that oversees public institutions' expenditures, almost immediately blocked the use of those funds. Gabriel Fuentes, a member of the DTS at the time, recalled the situation:

[Azócar] had problems with the Contraloría because the Contraloría had blocked in the past, rejected, marketing campaigns for programs that were not already func-tioning. Do you remember the AUGE? When [health minister] Artaza appeared with a baby in his arms saying "The AUGE is going to keep this child healthy" and I don't know what more? It was a mess, they almost kicked out Artaza ... then the Contraloría was very serious, blocking the use of money for political objectives, for propaganda objectives.

As Fuentes here recalls, the Contraloría blockage was triggered by a controversy regarding a media campaign for a public health plan known as AUGE[4] that had happened some months earlier. This media campaign, based on a television ad showing the health minister Osvaldo Artaza carrying a baby, was focused on explaining the future benefits that AUGE would bring to the population when it started in 2005. The Contraloría objected on the grounds that, according to article 16 of law 19.774, none of the conditions in which public services can spend on marketing were met; the campaign was neither "necessary for the fulfillment of its duties [nor] ... has the objective of informing users about the way to access the services they offer" (CGR 2002). Discarding from the start the argument that the campaign was "necessary and essential" for the fulfillment of the Ministry of Health's duties, the Contraloría focused on the matter of when it is permissible for a public service to engage with users of public programs. After summarizing the existing legislation on the matter, they concluded:

[The] marketing and diffusion ... of activities or programs that public services "want to make" in the future ... is not allowed in accordance with the regulations. Besides ... the regulations regarding marketing and diffusion do not authorize doing research on taxpayers' opinions about projects under development or strategies to overcome possible resistances by those affected. (CGR 2002)

This paragraph is interesting because it shows how deeply ingrained inside Chilean policy assemblages are devices (such as regulation and its interpreters) that enact one, and just one, particular kind of active citizen. What the Contraloría was criticizing was not the devoting of funds to public participation as such (tellingly understood as "marketing"), but the timing of such a process. In this regard their position was that a public engagement mechanism could only be introduced after the proposed plan had already started. As the second quoted sentence shows, even carrying out research about the "opinions" or "possible resistances" of future users was forbidden. Assigning funds to such practices was seen as unlawful, on the grounds that the government would just be making political propaganda about a service that doesn't yet exist.[5] Thus citizen participation is synonymous with giving information to passive recipients, and it must be implemented only when infrastructuration has been finished, a position that practically canceled any attempts to include Santiago's population in earlier phases of the policy assemblage, even as merely passive receptors of information.

Azócar contested the blockage in a meeting with the Contraloría's director.

I said, "Look, this thing is a revolution from every point of view ... after decades of people's dealing in one way with public transport we are going to change it, I mean, we need another kind of user that thinks differently, that rationalizes, that sees with a different logic a system that has a completely different logic than that of the former system, so we need to prepare the citizenry to make profitable this huge investment that we are going to make, we have to make them understand this right away." Luckily they understood, "Look, if we don't start right away we are going to waste a huge amount of public money for the equipment, for the studies, and for everything else, and this thing can fail because of this" ... and the money was approved.

Reversing the position stated in the PTUS, Azócar started by acknowledging the existence of habits in using public transport in Santiago. Then he moved to the more usual transport planning frame in which habits are something that could be changed if a new kind of user is produced, one that "rationalizes" and understands the "different logic" behind the plan. In this process the CGTS had a central role to fulfill; otherwise, taking the Contraloría's perspective, it would have been guilty of "misus[ing] public funds" because a huge public investment would have been wasted. This strategy is interesting, because the argument was won not by challenging the Contraloría's performance of the users as merely receptors of information when the policy is working, but by showing such training/education processes to be "necessary for the fulfillment of [CGTS] duties." Thus in the end the lifting of the blockage did not challenge the Contraloría's usual performance of users, but merely extended it to the infrastructuration process.

After the funds were available, a proper citizen participation unit was set up inside the CGTS, as López recalled:

My first task was to set up a citizen participation plan, and ... this plan of citizen participation had to be defined along with a group of different actors. In December we had a workshop where we invited all the environmental and citizen organizations of the region, and the question we worked with in this workshop was what the citizen participation strategy of an urban transport project like this should be. ... At the beginning the objective was to have a permanent working relationship with them in order to establish a tendering mechanism, and clearly for us, from the state, we were not going to create the participation directly but have a tendering mechanism in order for others to carry out this process, but based on a consensual call for tenders.

Following the usual "growth with equity" mandate of looking to third parties to run policies, NGOs were performed as the main actors in charge of territorializing the knowledgeable user of public transport. By establishing a tendering mechanism the government was going to transfer funds and the responsibility for such processes to the NGOs, in the understanding that they, as "experts" in participation, would be able to do a much better job than the CGTS, which would only retain secondary tasks in the matter.[6]

In order to set up this arrangement, a workshop took place on December 19, 2002, in which 21 NGOs participated. The work plan was first to present the main measures of the PTUS and then to talk about the strategy for public participation and what roles the NGOs could have in it. The discussion produced a series of proposals from the NGO actors about mechanisms to educate and involve the population in the plan, who was going to make the call for participation, who would be the actors involved, what would be the specific methodology, work plan, registry, etc. (CGTS 2002c), more or less in line with the initial expectations of the people from the CGTS.

In parallel, however, the NGO actors resisted the kind of script offered to them, the assigned role of mere executors of this educational plan. Guillermo Herrera, the head of one of the most active NGOs in urban matters in Santiago, recalled this issue:

We had a very fluid conversation with Pablo Azócar, whom we knew and had been working with for a long time and ... then there was fluid interchange ... and then we asked for a place in ... what was it called? ... in the transport directorate, but they never answered us, we even presented a legal petition for it. ... Now the idea, it wasn't a place for us, it was a citizens' place, and we were going to see how it was defined, how the citizenry was going to define a representative for this place. ... Azócar found it interesting, the only thing that he asked us is that the interlocutor should be someone relatively prepared, who could carry the citizens' voice. He thought it was interesting and this could have been something different, because this would have forced the citizens' representative to set up an assembly in which users and other organizations participated, and it would have to include the disabled population, it would have to include a gender perspective, it would have to include students' associations, etc., etc. I mean, we had some more or less clear ideas, if they agreed with it, about how we were going to organize it and the profile of the person who would occupy this position, the citizens' seat, but nothing happened at last.

After years of being actively engaged in dealing with multiple urban issues, the NGOs felt they had a right to be considered not only as experts in carrying out citizen involvement schemes but also as carriers of a certain knowledge that could actively contribute to the good infrastructuration of the PTUS, and that they should be delivered directly.

In order to advance in this direction, they proposed a complementary human device: a "citizens' representative." Such a device was going to embody the active citizen and be physically present, and with the right to speak, in the meetings of the DTS, the space in which the key decisions regarding the infrastructuration of the PTUS were taken. The embodied character of the citizens' representative would give a whole new presence to the knowledge carried by the NGOs in the planning process, allowing them to (at least theoretically) match the one coming from actors with technical credentials. As Herrera recognizes, to select a particular person to fill this role was not a trivial matter, because it had to be someone qualified to speak in technical language but also able to represent the interests of highly diverse groups of users. In itself the citizens' representative was going to function as an intermediary, connecting the "technical" realm of discussion at the DTS with the plurality of experiences of users on the streets and their particular forms of knowledge.

Even though the members of the CGTS received this proposal positively, they also had apprehensions about it, as López acknowledges:

They [members of NGOs] wanted this space [the DTS] to have a citizens' seat. For us it was complicated not because the citizens should not be in this space but because what were the mechanisms of representativeness? Or who was going to define which citizen, which citizens' institutions should be there? Do you understand me? Then finally what advanced in this workshop, I would say, was the logic of installing a permanent consultative committee.

For the CGTS the main issue was the representativeness of such a figure, how it was going to be selected from among the variety of NGOs with stakes in the issue. This was not a minor issue, because they feared that such a position could be taken over by the biggest stakeholders, excluding the less powerful or less organized actors.

In order to avoid such a situation, instead of the citizens' representative the CGTS proposed to constitute a Consejo Consultivo Ciudadano (Citizens Consultation Council), a permanent scheme in which the representatives of different organizations and groups of users would meet regularly to discuss different technical matters related to the implementation of the plan. But, as López acknowledges, this was only going to be a consultative entity, without the capacity to participate in the decision-making process as a citizens' representative would have. In proposing this model of engagement, finally, they were adhering again to model 2 identified by Callon (1999), with these actors as validators of knowledge produced elsewhere, but without clarifying whether they would also have the capacity to produce knowledge themselves or how their validation (or, especially, refusal) would impact in the general decision making of the process. This council was originally scheduled to start its work in March of 2003.

In the meantime, and as a result of the discussions of the workshop, at the end of December the public participation section presented a general plan for public participation in the implementation of the PTUS (CGTS 2002a). This plan enumerated a series of general objectives, adding to the educational campaign (seen as facilitating "a change of behaviors that warrants the plan's sustainability") a mandate to properly "involve the citizenry in the design and implementation of the plan." These objectives were mixed with some quite diffuse claims dealing with the general quality of life in the city, including photographs of the city, children's drawings, images of a family, and some highly idealistic phrases ("To reclaim the desire to be happy," "to make dreams explicit, the soul of Santiago"), as shown in figure 2.1.

This plan constituted the only instance in which the multiple ways to conceive an active citizen were mixed, with relative success. However, it was never properly applied nor even further mentioned, because of a controversy happening at the time that completely transformed the place of the active citizen in the infrastructuration of the PTUS.

Welén

An ad appeared in Chile's four biggest newspapers on September 15, 2002, inviting submissions of proposals for a name, logo, and slogan for the future Public Transport Plan for Santiago, explicitly stating that "all natural or legal persons, Chilean or foreign, may participate in this contest who wish to do so," even those with no previous experience in the matter. The relevance of such a contest for the actors at the CGTS went well beyond selecting a particular branding for the PTUS. Above this it represented the first of the (expectedly) many ways in which the fully active citizen was going to be brought into the infrastructuration of this policy assemblage.

In a later presentation, Azócar recalled this emphasis:

Figure 2.1
Presentation of Public Participation Strategy (CGTS 2002a), final slide. Image reproduced with permission from the Directorate of Metropolitan Public Transport of Santiago (DTPM).

We made a public competition to define the corporate image of the plan, a competition of which I'm quite proud because it was completely citizen-led. We didn't charge for the call for tenders, it was even open to design students. There was a queue that circled around the streets of downtown Santiago where our offices were located in order to retrieve the tenders. Design schools, universities, research centers, consultancy firms came to retrieve the tenders. 819 copies of the tenders were given out and 420 proposals were presented.

As he recalled, the high level of interest and ultimate participation was widely seen as a success, a confirmation of the citizenry's interest in getting actively involved in infrastructuration when asked to do so.

After receiving more than 420 proposals, a committee of people with expertise in marketing and design was assembled to choose the winner. After reviewing all the entries, they decided none of them fully embodied the three preestablished attributes that a brand for the plan should have,[7] so they decided to produce a winner by mixing elements from three different proposals. The result of this mixing, consisting of a name, a graphic isotype, and a slogan, can be seen in figure 2.2.

welén

Un transporte como la gente

Figure 2.2
Winning proposal for the PTUS brand (first contest). Image reproduced with permission from the Directorate of Metropolitan Public Transport of Santiago (DTPM).

Welén was the pre-Hispanic name given by the Indian population to a hill that stands in the center of Santiago (currently known as Cerro Santa Lucía). By choosing this name, as Ignacio Montes, an architect from the CGTS who oversaw the process, recalled, the members of the committee wanted to "territorialize [the plan], connecting it with the foundation of Santiago." Thus the name was explicitly aimed at showing how the plan would territorialize something new, a new foundation for the public transport system of the city. The shape and colors of the isotype, resembling a semaphore, were meant to be "very close, quite easy to understand ... and besides it has a diversity of colors, thus we thought it generated an empathy with the people that was quite strong," Montes continued.

Finally the slogan "Un transporte como la gente" (literally "a transport like the people") had a double meaning. First it suggested a transport system that had improved; in Chilean slang the expression "como la gente" means something that is rather good. Second, the phrase had the aim of making each single passenger conscious of her responsibility in the system. If the system is to be "like the people," then the final results of the plan, either good or bad, were not only a matter of good or bad policymaking but also "depended on the user," as Montes said: "the user makes the transport [system]; if the user was dirty, the transport would be dirty, if the user was nice, the transport would be nice, etc. etc." Then along with being a recognizable brand, this particular slogan looked to operate also as a ubiquitous disciplinary device (Ureta 2013), reminding users to self-govern every time they faced a device carrying it.

When this brand proposal was presented, in the next meeting of the DTS in December 2002, things did not go as expected, as Bonilla recalled:

When we went to present this [brand], Ignacio Montes, who was the head of communications for the plan, spoke for 15 or 20 seconds until Matias Lozano interrupted him and didn't allow the meeting to continue. As a result the directorate never saw the name or the logo, nothing, he interrupted.

At the time, Matias Lozano was a high authority in the Intendencia Metropolitana de Santiago, the local government of the metropolitan area, and for this reason a full member of the DTS. He also had extensive experience in marketing, having directed a successful marketing agency before arriving in the Intendencia. Given this position he was able to stop the presentation of the proposed branding, automatically signaling it as unacceptable, a motion that was seconded by several members of the DTS.

Lozano recalled his stark opposition to the proposed brand:

One of the problems of Santiago is its brand, it's a quite devalued brand in terms of public opinion and citizenry. ... From this perspective what we were doing in the Intendencia was that people assumed that they live in a city, so our workhorse was "Santiago: a world-class city," in order to develop the theme that we must make a change in what our city is, that cities are driven, managed; and for this reason ... we had a great influence in [the name for the PTUS], in that [the name] was Santiago. ... If we were going to modernize public transport this was something people could positively identify with, and no Welén, man! That was [the name] Pablo Azócar had made before we started working, they held a public competition and liked this name but only because they liked it, there was no background. We had a *communications brief* [that stated] what we were looking for, its identity, to make [public transport] our own, that people feel part of a city, that public transport is part of the place where they are living, not something strange to them. We had constructed a narrative in order to make the people feel it as their own.

Here again we can see "worlding" (Ong 2011) at work in the Intendencia's concept of Santiago as a world-class city, so central in the approval of the PTUS. This time it appears at the very center of a parallel policy assemblage being carried out at the Intendencia since the start of the Lagos administration: to relaunch the city as a dynamic, attractive, and modern urban center for business, tourism, and living.

For Lozano the brand of the new plan occupied a key position in this process. Given that the PTUS was to offer an up-to-date technological system, replacing one of the worst malaises of the *old* Santiago, it was central that it could be directly associated with the new version of the city the Intendencia was championing. Such an association should be made mainly through the inclusion of the word "Santiago" in the brand of the new system. Such an option was supported by a *communications brief,* a technical device extensively used in marketing and advertising to detail the components and targets of a proposed campaign. In contrast, Welén did not appear to him to have any support beyond the opinions of the evaluating committee. Besides, the whole promise of the PTUS was about the future, about what it would be, not about the city's past, especially its despised indigenous past. So Lozano decided from the outset that Welén must be discarded, rapidly gaining the support of several members of the DTS on that point.

After that, a new process for choosing the brand started, as Azócar recalled:

Lozano ... criticized everything very strongly, that he had never, never seen work so unprofessional, so little here, so little there ... Lozano was an expert ... and [said] that this was unprofessional and bad. ... Then a period of negotiations started between Lozano and myself, and we agreed on a methodology. This was in the last days of January and I then took a two-week holiday in February, and taking advantage of my being on holiday Lozano called an extraordinary meeting of the directorate and took the decision to change the methodology in my absence. Afterward when I returned from holiday I found a completely different scenario, now we weren't going to validate [the first contest], we weren't going to find a method to validate what I had done in order to strengthen it, but they asked four leading marketing companies to give proposals about what [the brand] could be, a completely irregular thing, without tendering, nothing, completely irregular. ... They forced me to attend a meeting which I didn't want to attend where [the marketing companies] ... made presentations, each one of them, then the directorate became the technical committee, the companies presented, went out, and the directorate discussed. I remained silent, I didn't participate in this, I was present because otherwise I would have had to resign right away; then they took the decision to choose one, "OK, this one who proposed Transantiago" everyone thinks is ok. I didn't say a thing.

The new contest proposed by Lozano in the special meeting of February was different in two key aspects from its predecessor: only four big marketing agencies were invited to participate, and the characteristics of the proposals had to strictly comply with the guidelines set out in the *communications brief* made by experts in strategic communication. Thus the role of active citizens as creators of the basic components out of which the brand would be made was discarded, replaced by a procedure based only on traditional expertise in the marketing area.

In a meeting in March of 2003 four companies presented their proposals and a winner was selected. The winning company proposed the name "Transantiago" for the plan, along with an isotype formed by a green square with a white arrow in its interior (figure 2.3). As a slogan they simply included the word "Súbete," meaning "go on board" or "step in."

Figure 2.3
Winning proposal for the PTUS brand (second contest). Image reproduced with permission from the Directorate of Metropolitan Public Transport of Santiago (DTPM).

Transantiago was a neologism formed, obviously, by a combination of the words "transport" and "Santiago." For the organizers of the first contest this name was nothing new. As Ignacio Montes recalled, "in the first competition 13 or 16 people, I don't remember how many, proposed 'Transantiago,' and we discarded it because it was like 'Transmilenio.' 'Transantiago' was very little creative, it had an absolute obviousness." Transmilenio is the name of a bus rapid transit system started in 2000 in the city of Bogotá, Colombia. Since opening it rapidly became a "success story" in the media, an example of innovation in the transport field coming from developing countries (Valderrama 2009). Given this, for Montes to choose "Transantiago" would have been to diminish the uniqueness of the Chilean project.

But Lozano made a completely opposite reading of this connection.

The "Santiago" theme, the "city" theme, the theme about making it our own, the theme about generating instances for improving the city, identity, international positioning … Transmilenio is a much smaller project, even, than the Metro of Santiago. Transmilenio in Bogotá has been sold quite well and has positioned Bogotá as an example of transport innovation. Well, then, instead of giving it a fancy name let's associate [the PTUS] with the city, because this was a much bigger project.

Thus in the end the name Transantiago appeared to have properties that Welén never had. While Welén only established a connection with the city's past, Transantiago connected the plan with the city and some desired future development, with global "success stories" and innovation, with modernity;[8] it could be "sold" much more nicely in the market of global cities enacted by worlding projects.

On the same day the name Transantiago was made public in a press conference, Azócar resigned as director of the CGTS, ending his involvement with the plan.

Weakness

The brand controversy was the culmination of a year in which the meetings of the DTS had been plagued by multiple controversies regarding the definition of several key aspects of the plan and power struggles among its members.[9] For this reason the controversy was not only about which brand seemed to reflect better the proposed plan, but also a way for certain DTS actors to take revenge on Azócar for deeds of the past months.

A central element in these tensions was a disagreement about the focus taken by the CGTS since the beginning of the year. Gabriel Fuentes from SECTRA, one of the key members of the DTS at the time, summarized the critiques of Azócar this way:

We didn't advance that much and then the conflagration was more or less big. … I'm sure it was a consensus, I realized that all the guys gossiped about Pablo [Azócar], "This guy doesn't give us trust," there was no trust, no trust, they didn't trust in what the director said to them, the ministers. … The mess was enormous especially because we didn't advance fast enough, we lacked an economic vision. … Many times I criticized him … because we didn't have a model for the buses, I saw a lot of people from transport [areas], a lot of philosophy, a lot of things about citizen participation, pure crap, very remarkable and laudable but here we needed someone to make contracts, someone to buy buses, and this thing required a business model.

Another member of the DTS, Horacio Garcia from the MOPTT, recalled the situation in a quite similar way:

Between May and December of 2002 in everything that came [from the CGTS] you saw nothing, the only thing that they gave you was that they had meetings with the "live forces," with the drivers. … Everything was a draft and what we needed to know was which were the routes, we wanted to know which kind of vehicles we were going to have, what was going to be the situations with the exclusive lanes, … how they were going to integrate … it was a technical issue and they gave us [things] dealing with the support of the people, let's say, and they had meetings with neighborhood associations and they spent an enormous amount of time [on that], but when it was demanded that they put things on the table, the truth is that there was nothing, or very little.

Thus the final controversy over the brand was related to a general critique about the approach that the infrastructuration had taken to that point, with an extensive perception among the other members of the DTS that the emphasis on citizen involvement and other "philosophical" elements was made at the cost of leaving aside the development of key technical devices of the plan. A business model, drafts of the contracts, new designs for buses: all of these were largely seen as the most urgent issues, and Azócar was perceived as not dealing satisfactorily with them. Given this, the emphasis on developing human devices to perform active citizens was seen, in Fuentes's words, as "pure crap."

As a consequence the departure of Azócar, followed by a large group of the people he had brought in, meant that no further serious attempt to enact human devices performing active citizens was ever considered in the infrastructuration of the recently christened Transantiago.[10] The active citizen was effectively, and quite comprehensively, deterritorialized.

The reasons we might pose to explain such an outcome are manifold. The most obvious, supported by many of the people who left with Azócar, was that the actors from the different state agencies (mainly the DTS but also the Contraloría and the Intendencia) were full-fledged technocrats who acted quite effectively to deterritorialize the active user, and its representatives, from the infrastructuration of the PTUS. Such an argument, however, does not explain completely the ultimate weakness of the active citizen, how after occupying such a prominent position for a while she could be deterritorialized so easily from the assemblage in a relatively short period of time.

A second element that could explain this weakness was the uncoordinated multiplicity that characterized the efforts of the members of the CGTS to enact the active citizen. Derived from the lack of previous experience in the transport area, the CGTS implementation of human devices to enact active citizens was characterized by assembling a high diversity of actors, both human and nonhuman, several of them carrying different scripts of what being "active" meant. As Mol (2002) explores, such a multiplicity is not in itself a problem. What made it problematic in this case was the complete lack of any real effort to develop coordination mechanisms between these contrasting human devices.[11] As a consequence, the active citizen became a mess of contrasting human devices, almost completely isolated in the different locations in which infrastructuration was carried out. When speaking at the Contraloría she became a relatively passive citizen needing instruction, when dealing with the NGOs she became a carrier of knowledge who pushed to be taken into account, and so on. As a consequence the multiple versions of the active citizen stood for the same thing only in name, while in practice they were not only different but actively resisted or competed with each other. More crucially, when under attack such a fractured entity proven to be quite weak, being deterritorialized with ease.

Finally, a hint about a third element that contributed to enacting the weakness of the active citizen was given by Azócar himself in an interview to a newspaper shortly after his resignation:

> I have been self-critical ... maybe I didn't have the capacity to convince others, maybe I should have lobbied more the other authorities' members of the directory, but the truth ... is that it seemed to me a little bit ridiculous to lobby people with whom we share the same government responsibilities. I thought that I would have to lobby the ones that I had to defeat, the opponents, the ones you are affecting with the policies you are developing, not those on the inside, and that was certainly a mistake on my part.

Although he refers to his whole work as head of the CGTS, his words appear especially apt for the case of the active citizen.

Given their personal commitment to the issue, for Azócar and several other members of the CGTS the relevance of the active citizen was so self-evident that they didn't see it as necessary to mobilize the support of other members of the DTS in this matter, to do politics as usual with all its bargaining and compromising. However, as a long line of STS studies has shown, no single technical or scientific claim will "shine with its own light" (Shapin 1995, 305). To be properly territorialized, sociotechnical devices need to involve a high diversity of entities, need to make heterogeneous alliances, especially if they represent novelties and challenge existing arrangements. Otherwise the device being mobilized is doomed to fail, no matter how much technical knowledge has been embedded in it. In contrast, several members of the CGTS took a quite "purist" approach to the issue, not really trying to mix their own human devices with others (for example the ones performing the user as a consumer or an ODS) in order to gain wider support among the actors involved. In this sense they usually tended to act more like religious acolytes than policy practitioners, proposing quite idealistic schemes of public participation (such as the one seen in figure 2.1) and expecting them to *naturally* rule over any other kind of human device.

In all, we can conclude that Transantiago was born without active citizens and remained so for a long time, until the system started to carry people in February of 2007. Such an outcome posed a big question mark over the kind of political power that the PTUS proposed originally to enact, a governmentality in which human beings were going to be active not only as ODS or fare-paying consumers but also as epistemic actors, producing and mobilizing knowledge that complements, and challenges, the knowledge produced by experts. Instead, the infrastructuration turned to the business-as-usual governmentality of transport planning, as we will see in the next chapter.

3   Infrastructuration II: Modeling Consumers

Quantifying Transantiago

The main reason given for the deterritorialization of the active citizen, as we saw in the previous chapter, was that enacting the active citizen represented an unnecessary distraction from decisions about key aspects of the recently christened Transantiago, such as the redesign of the future bus route network, the number of buses and companies needed to run it, the general financial structure, and so on. For the actors involved, these decisions could not be based only on conceptual or theoretical elements such as the ones included in the PTUS. Although widely shared, such concepts were still too broad and diffuse, too soft. What infrastructuration needed at this stage were commensurations: to transform such "different qualities into a common metric" (Espeland and Stevens 1998, 314), and, by doing this, to "reduce and simplify disparate information into numbers that can easily be compared" (316). In order to be properly infrastructured, the dozens of highly heterogeneous elements contained in the PTUS needed to be embedded into a common metric, even the most uncertain of them. Once this process was done, or so this logic states, the elements could be compared and concrete decisions taken.

In particular, the members of the DTS were greatly interested in the production of economic commensurations, from establishing indicators regarding the detailed demand for public transport to putting prices on the different needed investments. As was widely recognized, the main reason for the crisis of public transport was a system constituted during the dictatorship in an utterly irrational way. However, the preferred alternative was not to return to the former predominantly state-owned system but to produce an "optimized" version of it that would materialize the double aim of requiring no public subsidy and offering better service. To successfully infrastructure such a new organizational and financial ordering, including a mixture of new and old entities, it was necessary to take into account (meaning to quantify and assign their rightful value) all the relevant actors, matters of concern, and/or externalities.

From the very beginning such a task was assigned to a particular kind of device: models. Following the classic definition of Van Fraasen (1980), models can be defined as "specific structures in which all relevant parameters have specific values" (44), values that are expressed in a common metric, making them easily comparable and interchangeable. When applied to concrete issues, models allow the analysts "to gain understanding of a complex real-world system via an understanding of a simpler, hypothetical system that resembles it in relevant respects" (Godfrey-Smith 2006, 726). Models are usually treated as some sort of middle ground, "separate from, and partially independent of, both theory and data" (Morrison and Morgan 1999, 15). For this reason, for the members of the DTS the creation of models in which they could commensurate and compare the different elements of the system was the most central task to which they had to direct their efforts. In doing so, and in contrast to the fractious year under Azócar, they hoped to move infrastructuration beyond politics, to a realm of exactitude where truly rational decisions could be taken about the concrete characteristics and costs of the future Transantiago.

This seemingly apolitical character of models was especially appreciated when it came to the inclusion of individuals and populations in the planning process. Instead of the expected messy and complex participation of active citizens, with all their demands and lack of proper knowledge, models seemed to offer an alternative (but no less valid) path. Through the use of sampling procedures and other already legitimized statistical procedures, modeling promised to simplify such involvement to the very basic activity of producing scripts in the form of "individual human agencies capable of calculating their interests in one way or another" (Callon 2007, 345). Once these calculative agencies were produced, they could be put into commensurable relations with the other entities included in the model and rational decisions could be taken, leaving aside all the "crap" associated with the active citizen (quoting again Fuentes).

However, before this ideal moment could be reached, proper models had to be produced. This chapter will explore the role of these modeling practices in the performance of the script of the future user of Transantiago as a *fare and time optimizer*, a rationally calculating, low-income consumer who always prioritizes low fares and shorter traveling times when using public transport. This script emerged from effective coordination between the two other main kinds of human device included in the PTUS besides active citizens: ODS and consumers. We will study this process by analyzing the development of the two main models behind the plan: the *design* model developed for the redesign of the bus route network, and the *business* model developed to establish the financial structure of the new system.

Rational ODS

Two years before the events described at the end of the previous chapter, in February of 2001, SECTRA made a call for tenders for the study "Análisis de modernización de transporte público, V etapa" (Analysis for the modernization of public transport, stage V). This particular study was intended to "redesign the current physical and operational structure of the surface public transport system of the city" (MIDEPLAN 2001, 5). More particularly it was to produce a concrete model of the current public transport network of the city from which different future policy scenarios could be constructed and evaluated. The resulting model, to be known as the "design model," was going to be the backbone for any concrete transformation of the existing public transport system of Santiago.

As its name reveals, such a study was the latest in a line of research initiatives funded by SECTRA since the early 1980s to study different options for transforming the public transport system of Chilean cities, especially Santiago. In this task several transport engineers occupied central places, moving almost seamlessly between the government and academia.

As seen in chapter 1, during the dictatorship transport engineering flourished in the universities and at particular governmental offices dealing with transport issues. By the return of democracy it has reached a high level of sophistication and prestige,[1] not least for the conceptual innovations developed as part of the universities' collaboration with SECTRA on this series of studies. Up to this point, however, the application of these tools to properly deal with the crisis of public transport in Santiago had been limited to introducing tendering mechanisms for routes and other specific modifications in the early 1990s. The grand plans of radical transformation lying behind these particular measures, out of which the discipline of transport engineering was born,[2] had been unable to be properly implemented.

In June of 2001 the study was awarded to a consortium formed by the Chilean transport engineering consultancy firms Fernández y de Cea Ingenieros (FDC) and CIS Asociados Consultores en Transporte. In this consortium CIS was mostly in charge of collecting the data while FDC was to be in charge of the central aspects of the modeling process. The latter firm was headed by two highly respected academics in transport engineering who had been working both as functionaries and as consultants with SECTRA and the MTT since the mid-1980s, and had also been in charge of the previous phases of this study. The difference now was that the inclusion of the study as one key component of a proper policy such as Transantiago would provide the consultants with an opportunity to finally test in reality the sophisticated conceptual devices they had been developing for more than two decades, and for which they had received significant academic recognition.

Felix Castillo, a transport engineer working on SECTRA at the time, recalled the relevance of their involvement in the study in the following terms:

[These studies] have been developing for many years, a lot of methods, a lot of research; and a lot of applied research has been developed looking to explain the behavior of users in a transport system, and many computational models have been developed, mathematical algorithms that tried to explain this behavior. ... For this reason if you ask me about the process of Transantiago I think it started well before the Lagos government, it initiates with ... I don't know, in order not to go too far away, in the eighties, when the first transport models were developed and calibrated here in Chile, there was a huge amount of work at the universities, at the [University of] Chile, at Catholic [University], by many academics from the departments of transport engineering that participated in this.

His words elicit the very intimate relation between policy proponents and their technical counterparts that characterizes the transport planning area in Chile.[3] Such intimacy recalls what Van Egmond and Bal (2011) label *boundary configuration* or "strongly situated interconnections between science and policy institutions that share a specific approach to problem definitions and methods and that are embedded in, and at the same time embed, specific social, discursive, and material elements" (108). Besides easing everyday collaboration, such an arrangement has the key political effect of excluding any actor and/or human device that is not able to *talk* in the specific kind of language developed by the consultants/policymakers over the years, practically insulating them from any criticism coming from outside the core of the research team. In practice there was such a symbiosis between these transport engineering academics and the technical personnel from MOPTT and SECTRA that the entrance into the design process of third parties carrying a different kind of expertise became almost unthinkable; they had built a very strong boundary of concepts, academic papers, mathematical algorithms, computer software, and so on that no other actor was able to get past.

The first task the consultants had to deal with in order to develop the model was to have a valid commensuration of the main elements of the current system, in particular public transport demand. This they developed by implementing transport engineers' preferred research tool: an origin-destination survey. This survey, known as EOD-Buses, consisted of the application of a questionnaire to users of public transport buses while they were traveling on them. Fieldwork was carried out in two waves (October-December of 2001 and March-May of 2002) and ended up collecting more than 110,000 individual inputs, each one corresponding to a complete journey. For most participants in the process, a sample of this size along with the application of sophisticated sampling methods gave the resulting dataset an unquestionable validity as speaking for the real users of surface public transport in 2001–2002. As Felix Castillo concluded, with this approach "you have completely characterized the demand" for this period.

Castillo's statement can be seen as a good example of what Desrosieres (2001) calls "metrological realism," or an attitude toward data and statistics that rests on the belief in "the existence of a reality that may be invisible but is permanent ... above all, this reality is independent of the observation apparatus" (341). In connecting this objective reality with the scientific data, the law of large numbers occupies a central role, serving "as an operator for the transformation and transition from the world of observations to the world of generalization, extrapolation, and forecasting" (ibid.). Thus in this case the size of the sample, and the rigor in the application of method, appeared to warrant "that this was an objective process which would produce a socially and technically optimal solution, freed from stakeholder politics" (Goulden and Dingwall 2012, 4). Along with the strong boundary configuration of the research team, metrological realism gave a layer of facticity to the dataset, making it almost unquestionable to any external actor, even to the members of the DTS.

However, as an analysis of the reports produced by the consultants reveals (FDC and CIS 2003), the production of the dataset was neither automatic nor straightforward. Consider the problems found in applying the main object through which data collection was carried out: the EOD-Buses survey questionnaire. As can be seen in figure 3.1, the questionnaire asked the person being interviewed to provide certain information about her trips and other details. But this information had to be provided in a very particular way in order to be able fit into the questionnaire and, by doing this, perform a valid ODS.

First, and in relation to geographical space, ODS always travel from one delimited origin to a particular destination, the route being irrelevant as long as it is the fastest and/or cheapest available (Schiefelbusch 2010). For this reason, in order to perform an ODS the interviewee had to provide exact information regarding the points of origin and destination of her trip: the closest street intersection and the borough of the point where she started her trip, the point where she boarded the bus (in which the interview was being carried out), the point where she was going to leave the bus, and her final destination. In the second place, she had to provide exact information about the hour at which she started and was expecting to finish her trip, to the very minute. Finally, she had to choose among three reasons for her trip and provide an estimate of her family income.

To perform such calculative agency was not easy for an important number of interviewees, as shown in the summary of the survey pre-test (FDC and CIS 2003, ch. 4, 21–37). First, for many of them it was difficult to differentiate between the overall starting/ending point of their trip and the point at which they took/left the bus, with the consequence that "49% declared that their origin or destination corresponds with the point of getting on or off the bus" (ch. 4, 34). Along with this, "in many cases the intersection [provided by the interviewee] did not appear in the available geographical grid" (ch. 4, 46), forcing the actors in charge of the fieldwork and coding to translate these answers into points that could be added to the dataset. Second, in regard to time, the pre-test revealed that it was difficult for interviewees to provide the exact times at which they started their trips and/or the times at which they expected to finish. Most of the interviewees had "a tendency to state the values of their start of trip as multiples of 30 minutes (7:00, 7:30, 8:00 and 8:30 minutes)" (FDC and CIS 2003, ch. 5, 17). This situation, labeled as a "problem of perception" on the part of the users, ended

MINISTERIO DE PLANIFICACIÓN Y COOPERACIÓN · MIDEPLAN
COMISIÓN DE PLANIFICACIÓN DE INVERSIONES EN INFRAESTRUCTURA DE TRANSPORTE
Secretaría Ejecutiva SECTRA

ENCUESTA ORIGEN - DESTINO A PASAJEROS DE BUSES

1. DATOS GENERALES

Fecha		2001	Código de Ficha		N° Encuestado	Hora Encuesta	:

2. DATOS ASOCIADOS AL ORIGEN DEL VIAJE

At what corner did you take the bus? → ¿En qué esquina se subió al BUS?

| Calle1 | | Comuna | Cod. Zona |
| Calle2 | | | Cod. Comuna |

What is the closest corner to where you started your trip; NOT where you took the bus, but where you initially started? → ¿Cuál es la esquina mas cercana dónde inició su viaje; NO donde se subió al BUS, sino donde inicialmente partió?

| Calle1 | | Comuna | Cod. Zona |
| Calle2 | | | Cod. Comuna |

At what time did you start your trip? / Did you reach the bus by walking? → ¿A qué hora inició su viaje? : ¿Al bus llega a pié? 1. si ☐ 2. No ☐

If not by walking, how did you reach it? → ¿Si no llega a pié, como llegó? 1. Auto ☐ 3. Metro ☐ 5. Bus rural ☐ 7. Metrotren ☐ 2. Taxi ☐ 4. Bus ☐ 6. Taxi colectivo ☐ Cod

3. DATOS ASOCIADOS AL DESTINO DEL VIAJE

At what corner are you going to leave the bus? → ¿En qué esquina se bajará del BUS?

| Calle1 | | Comuna | Cod. Zona |
| Calle2 | | | Cod. Comuna |

What is the closest corner to the place where you are going to finish your trip? → ¿Cuál es la esquina mas cercana dónde terminará su viaje?

| Calle1 | | Comuna | Cod. Zona |
| Calle2 | | | Cod. Comuna |

At what time do you normally finish your trip? / Will you reach your final destination by walking? → ¿A qué hora normalmente termina su viaje? : ¿Al destino final llega caminando? 1. si ☐ 2. No ☐

If not by walking, how will you reach it? → ¿Si no llega a pié, como llegará? 1. Auto ☐ 3. Metro ☐ 5. Bus rural ☐ 7. Metrotren ☐ 2. Taxi ☐ 4. Bus ☐ 6. Taxi colectivo ☐ Cod

4. CONSULTA DEL NIVEL DE INGRESO FAMILIAR Y PROPOSITO DE VIAJE

What is the reason for your trip? → ¿Cuál es el propósito del viaje? Estudio ☐ Trabajo ☐ Otro ☐ Cod.

What is your family's income range? (only WORK and OTHERS) → ¿Cuál es el Rango de Ingreso Líquido del Grupo Familiar? (sólo TRABAJO Y OTROS) Cod.

0-55.000	☐	250.001 - 350.000	☐	800.001 - 1.000.000	☐
55.001 - 105.500	☐	350.001 - 450.000	☐	más de 1.000.000	☐
105.501 - 160.000	☐	450.001 - 600.000	☐	No Sabe	☐
160.001 - 250.000	☐	600.001 - 800.000	☐	No Responde	☐

NOTA: La información solicitada es confidencial y sólo se utilizará para fines estadísticos.

Figure 3.1
Origin-Destination Buses survey questionnaire. Image reproduced with permission from SECTRA; translation by the author.

up producing entries that were deemed "not adequate to correctly deduce the intervals of analysis" (ibid.). Finally, most interviewees had problems in providing their family income; as the study recognizes, "this is the question that … presents the highest rate of omission" (FDC and CIS 2003, ch. 4, 31).

Then, "contrary to what the etymology of the unfortunate term 'data' suggests, very few 'data' are actually 'given.' … Coding always involves sacrificing something with a view to the subsequent use of a standardized variable" (Desrosieres 2001, 347). Coding, and commensuration in general, always involve transformations in order to make decisions and judgments, and this particular survey was no exception. As with any other mobilization, becoming a valid entry in the dataset demanded that the people interviewed perform a very particular kind of user of public transport, a highly calculative agency able to rapidly provide quite detailed information about several aspects of her trip, including quantifications. Any failure to do so resulted in being excluded from the dataset: "incomplete listings, and others that could not be located in the dataset of the field map, were eliminated" (FDC and CIS 2003, ch. 4, 52).

The result of applying this particular technical device was the enacting of an individual who behaved in the way transport engineering's theory on user behavior (a part of which was developed by Chilean practitioners) expected her to behave: as a calculative agency whose movements from single origins to single destinations in the city were the result of a sequence of choices guided by rational judgments of time and costs involved. Such a position was clearly stated by Jorge Bravo, an engineer working for FDC:

The models of user behavior are more or less standard; for example there are different decisions to make when taking a trip. Whether to take or not to take the trip is a decision of trip generation, and once you have decided to make the trip you have to choose your destination, a decision of trip distribution, and once you have decided the destination you have to decide, and this does not mean that these decisions are sequential, by what mode you are going to reach it, the modal partition of the trips, and once you have decided all these you have to decide what route of the corresponding network you are going to use. The sum of all these decisions by the user is modeled.

These sequential judgments are always ultimately directed toward using "the services provided such that [the users'] own private utilities are maximized" (Fernández, de Cea, and Malbrán 2008, 953), meaning in practice that the ODS will always select from the available transport means the one that offers the fastest and/or cheapest way to link two clearly defined locations.

Such a conclusion confirms Breslau and Yonay's (1999, 327) assertion that "external reality is not the starting point for building the model but is drawn on selectively when it can strengthen an assumption in the math." Any user not able to provide the exact data that would constitute an ODS was automatically transmuted into an invalid case and hence deleted. Such a deletion was only relative, though. Given its claims of being representative of the whole population of the city, we can see the dataset as standing not only for the interviewees who successfully completed the questionnaire but also "for the unruly or opaque, though also for the incomplete" (Sismondo 1999, 248), who are then normalized through the claims for metrological realism made by the consultants and their technical counterparts.

Once this population was available in the form of a large dataset, it was time to move to the next step: constructing a general model that would provide a valid representation of the public transport system of Santiago in the year 2001.

Such a task started with a conceptual phase, internally known as "physical design," in which the general characteristics of the system to be planned were set. This is the space in which the previous stock of knowledge about the issue was integrated into the process to provide guidelines for the structuration and calibration of the empirical data into a particular model configuration. Existing knowledge about the characteristics and problems of Santiago's public transport system was augmented by brief analyses of the public transport systems of a number of other cities. In general the process of setting these qualitative elements was quite easy, not least because of a boundary configuration that excluded any kind of controversial position.

Probably the only aspect that was, briefly, controversial at this stage was the issue of transfers. Unlike the existing public transport system, the proposed network structure would necessarily require passengers to transfer between trunk and feeder bus lines and Metro lines in order to reach most destinations. The people at SECTRA were aware that these transfers were going to represent a novelty many users would resist and were initially worried about their effect on the general performance of the system. In particular, they initially feared that numerous users were going to give up on the system, preferring other means of transport (mainly cars), which would create a financial black hole. In the end, however, such a possibility was canceled by introducing one particular assumption into the modeling process: the concept of the user as *captive* of the public transport system. This meant that the user was performed as someone who did not have any alternative to using public transport for her daily trips, a point already made in the original PTUS proposal. This was explicitly stated in the call for tenders with the affirmation that the new system reconfiguration "will not produce any significant changes in the public/private modal partition, nor in the distribution of trips in public transport" (MIDEPLAN 2001, 9). In practice this assumption made irrelevant for the modeling process any question regarding the reaction of users to the new system, especially in terms of possible resistance to transfer between different services. Whether the users liked it or not, they were going to demand public transport in more or less the same way as before. In the end, the possible negative reactions were introduced as a fixed extra amount for each transfer in the total travel cost experienced by the users.

Along with settling these conceptual issues, a key task was to quantify several components of the proposed integrated system, mainly in terms of the numbers of main routes to be served by the trunk buses and the number and grouping of the feeder services. Taking as a basis the data from the EOD-Buses, a new bus route network was proposed based on assigning a bus route to each origin-destination arc with a certain level of demand. After testing different options, the network was divided into 10 zones, each served internally by feeder lines and interconnected by trunk lines.

During a subsequent phase, known as "operational design," the idea was to determine the best frequencies and the size of the fleet necessary to run each route. These frequencies were going to be found at the point at which the implementation of the system reduced the social cost to its lowest levels.[4] In order to calculate these social costs, three different sets of elements were needed: (1) the production costs of the services, (2) the value assigned by users to their travel times, and (3) the value of the externalities produced by the system, like accidents, congestion, or air pollution. After that, and taking into consideration each element at different magnitudes, the idea was to arrive at a certain future scenario that minimized the general social costs of the system through a selection of determinate frequencies of service and number of vehicles with a certain capacity for each bus route of the city.

In relation to users, the design model needed to commensurate exactly how the demand was going to be distributed among the different bus and Metro lines of the network. In order to provide these quantities, a specific model was produced to simulate user behavior, known as a "model for the assignation of multimodal public transport networks," based mainly on previous work by the consultants.

In this model the user was scripted as someone who was going to select her route of travel based on her rational appreciation of the costs involved in the process, with the aim of minimizing them as much as she could. These costs were represented in terms of the money spent for each trip (through fares) and the time involved in all the stages of it, from departure at the origin to arrival at the destination. The equilibrium was found at the point at which "for each origin-destination pair, all the used routes will have the same generalized (minimal) costs and all the nonselected will have the same or bigger generalized costs than the minimum" (FDC and CIS 2003, ch. 2, 18). Thus the user appeared as a perfectly informed non-cooperative rational actor who always chose the route that minimized her costs, costs that were mainly a translation into standard monetary units of the time used.

This model, represented in figure 3.2, can be read as follows: the users' selection (Cg^{modo}) of each particular route/arc of transport, whether bus or Metro, is a function of the value of the sum of traveling times (*tv*), the relative weights of waiting times (*pwait*) multiplied by a function of waiting times (in brackets), the relative weights of walking time (*pwalk*) multiplied by the absolute walking access time (*tc*), and the fare (*tarifa*) divided by the traveler's value of time (*vtime*) of each particular means. The main operation of this human device is to provide a mechanism to sum up the time each user devoted to traveling from one origin to one destination and a particular fare, producing a user's valuation for each route of public transport that could be used to predict the demand each route would face.

The first interesting aspect of the assignation model is that it presupposed that users experienced time in different ways while traveling. In the model this difference was materialized by the relative weights of *pwait* and *pwalk*, while traveling time (*tv*) was introduced without a weight. The relative values of waiting time and walking time were mobilized from the consultants' previous research on the topic, as can be seen in figure 3.3. What this little box did was crucial. It performed a user of public transport who perceived time in three different ways while traveling, waiting for a bus/

$$Cg^{modo} = tv + pwait \cdot \left[\frac{\alpha}{d_s} + \beta \cdot \left(\frac{V_s + \widetilde{V}_s}{K_s} \right)^n \right] + pwalk \cdot tc + \frac{1}{vtime} \cdot tarifa$$

Figure 3.2
Model for the assignment of multimodal public transport networks. Image reproduced with permission from SECTRA.

Tabla 6-5: Parámetros calibrados

vtime_nml	3,62
pwalk	1,93
pwait	3,63

Fuente: Elaboración propia.

Figure 3.3
Parameters of walking and waiting times. Image reproduced with permission from SECTRA.

Metro to come, and walking between transit stop and origin or final destination. Also, and probably more important, it assigned a quantification to these different perceptions. Under the heading "calibrated parameters" it assigned an average value of 3.62 to traveling time for bus users, while the relative weights of walking time and waiting time were set at 1.93 and 3.63 respectively. Given these commensurations, the user of public transport performed by the model was someone who perceived walking and waiting time as two and almost four times longer than the time involved in properly traveling.

Even though it was central for the modeling of Transantiago, very little information was provided in the report about the origins of this commensuration. There were no complex functions, no conceptual discussion, just an earlier box stating the different values of time for bus and Metro users (from which the value of 3.62 was taken) that also had no major reference. The box, and the crucial information contained in it, were only supported by the note "Source: made by authors" at the bottom and a mention two pages earlier that several elements of this section were based on previous research by the consultants for SECTRA (especially FDC 1997).[5]

The box and its contents were mainly supported by the consultants' expertise in these issues, an authority that allowed them to mobilize these commensurations as solid, self-explicating entities. This mobilization clearly shows us the model functioning as an "inscription device" (Latour and Woolgar 1986) that had become increasingly black-boxed with each successive use, leaving behind its origin as the result of the application of particular methods in particular locations and becoming almost undeniable *fact* about society. This black-boxing implied that, for several of the participants in the process, the values provided by the consultants became the *real* temporal perception of public transport in Santiago by its users.[6] As a consequence, these users would always tend to select bus and Metro lines that involved little walking time and, especially, waiting time, even if their absolute traveling times were longer than they would have been with alternative routes.

Applying these commensurations to the original model, the consultants produced an estimate of the likelihood of users selecting different bus or Metro lines. This modeled user was finally performed as a rational consumer of public transport who had perfect information about her whereabouts, was differentiated by her family income and reason for travel, was probably angry about transfers but "captive" of public transport, valued public transport only as a matter of lesser monetary/temporal cost, and perceived time in differentiated ways, along with a few other attributes.

After this model was tested by producing a description that was deemed accurate for the current public transport network of the city, the next stage was to start producing different "scenarios" of future configurations of the public transport network to guide the decision-making process. But in order to decide between these different scenarios, a complementary model was necessary: the business model.

The Low-Income Consumer

The business model had the main aim of sketching a new financial ordering for the public transport system of Santiago, including all the relevant innovations planned by Transantiago: feeder and trunk bus lines, a single fare, total integration with the Metro, etc. Compared to engineering models, business models are less focused on commensuration and more on providing "a set of generic level descriptors of how a firm organises itself to create and distribute value in a profitable manner" (Baden-Fuller and Morgan 2010, 157). In doing so, this kind of model aims at "demonstrating its feasibility and worth to the partners whose enrolment [was] needed" (Doganova and Eyquem-Renault 2009, 1568).

In particular, the business model of Transantiago was given the key role of being the device through which private actors would be enrolled to run key components of the system, especially trunk and feeder bus fleets. Eduardo Cano, a high authority of the MOPTT at the time, recalled some of the complexities involved in this operation:

The difficulty that we had in the DTS was how we could set up a business, a tendering process in which the serious companies of the world and Chile would participate, and how we could manage it so that the current micreros took it seriously and organized to participate, because we found it a little unrealistic to make tenders in which all the micreros collapsed and the big French company arrived ... or we found it little palatable in political terms, besides being risky for the government, because we didn't want to end up in the hands of a French company ... so we advanced little by little, amidst everyone we polished a business model.

This suggests that the business model of Transantiago was performative in a double sense, because it looked not only to build a representation of the new financial structure of the public transport system but also to enact "the public of the demonstration" (Doganova and Eyquem-Renault 2009, 1568), the professional transport entrepreneurs who would run the system, ideally a mixture of "civilized" micreros (now operating as conventional public transport companies) and foreign companies.

In order to implement the model, a group called the Business Unit (BU) was set up inside the Coordinación de Transantiago (CdT).[7] This unit was formed mainly by actors with previous experience in running tendering processes for infrastructural projects from the MOP during the 1990s, an experience widely perceived as a success (Engel, Fischer, and Galetovic 2000). Before it started properly working on the model, the BU focused on clarifying the main standards that were going to frame it. Besides the ones coming directly from their previous experience, there were several others proposed by the members of the DTS, such as the need to create competitive and transparent tendering processes, and the need to introduce new buses, less polluting technologies, etc. Above these particular issues, there were two key restrictions coming directly from the central government that had to be respected at all costs.

On the one hand, there was a limit on the level of the government's involvement. As stated in the PTUS, and in accordance with the neoliberal component in the "growth with equity" model, under no circumstance would the government directly provide any kind of surface public transport services. Along with this, and especially relevant for the design of the business model, the government would not set any kind of temporary or permanent subsidy, so perforce the new system had to be financially autonomous in the long run. In practice this meant that the business model had to enact a financially self-contained system, a system whose revenues covered, at least, all its costs.

Patricio Fierro, an engineer from the BU, explained the other restriction in the following terms:

There was also the presidential mandate that the fare would not increase ... that on average the Chilean family wouldn't pay more. ... Maybe the people would have been willing to pay slightly more for something better, but this was never an option, we never thought about it, because the president said that the cost [of public transport] in relation to the income of Chilean families would not increase, and it is difficult to say "No, the president is wrong" [laughs]. It was complicated ... besides it was also a matter of how arrogant we were. ... When there is technocracy ... it is difficult to say "I can't," and you will never have proof that it wasn't possible. So you fight, you keep fighting to see if it's possible. ... I mean, "Look: what we want; what we have" and how we mix up these two things in order to become a single unity ... I have a system that has 7,000 buses, ok, and I want new buses and I want a different fare collection system because it's more safe, etc. etc., but all of this has costs; how can you increase the costs and maintain the fare? Well, by reducing the costs somewhere else, so what we did was a design that made the system more efficient, that cost less, then you could invest, reduce the costs and keep this [the fare] stable.

As Fierro recognizes, the second key standard, coming directly from President Lagos and much closer to the social democratic component of "growth with equity," was that the average fare of a trip must not increase compared to the existing public transport system. This limit was based on a performance of public transport users as largely low-income consumers who could not afford to spend more on public transport, a version similar to the one included in the diagnosis made in the PTUS. Given this situation, this restriction looked to protect them from the worsening in their quality of life that such extra expenditure would certainly have meant.

As the latter part of Fierro's comments recognizes, the acceptance of both restrictions by the actors from the BU was not only based on their imposition from the central government. Besides this they were taken as a technical challenge, as a way for the BU to prove its capacities by delivering an improvement in the system's functioning based only on rational planning. The basis of the business model was an argument about inefficiency and how optimization could improve things. The starting point was the widely shared crisis diagnosis of the former system as highly inefficient in economic and technical terms. Given this, its complete optimization as proposed by the PTUS would be able to free enough funds to implement all the necessary improvements in the system without the need of either a permanent public subsidy or a rise in passenger fares.

Taking these restrictions as given, the BU actors produced several drafts of the business model that were discussed with the DTS and external consultants; then they returned to the drawing board to rework the model in accordance with their suggestions. Finally the sixth draft, produced in July of 2003, was accepted. Like most business models it was formed by two key elements: a "narrative [that] draws a world and justifies the selection of the entities to be taken into account ... [and a] calculation [that] detaches and associates these entities to create new ones, which are then stabilized and transformed into the characters of the story told" (Doganova and Eyquem-Renault 2009, 1567).

The narrative part, after describing Transantiago in general terms, proposed the business model as an "operational scheme of the system" (CdT 2003, 16). This operational scheme was formed by multiple entities grouped into costs (running costs, infrastructures, etc.) and revenues (fares). Both components were then located in a common frame defined by the assertion that "the relationship between revenues and costs must be as close as possible to equilibrium" (CdT 2003, 18). Such equilibrium was especially relevant for a situation in which costs were bigger than revenues, because it would force the state to directly intervene, providing the funds lacking, given its position as guarantor of the economic feasibility of the system for the private entrepreneurs who were going to run it.

After this narrative, the business model was presented in the calculative form shown in figure 3.4. This model can be read as follows: the fare paid by users (t_i^T) multiplied by the demand for public transport over a certain period T (Q_j^T) is equal to the sum (C_i^T) of the variable (CV_i) and fixed (CF_i) costs of the period T plus payments for former deficits (P_{i-1}) minus other revenues of the period (OI_{i-1}^T). This calculation then stabilizes the claim for equilibrium between the revenues and the costs of the system outlined in the narrative. To be viable in time, the system must necessarily find a way

$$t_i^T \cdot Q_j^T = C_i^T - OI_{i-1}^T \ (1)$$

$$C_i^T = CV_i + CF_i + P_{i-1} \ (2)$$

Figure 3.4
Mathematical formulation of the business model of Transantiago. Image reproduced with permission from the Directorate of Metropolitan Public Transport of Santiago (DTPM).

to balance revenues and costs internally, meaning without the intervention of the government, through variations on the included components. Given the expected reductions in the costs of the system through optimization, this balance should also be reached without increasing the system's fare, thus without affecting the incomes of the low-income consumers whom the government looked to protect.

In a later publication the business model was visually presented as in figure 3.5. This image again presents the system as operating in equilibrium mode: each passenger (presented here as "customers") pays a certain amount of money (fare) for each trip. These fares constitute the revenue of the system and are administered by a central entity, the Financial Administrator of Transantiago (AFT in Spanish), which uses it to pay for the system costs to the providers of services. The only difference with the model seen above can be found at the bottom of the image, where a mechanism to warrant the financial equilibrium of the system is included. This mechanism is based on a balance between revenues and costs in accordance with which

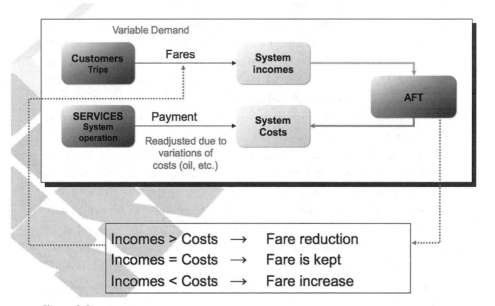

Figure 3.5
Visual representation of the business model of Transantiago (January 2004). Image reproduced with permission from the Directorate of Metropolitan Public Transport of Santiago (DTPM).

fares will increase or decrease in response to costs, securing the long-term financial sustainability of the system.

In practice, however, this mechanism was not always going to function this way. As we have seen, there was a presidential mandate that the fares of the system must not increase above their current levels. Thus the mechanism would only work as represented if the costs were less than or equal to the fares paid by users, paying the same fare for using Transantiago as they paid in the current system. If the fares were not enough to cover the costs of the new system, the only possible solution would be to reduce these costs. Then in practice the equilibrium mechanism of the business model was not a fare that went up and down in accordance with costs, but costs that must always be lower than or equal to the system's revenue.

Bad Habits

After the design model was tuned with a representation of the current situation, it started to be used to produce scenarios of possible future public transport system configurations. Each scenario mixed in different ways the multiple components of the future system identified in the "physical design" phase, such as the amount of infrastructure available, the number of transfers per trip, the fares, the size of the buses, the waiting times of users, etc. The scenario finally selected was going to become the blueprint out of which the exact number of buses needed to run every bus line would be determined, the most important component of the soon-to-be-published call for tenders for the management of each trunk and feeder bus area.

The FDC-CIS consultancy (2003) ended up producing eight scenarios for 2005, the year in which Transantiago was supposed to start. The last proposed scenario, labeled with the number 5.5, included all the characteristics of the new public system and established that the number of buses necessary to run the system was 5,152. However, the consultants stated clearly that the final choice of scenario could not be made solely based on the data from the EOD-Buses. Such data, they argued, had to be contrasted with information coming directly from the daily operation of the system in order to check whether the estimations were realistic. Or, in other words, ODS alone could not be used as spokespersons of the users of public transport. In order to produce accurate scenarios they had to be joined by other human devices, especially the ones produced by the inputs collected directly "on the street."

In mid-2003 the Transport Services Unit (TSU) of the CdT, formed by several engineers hired by Azócar, was put in charge of this task. Sylvia Miranda, a member of the unit, recalled the task in the following terms.

The first [scenarios were] ... a very engineering thing, very mathematic and hard, ok, these are the routes, or more or less this is the structure that the services must have. But we realized that we needed to take this to the field. What you made in the model is one thing; and another, very different, especially if it's a project that deals with people, is what happen with the users, the people. Then ... we started to work with the boroughs in order to ground the routes, to take them to the street. ... The model considered only a few streets in each area ... only the most important ones really. When you want to make a public transport system you have go to the small streets, where people really take the bus. We based [our corrections] on the networks existing before Transantiago ... because people are used to having the bus pass there, because people like to take it there or it's a habit ... but as I'm telling you, this means that the quantity of buses that you were going to use was bigger than what the model originally predicted because ... the real network was not covered by the number of buses [included in the available scenarios].

As Miranda recognized, the model was grounded by checking at the street level whether the broad parameters for each bus route included in scenario 5.5 were really offering a service of at least the same quality as the one already on existence. This exercise, based on field trips and meetings with both users and local authorities, ended up producing an alternative script of the user of public transport as a carrier of habits, as an individual who already had long-established ways of using public transport (regarding the amount of walking necessary to reach the bus stop, the average time needed for the next bus to come, etc.) that she didn't want to change.

Such a performance of the user was not trivial but represented an open challenge to the ODS. In line with most policymaking, transport planning has a strong negative conception of habits, regarding them "as something that attests largely to man's animal nature" (Grosz 2013, 233), a "mechanistic and automatic repetition of the same, which veils us from the world, inhibiting self-knowledge and understanding" (Bissell 2015, 129). Given this conception, "in much of ... transport research habit is frequently positioned as prohibiting informed decision making" (Middleton 2011, 2858) and thus becomes a major focus of reform in order to advance toward more rational orderings. Thus the ODS was expressly enacted as an entity without any kind of habits, a fully rationalized individual who was always willing to change her behavior in accordance with the available information and a cost/benefit calculation.

In contrast, the version of the user proposed by the TSU presented habits more "as resources for how people frame their everyday experiences ... as opposed to being shaped and informed by processes of rational decision making" (Middleton 2011, 2872). Habits in this view were part of a "virtual infrastructure" (Bissell 2015) that, like any other kind of infrastructure, had a certain obduracy (Hommels 2005) in the sense of resisting radical change no matter how much information was provided about the benefits of a change. For this reason any realistic scenario had to contemplate such habits, had to find a way to take them into account, to make then quantifiable, in the modeling process. Based on this approach, in August 2003 the TSU ended up producing scenario 6-200R which affirmed that, for the new system to offer a service of at least the same characteristics as the current public transport system at the local level, a fleet of 6,551 buses was needed.

The BU had a contrasting approach to this issue, as Fierro recalled.

The ones who had the leading role [in selecting the necessary bus fleet] were the Transport Services Unit, because they were translating the scenarios into something more tangible; these are going to be the routes, etc. etc. ... Then the truth is that at this moment we [the Business Unit] did not participate much. Later, when the business model started to settle in the call [for tenders], we started to have more relevance because ... transport designs have costs. ... Of course when we were making the balance of what goes in and how much it costs, we started to have more relevance regarding what [bus] frequency we were going to demand [from the proponents], why we were going to ask that much, etc., and then we started to have a more conflictive work, I would say, regarding what they want, how we can achieve that, and what we are able to pay.

For the BU the most important thing was to respect the business model, so the costs of the system could not exceed its revenues. This was based on the double restriction of a system without public subsidies and maintaining the same fare. However, based on their calculations, implementing and running a fleet of 6,551 buses would necessarily mean that the costs of the system would be higher than its revenues, forcing it either to increase the fare or ask for a subsidy. As neither option was feasible, the most probable outcome was that the system would operate in a situation of permanent financial default, making it highly unlikely that any private entrepreneur would be interested in running it. Thus scenario 6-200R was actively resisted by the BU from the very beginning.

Once the controversy was fully declared, the position of the BU in the organizational architecture of the CdT gave them an important advantage, as Miranda recalls.

When the people of the Business Unit arrived, [the CdT structure] started to be like a pyramid, I mean, it was the coordinator [on top], then came the Business Unit and then the rest … do you understand me? Then we were left below, it was like we depended on what the Business Unit said. … It was enraging but we could do nothing, we were there, we had an obstacle in the Business Unit, which should have been located on the same level as the rest, but it was up there. … Besides, they worked a lot with SECTRA; for example, even though we were the design area and I was seeing everything related to the model, [when the BU needed to know] the results, the demand and all these things, they didn't ask me, they went and directly asked SECTRA.

As the key actors in charge of setting the financial sustainability of Transantiago, the BU had privileged access to the head of the CdT, SECTRA, and the DTS, having constituted with them a further "boundary configuration" inside the organization, this time excluding other areas of the CdT. Given this, it was not difficult for its members to mobilize support for their position on the controversy, as recalled by Caridad Manzano, another member of the TSU at the time.

[We] designed Transantiago with more than 6,500 buses and with an important level of detail … but the result was that the numbers did not match, that the fare would be too high … and then … came [to CdT's offices] … an adviser of the MOPTT minister … and said to me in front of the coordinator that our team wouldn't keep doing designs, ok, that what we had done with these 6,500 buses was wrong, besides we were a bunch of fools because we put in so many buses, that [our scenario] was going to the rubbish bin and that SECTRA was going to make the designs from now on.

After discarding scenario 6-200R and working with FDC again, in August of 2004 SECTRA produced scenario 11, whose main novelty was that it "incorporates a series of modifications that were specified by the Technical Counterpart, aiming at adjusting the offer to the demand, improving the reach of the system, and correcting detected mistakes" (FDC 2004, 4). This adjustment was made by including the following standards in the model:[8]

I. Eliminate the excessive concurrence of trunk and feeder services in some sectors of the city.
II. Maintain the spatial coverage of the public transport network, widening it in some peripheral sectors.
III. Relax the minimum frequency criteria (from 6 to 5 vehicles per hour) in order to diminish the running costs.
IV. Diminish, as much as possible, the operating costs of the fleet (smaller fleets).
V. …
VI. In the peripheral zones, some services with a frequency less than the minimal (4 vehicles per hour) are going to be considered.

Thus the aim of "adjusting the offer to the demand" in practice meant that several quality standards present in scenario 6-200R were reduced or simply eliminated.

The main casualty from such an arrangement was the user as carrier of habits performed by the TSU. The system proposed by scenario 11 would be quite different from the existing one, especially in terms of a substantive reduction in the number of buses and the consequent increase in waiting times at bus stops. But, and following the ODS performed by the design model, this longer waiting time would be compensated by a network that "maintains the spatial coverage of the public transport network, widening it in some peripheral sectors." Thus there was not going to be an increase in the walking time of users. Such a situation, along with the expected improvements in travel times, would compensate for the increase in waiting times, maintaining the social costs of the new system. Given that the ODS has no habits, it was never asked whether all these changes in travel routes could cause any kind of resistance on the part of users.

The smaller bus fleet of scenario 11 was going to have a second consequence in terms of the habits of public transport users: it would necessarily mean that they were going to travel in more uncomfortable conditions than in the existing system. Because of the substantial reduction in the fleet size, each bus was expected to carry many more passengers than in the existing system, so they were designed to have more standing spaces and fewer seats. As a consequence, and in contrast with an existing system in which it was relatively common to travel seated in sparsely occupied buses, the user traveling in Transantiago was going to face overcrowding, most of the time also involving standing up for the whole trip.

Such inconvenience was not perceived as affecting the general performance of the system because the design model did "not include overcrowding in the calculus of the social benefit. Thus, it was not able to 'see' that a solution in which people travel with less overcrowding is better for users than one in which the vehicles travel at full capacity" (Quijada et al. 2007, 45). If overcrowding (or any other commensuration of discomfort) does not exist for the ODS, then the fleet can be reduced until the costs of running it become equal to the revenues of the system (because, as we have seen, the demand was "captive" no matter the service given) without the social benefits of the scenario being affected in any way.

All these adaptations were possible thanks to a key characteristic of models: even though they usually "do not meet criteria for realistic correspondence, [models] ... might still be empirically adequate to a restricted set of data" (Sismondo 2000, 246). Given this, models and their results are evaluated as good and functional if their predictions match with the set of data used to produce them, even if such data collide with other representations of reality available. This is what Boumans (1999) refers to as the built-in justification of scientific models, meaning that the acceptance of the results of a certain model is not derived from the mere *concordance* or *fit* between the model and all kinds of data (understood as different versions of reality), but is produced along with the results that the model offers. In practice what is relevant is the model's internal consistency, the way a model relates and coordinates the particular set of entities (data, visions of the world, actors, etc.) involved in the modeling process. Whether it is able to enact realities beyond such a process is ultimately secondary.

This is especially so in fields like transport planning, as Goulden and Dingwall recognized:

In fields like transport, with distant time horizons, the accuracy or otherwise of predictions can often only be determined long after the planning exercise has ceased to concern policy makers. The crucial goal is the legitimation of decision-making in the present that can justify the investment decisions that need to be made if the future is to happen at all. The important criterion for evaluating approaches to modelling is, then, their ability to generate a perception of accuracy: the futures created must appear plausible, both within their own logic and within that of a contemporary audience. (Goulden and Dingwall 2012, 8)

To be successful, models don't need to be accurate in the long run, but they need to convince the current audience about the accuracy of the scenarios/futures they project. In this case the prestige of the consultants involved, the boundary configuration of their working practices, and the metrological realism given to the data were more than enough to lend the model an aura of accuracy difficult to challenge, even by actors with significant political power.

In the end the actors from the BU plus SECTRA and FDC were able to simply exclude any human device that did not match the ones embedded in the design and business models, such as the one enacting users as carriers of habits. Their only limit was that the proposed scenario had to match with the EOD-Buses dataset and the restrictions embedded in the business model (no subsidy, no increase in fares). And given that they had produced such data themselves, their only task was to increase and decrease the number of buses necessary to run the system until reaching a point of "equilibrium": scenario 11.

Scenario 11 was able, at last, to coordinate the two main human devices behind the plan, a rational ODS and a low-income consumer. Out of such coordination emerged the most pervasive script of the user of Transantiago, at least until February 10, 2007: the *fare and time optimizer*, or a calculative low-income individual who always prioritized low fares and traveling times when using public transport, having no habits or comfort demands whatsoever. For the fare and time optimizer the arrangement proposed by scenario 11 was ideal, because it would allow her to pay the same fare as in the previous system for using a completely new public transport system, with the only cost being longer waiting times that would be compensated with shorter traveling times. The expected overcrowding was irrelevant, since the fare and time optimizer was unable to put a value on it.

Finally, scenario 11's reduction of the fleet to 4,532 buses was considered enough to warrant that the system's revenues would at least equal its costs without the need of increased fares, so it was approved by the BU and then taken as the basis for the definitive call for tenders for the management of bus routes that was published in November of that year. In January of 2005 the management of each of the five packages of trunk lines and the ten feeder areas was assigned to a mixture of former micreros reorganized as "modern" companies and prestigious foreign companies, the whole process being evaluated as a great success.

However, and given that we are here analyzing Transantiago in several different configurations, the "success" of the modeling process cannot only be evaluated internally. As Sismondo (1999) noted, models travel, they usually move to different places, some of them quite unexpected for their creators. In policy assemblages such mobility is usually related to models moving from infrastructuration to other configurations of the assemblage, especially the ones involving the territorialization and deterritorialization of the futures proposed during the modeling. It is during these mobilizations that the ultimate "success" of models should be evaluated, in their capacity to perform the futures they describe. In this case such success was going to be found in a public transport system that, functioning without subsidies and fare increases, was populated by fare and time optimizers who were always making calculations about the better way to travel. Such a system would deterritorialize, once and for all, any traces of habits, with the users enthusiastically able to change any aspect of their trips (even comfort) if certain gains in terms of time and money were involved. Such a new ordering would allow the proper enacting of the governmentality promised by the PTUS (minus the active citizen part): a world-class public transport system populated by different kinds of happy users and governed by a watchful, but not too nosy, state, the perfect world-class society. The rest of the book will be devoted to seeing to what extent such a future was (de-) territorialized.

4   Disruption

A Human Sea

With the passage of time the launch date of Transantiago started to be seen with increasing levels of anxiety by the actors involved. It was becoming clear for them that to assemble a system of this scale and complexity was a task much more challenging than expected. Not only had several single key components proven quite difficult to produce on their own, but also there were many doubts about how they would work together. Besides, given temporal and financial pressures, in most cases there was no chance to set up experimental laboratory-like tests to try them beforehand. In practice Transantiago was mostly going to be an "in vivo" experiment (Muniesa and Callon 2007) whose ultimate results were quite difficult to predict beforehand.

For these reasons the launch date was postponed twice, a couple of months each time, in order to have more time to deal with some critical issues. Some of the actors involved even claimed that more time was necessary, that there was no way to solve all the existing problems in just a few extra months. But at that point the system had acquired such a degree of momentum, in Hughes's terms, that it reacted "against abrupt changes in the line of development" (Hughes 1983, 465). There were ads on TV, contracts to respect, international visitors scheduled. So the final starting date was set for Saturday, February 10, 2007, not a day later.

Given this, the only hope for the actors involved was to "cross the desert" as soon as possible, as a high authority of the MTT[1] at the time claimed in our interview. They knew the first days and weeks were going to be difficult, not only for the users but for a whole city that would have to learn to live with a completely new way to organize public transport from one day to the next. So several contingency measures were introduced to deal with the expected problems, like having an extra number of police officers on the street and developing security measures to deal with massive use of the Metro. With them, along with the fact that the level of public transport use was reduced by 60% due to the summer holidays, the government hoped to be able to contain and correct the emerging issues relatively fast and reach a normal state in a matter of months, at the latest.

But the situation they found after just a few hours of functioning was beyond their grimmest expectations. As an example we can see the testimony of Cecilia Prieto, a transport authority of the borough of Lo Barnechea, on the east side of the city. This borough, with a mix of high- and low-income population, tends to receive an important amount of service workers during the weekend. For this reason on that morning she went to Cantagallo, the busiest node of the borough, to check the situation.

I remember perfectly that around 8:30 in the morning of that Saturday the first trunk [bus] arrives full, full, but full, full up to the roof ... it started on a Saturday, where it was understood that on Saturdays people rest, but they didn't realize that Saturday is a day that has a lot of movement and [the trunk bus] arrives full, full, full and then one of these little [feeder] buses arrives, this was like David and Goliath, and then all the people at Cantagallo ... I swear that I had the sensation that the people crashed and it was the survival of the fittest, and I'm telling you that it was 8:30 in the morning of the first day, and then I was expecting that they were going to flip over the bus, then some were able to go inside the bus and it started, carrying three-quarters of the passengers outside ... I stayed in Cantagallo until 9:00 at night, Cantagallo was a human sea and the people didn't know how to travel.

It wasn't a "desert," then, that the system had to cross toward normality, but "a human sea" that flooded almost immediately the very limited buses and Metro trains available, leaving thousands of users without any means of travel.

Such a situation, repeated in almost exactly the same terms throughout the city, transformed Transantiago almost immediately into the biggest disruption the transport system of Santiago had ever experienced. From the very first hours the actors in charge of the process faced dozens of serious overflows as several components of the system started to behave in unexpected ways or were simply missing: there were not enough buses on the streets, the software to control the bus fleet was not operational, the contactless payment card failed massively, people had very little information about how to use the system, and so on (for a summary on the technical failures experienced by the system see Muñoz and Gschwender 2008). The situation was made more critical given that several of these issues cascaded into each other, resulting in almost every aspect of the system being affected. As one high authority recalled in our interview, even actors who had been involved in the plann ing of the system for years experienced a sensation of "brutal disorientation."[2]

Given these circumstances, it was hardly expectable that the human device in-scripted during infrastructuration, the fare and time optimizer, was ever going to emerge. In its place, and intimately connected with the overflowings of the system, the contact between the city's inhabitants and the system enacted two particular human devices. The first was the "flesh and blood" user enacted by the millions of inhabitants who wanted to travel through the city using the technologies of the plan. The second was the "mediated" version of the user enacted by Chilean and international media outlets in their coverage of the situation. As we will see, both were deeply ingrained in the transformation of Transantiago from a public policy of the transport area to one of biggest controversies that any Chilean government has faced since the return of democracy in 1990.

Discomforted Bodies

Such feelings of brutal disorientation were shared, using the widest possible selection of synonyms, by the daily users of public transport who participated in the fieldwork on which this book is based. Almost without exception they recalled their first days and weeks using Transantiago (in most cases up to the moment when fieldwork was carried out, several months later) as an utterly confusing, even nightmarish, period. To the critical lack of buses on the streets were added several other problems that made reaching their usual destinations, even with hours of delay, quite challenging. First they had to acquire and put some credit on a new contactless card called a Bip! card to pay for their trips, replacing the usual payment in cash; top-up places for the Bip! card were quite scarce (especially in the periphery) and few users knew where to find them. Then they had to make sense of a completely reshuffled route network in which all the previous bus routes had been replaced by new ones, usually involving combinations between different kinds of bus lines and/or the Metro. Once on the street, they had to walk to newly established bus stops, usually located quite far away from each other, to wait for their buses, ending the micreros' long-established practice of just stopping the bus at any point on its route, even in the middle of a street crossing. Once at the bus stops, they had to deal with a completely new, and quite complex, graphic information system to obtain any extra information. Then they had to wait, uncertain when the bus was going to come or whether it was going to come at all. As the bus finally approached, usually after they had been waiting several minutes, they had to fight with the other people at the bus stop to reach its doors and enter. If they were lucky enough to get inside the bus, they needed to hope that the device validating the availability of funds on the Bip! card was functioning and after that travel the whole way standing up, with the bus usually completely packed. Then at some point they would have to get off and transfer to another of the new bus lines and/or the Metro, starting the whole process all over again.

In all, for most users the start of Transantiago shattered the habits they had developed during years of using public transport in the city, forcing them to rebuild them anew from one day to the next. Even a short local trip carried high degrees of uncertainty, not only regarding the time of arrival but almost every aspect of it. What made everything more difficult—and in this sense the script developed during infrastructuration was quite right—was that most of them really did not have an alternative to using public transport, at least at the beginning. They were utterly "captives" of Transantiago and experienced this in the most straightforward sense: as a forced suppression of liberty that they had to endure somehow.

When they were asked about the experience of "incorporating" (Hayles 1999) Transantiago, there was one particular critique that appeared time and time again, occupying the most prominent place in their narratives. However, and contrary to the scripts developed during infrastructuration (especially during the modeling process seen in chapter 3), this critique had nothing to do with time or money. Although from the very beginning Transantiago operated with speeds that were far lower than expected (even lower than the previous system's) and the fares remained unchanged, complaining fare and time optimizers failed to materialize when evaluating the plan. Instead, the valuation that rarely failed to occupy center stage when talking about the system was how *incómodo* (uncomfortable) it was.

Such a valuation commonly started out of a surprising judgment: how relatively comfortable the former system was. Contrary to the version of the user enacted in the PTUS, during fieldwork people usually remembered the former system with a certain fondness, even tenderness. Although they all recognized that micreros were a nuisance, several other aspects of the system received a very positive evaluation, especially in terms of comfort. Usually bus routes passed quite close to their homes, the frequency was high so they didn't have to wait long, they could stop and access/leave the bus wherever they wanted, they could negotiate with the driver if they had less money than the fare, and, especially, they were usually able to travel seated during the whole trip given the large bus fleets operating, without the need to combine with other buses or Metro along the way given that most routes crossed the whole city.

In contrast, Transantiago was usually seen as utterly *incómodo*. Walking to the bus stops was *incómodo*. Waiting for the bus was *incómodo*. Traveling in packed buses was *incómodo*. Making combinations between different lines and/or with the Metro was *incómodo*. The packed Metro trains were *incómodos*. With only one relevant exception,[3] every single component of the system was labeled as *incómodo* at several points during our interviews. Especially after a couple of weeks of functioning, when the brutal disorientation of the first days had somewhat receded, what was left of the experience of incorporating a user of Transantiago was how *incómodo* it was.

In order to explore these experiences of discomfort we are going to present the case of Lucía Santana (54) and her experience with the new bendy buses of Transantiago. Santana lives with her partner Marcos Lara (57) in a low-income neighborhood called Villa Chiloé in the borough of Puente Alto, southeast Santiago. Villa Chiloé is located on the very edge of the city. To the south it ends almost in the Maipo River, while on the east and west it is surrounded by other low-income neighborhoods and farming land. Given this peripheral location, and the impossibility of buying a car, both Santana and Lara depended heavily on public transport to access most locations outside their immediate local area.

The two made similar trips, traveling daily from their home to their workplaces located in the western area of the city. Nevertheless, they experienced the (dis)comfort of the new bendy buses quite differently, as recalled in our first interview.

[Ureta] Did you ever have any problem inside the buses?

[Lara] No, besides they never go so fast that you have to steady yourself, they are never fast ...

[Santana, interrupting]   It's because you're tall, dad! Myself, since I'm much smaller, even if I want I cannot reach them [bus handgrips], my hands cannot reach them, so I have to ask permission and grab a lady when I can't reach them … my arms are not long enough to reach up there and my arms are tired, and it hurts to travel all the way like this and you are delicate, as a woman you are delicate, he doesn't, he's lucky because he is taller, he grabs it and it's done, but not us, we end up like monkeys hanging from a tree. … It is almost as if they throw you a ring and you hang from there, you end up like a monkey and you don't know how to steady yourself! … I'm small, my husband is not, for him the things [handgrips] are ok, but I look like a key ring! They put me there and I hang like a key ring because I have no other way to steady myself! I'm small; I can't reach them.

As Santana recognizes, she and Lara are of quite different heights. While Lara reaches almost 1.80 meters (six feet) when standing up straight, Santana is barely 1.50 (five feet). Such a difference in their bodies made quite dissimilar their experience of riding on Transantiago's new bendy buses. Lara was generally satisfied with them, at least in comparison with other components of the system. Santana, on the contrary, complained loudly about how uncomfortable they were given that she could barely reach the handgrips, located about two meters above the bus floor. In order to steady herself she was forced to grab other people or hang from the handgrips like a "monkey" or a "key ring." As her passionate complaints reveal, such a situation was not experienced as casual or anecdotal, but generated an important amount of rage and impotence.

Santana's critical evaluation of the buses also included the seats:

I rarely sit on those buses because the seats are plastic and you keep slipping, you keep slipping and you have to go all the time [steading yourself], shit, as if you were in a rollercoaster! So you have to steady yourself all the time, so I rarely seat on those seats … they are plastic, I don't sit on the buses, I never sit because you slip, you slip. … [So I travel] standing up, otherwise you slip, it is very uncomfortable to sit there. … [Besides] there are some seats that are located quite high, so you end up [sitting] quite high, no, no, I never sit, even if it's empty, they are not comfortable, I use them to leave my stuff on but not to sit, they are not comfortable, either they are too high, or during summertime you perspire, and now in wintertime you slip, no, no chance with those buses … twice in the summer I traveled seated and I perspired, it was a horror, a fat lady perspiring, no, so I travel standing up.

Here again we find a narrative of discomfort, with Santana slipping and perspiring excessively while seated on the bus seats, an experience that ultimately caused her to choose to travel the whole trip standing up, with the substantial increase in tiredness this caused.

Her experiences while using the bendy buses highlight several interesting aspects of the practices involved in incorporating an infrastructure such as Transantiago. For one thing, they show how different bodies enacted different "passages" while traveling on buses (Moser and Law 1999). While for tall bodies the use of the buses remained mostly business as usual, albeit quite crowded, seemingly not something worth telling about (in our interviews Lara rarely referred to the buses when talking about Transantiago), for shorter persons such as Santana the experience of traveling by bus became a very visible source of discomfort, even pain, especially due to the design of seats and handgrips. It is interesting to note that such emotions were triggered not only by the characteristics of the buses in themselves, but mainly by how they showed the limits of her own body. As recalled by Becker (1997, 194), "when disruption occurs, people experience the body as if it belongs to a stranger, and there is a deep discomfort, indeed an agony, in this experience." Santana's body, which up till then had been able to travel by public transport, is now perceived as limited, even impaired to a certain degree, by the location of bus handgrips and seats, especially in comparison with her partner. She has become something strange, even to herself, something that does not fit inside buses.

Such an experience raises questions about why and how handgrips and seats ended up like this, how such discomfort was enacted into Transantiago. To answer such a query we have to step back a couple of years.

Along with the change in the physical and organizational structure of the bus network, one of the PTUS's central proposals was to replace the micros, as the typical kind of public transport bus working in Santiago were known. Micros, it was argued, were made by simply adding a body with the shape of a bus to a chassis of an average truck. As a consequence their floors where located more than one meter above the street level and had to be reached by the use of several steep steps. On its interior, the space was almost completely filled with seats, lined facing the front of the bus in groups of two only interrupted by a narrow aisle the length of the whole structure. Given this, micros were presented as old, uncomfortable, dangerous, too small, etc. Any positive aspect of the bus was mostly deterritorialized in order to make the PTUS's crisis argument. As a consequence, and along with the micreros themselves, micros were usually presented as the ultimate territ orialization of all that was bad with the former system.[4]

Thus in order for the new public transport plan to function properly, a new bus technology was needed, one that truly embodied the values and characteristics of the "world-class" public transport system to be enacted by Transantiago. In order to achieve this, in 2002 a study was commissioned by the MOPTT from a private consultancy firm called TEC to provide a draft for regulations setting a so-called "Transantiago standard" that would be made compulsory for public transport buses once the system started (TEC 2003). Later on, the study was used as the basis for a new regulation, known as decree 122, turning the proposed standard into law.

During this process, both the consultants and their counterparts at the MOPTT had one common assumption in mind, as recalled by Rafael Frías from the legal department of the MOPTT:

What was defined at the moment of generating the bus specifications was that this would be a regulation that established technical minimums that we considered reasonable. … Taking into consideration, as a reference, the existing international standards, *we were not going to invent the wheel; in these matters everything has been developed* [emphasis added]; then I would say that our fundamental approach was to take as the basis the European standard in relation to bus construction, some cases, some particular themes of the standards of Brazil and Argentina, and in some cases to rescue some elements that were already considered in the current norms.

As he recalled, the approach taken was based on the assumption that there was no real space to develop regulations just for Santiago or to "invent the wheel," because the international standards available were perceived as quite sophisticated and universal enough to be mobilized in other places. This was especially so with regulations made by the European Union, given that, as affirmed in the consultant's final report, it "has a multinational character and, as such, has been developed and perfected by technical teams that include representatives of each member country" (TEC 2003, 135–136). Thus such standards were taken as a backbone for the definition of several of the new Chilean standards, in particular directive 2001/85/EC of the European Parliament, published November 20, 2001, that fixed the conditions for buses to be used in public transport (EC 2001).

Trying to sort out what kind of argumentation went along with the mobilization of these regulations, I had the following interchange with Frías about bus seats.

[Frías] We didn't invent that the seat be … that the seat has a minimum height, we took the bus construction standards most used by bus manufacturers, that is, the

European standards, and said, "Let's take the same parameters." I really don't know if the height of seat is the same as in the European standards, but this is the spirit, to take always as a reference some norm already in existence.

[Ureta]   And what about the adaptation of these norms? Because the norm was made for Europe and we live in a different country, we are ... in a different context; how was this adaptation organized?

[Frías]   Why are we different? Why should we be different?

[Ureta]   Because there's a different society, different people, I don't know, the streets are ...

[Frías]   No, but we are people anyway, the European passenger doesn't have to be different in relation to the theme of comfort, the suspension, with the Chilean passenger, neither in the width of doors, maybe the height, but generally it's the same measure ... we don't have to invent the wheel, these things have already been developed.

Following Bissell (2008), we can identify Frías as taking a biomechanical definition of comfort in accordance with which it appears as an "inert sensibility" (1707) that is embedded into certain technical devices, no matter how and where they are used. Given this, most of the standards about devices such as handgrips and seats were taken without any modification from the European regulations because "the European passenger doesn't have to be different in relation to ... the Chilean passenger." So, if these regulations enacted comfort in Europe, they were going to do the same in Chile. Comfort travels along with the regulations, emerging in similar ways anywhere the regulations are enacted.

As a materialization of this conception we can compare figures 4.1 and 4.2. Apart from the titles both images are exactly the same. They show a diagram stating the measures that each single passenger seat should have in a bus. Figure 4.1 was included in the final version of the European directive 2001/85/EC, while figure 4.2 was included in the final version of the new regulations for Chilean public transport buses published in 2004 (MTT 2004), copying a similar image provided in the final report of the consultants (TEC 2003, ch. 4, 113), excluding in the process any reference to its European origins.[5]

In its mobilization from the EU directive to the Chilean regulation, this image did not travel alone. Like any other technical device it carried several other entities, among them the different human devices in accordance with which it was tested and established. Figure 4.1 in particular brought along

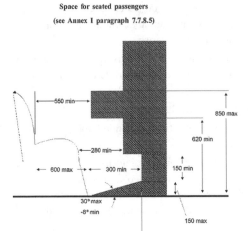

Figure 4.1

Diagram showing the space between seats in urban buses in the EU, according to Directive 2001/85/EC of the European parliament. Image in public domain. Source: http://eur-lex.europa.eu, © European Union, 1998–2014.

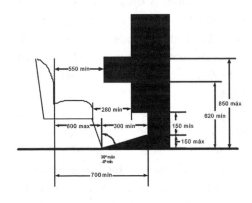

Figura 4: Espaciamientos de asiento

Figure 4.2

Diagram showing the space between seats in urban buses in Chile, according to "Modifica Decreto N° 122, de 1991. Fija Requisitos Dimensionales y Funcionales a Vehículos que Presten Servicios de Locomoción Colectiva Urbana que Indica." Diario Oficial de La República de Chile, Jueves 8 de Enero de 2004. Image reproduced with permission from the Directorate of Metropolitan Public Transport of Santiago (DTPM).

with it the script of the user used to determine its technical specifications. Such a standard European user, to put a name on it, was formed by different attributes that were included in the standards for bus seats, mostly in the shape of a prototypical European user body, but also in forms of physical behavior, consumer rights, taste, etc. However, as a body of literature on the mobilization of technologies and knowledge between different localities or times has explored (Akrich 1993; Baillie, Dunn, and Zheng 2004; de Laet 2000; Howlett and Morgan 2010), mobilizing such a script was not automatic. In practice, knowledge and technologies "can only be considered 'the same thing' as long as they remain in the same 'place,' that is, as long as they are in a place where they are made to refer to each other" (de Laet 2000, 163). Thus, this script can only be expected to be a representation of the bodies of users of public transport in the particular context in which it was developed, in Europe in the early 2000s. When mobilized in the Chilean standards it became something different, a script nonetheless, but not necessarily a script that matched with certain Chilean bodies.

The potential difference between the scripts of the user embedded into the Transantiago standard and actual users of public transport in Santiago was heightened by a lack of proper testing of the components inside the specific model of bendy buses that was finally selected for Transantiago, as recalled by Beatriz López of the CdT:

The bus that we tested was a Scania, that was the one we tested, Scania built a prototype and with that one we made all the tests, I'm talking about the year 2004 ... but then [in 2005] the tendering was adjudicated to Volvo and their bus was never tested. ... So you see in the Volvo bus the handgrips are quite high, I mean, in the European style, as if people's average height was 1.70 [meters], I mean the handgrips are not adapted to the Chilean standard, from the standpoint of the [user's] height, I mean, those things were not tested before starting the operation ... there was exhaustive work beforehand in terms of validating the bus, but it was with another bus, it wasn't the bus that was finally selected.

The situation described by López was a direct consequence of the fractured way in which the infrastructuration of Transantiago was carried out. Given the very limited time available to implement the plan, the teams in charge of its different components were given as much autonomy as possible, implicitly seeing coordination work as a waste of time. López and her team at the Transport Services Unit of the CdT were in charge of carrying out "exhaustive" tests on a prototype bendy bus produced by the manufacturer Scania, including some necessary adaptations to make it fit with the average user's body, which they perceived as smaller than 1.70 meters. However, the Business Unit of the CdT was in charge of the tendering for the bus providers. In selecting the best bid, they mostly took into consideration financial issues, not considering as a relevant issue whether the proposed bus has been tested in Santiago or with Chilean users.[6] Testing was irrelevant not least because, as seen in chapter 3, comfort was not included in the models, it was not an attribute that the fare and time optimizer would value. Thus in the end they selected Volvo over Scania, Volvo having made the cheapest offer and offered credit.

Given the lack of testing, the capacity of the Transantiago standard to truly materialize comfort rested ultimately on the assemblage formed by the technical characteristics of the new buses and the characteristics of the future users' bodies. For users such as Lara, leaving aside the discomfort of crowded spaces and traveling standing up, it worked relatively well, materializing a certain degree of comfort (at least in terms of having several handgrips from which they could hang and seats with wide space, especially suited for tall users). For users such as Santana, whose height is much more common in the country,[7] it became a source of further and frequent discomfort. Thus comfort proved to be never solely biomechanical but always a lived experience. Comfort did not simply travel along with objects such as regulations and seats but emerged, always briefly, as a lived experience between these devices and certain human bodies, among other entities (Bissell 2008).

In all, we can see that incorporating discomfort when using Transantiago was not circumstantial or the result of a faulty implementation, something that could be easily corrected by putting the system to work as designed, but was very much in-scripted into Transantiago through devices such as seats in bendy buses and new regulations. Such a process, again, was very much helped by the assumption of a fare and time optimizer that was not able to *see* discomfort to put any kind of value to it.

Above any other issue, it was through multiple kinds of discomforts that Transantiago became real to its users. And discomfort rapidly turned into rage. Such rage became thematized mostly as the sense of a certain kind of violence that the government was exerting over them with no reason or provocation on their part. It was felt as unfair, deeply unfair, and usually paired with arguments about socioeconomic discrimination, as concluded by Santana:

At the very end poor people are the ones who occupy public transport, in order to go and work for them, this is why they don't realize [how bad Transantiago is], because they go down by car, they have huge cars up there, even the smallest kid has a car with a chauffeur, this is why they don't notice, because the ones who use public transport are us, the people. ... Then this is a thing that is never going to change, [all the arguments about improvements] are lies, we are seeing that it is not changing. Transantiago is not going to change, never.

As recalled by Becker (1997, 192), "stories of disruption are, by definition, stories of difference. Disruption makes an individual feel different from others and can render social relationships uncomfortable and cumbersome." As Santana expresses, for most users this disruption was felt as just another demonstration of the huge inequalities existing between social classes in Chile. Given this perceived "structural" character, it was ultimately taken with fatalism, as a situation that was going to remain the same, no matter how many words were uttered about improvements to the system: "Transantiago is not going to change, never."

Sufferers

Transantiago occupied a space in the Chilean media from the very beginning. Ever since the press conference announcing the PTUS in 2000, the plan kept appearing with a certain regularity in the news. Usually connected with the "crisis of public transport," the policy was generally praised as a bold but necessary step to deal with a long-lasting urban problem. Such a discourse was heightened by Transantiago's frequent ads from mid-2006 featuring Iván Zamorano, one of the country's best-loved footballers, talking about the future wonders of the system accompanied by pictures showing all kinds of happy commuters, especially ones who had been discriminated against by the former system: women, the elderly, children, people with disabilities, etc. The media, with few exceptions, echoed this narrative, contributing to heightening the hype surrounding the system leading up to its starting date.

Such a narrative changed radically from February 10, 2007. As could be expected, the start of the operational phase of Transantiago occupied the most important place in the news of that day and remained there for quite a while. In order to explore the human devices deployed in such coverage, we are going to analyze the reports about Transantiago made on that day by Chilevisión Noticias, the main news program of Chilevisión, a Chilean television-based broadcasting company.

An example of the first day's coverage of the system's operation can be read in box 4.1. Following the traditional media strategy of letting "the images speak for themselves," in the first 15 seconds there is no voiceover or caption, just the image of a bus approaching a corner where dozens of people are waiting for it, who start screaming and stepping into the street to block its way. Then the voiceover starts by telling us that the "big day" has arrived but the results have not been good, with "people waiting for the bus for hours and lots of buses that were not in service." During the voiceover, the clip briefly shows images of completely overcrowded buses, policemen regulating access, a woman reading the newspaper seated on the sidewalk.

Box 4.1
Chilevisión Noticias coverage of the start of Transantiago, February 10, 2007 (1).
Made by the author based on video transcript.

> The clip starts with the image of a bendy bus arriving at a corner where dozens of people wait for it. They are shouting and whistling and, as the bus approaches, they move forward, blocking the street and screaming for the bus driver to open the door. After that there are images of people boarding the bus with the assistance of policemen, buses completely crowded circulating, a woman reading the newspaper sitting on the sidewalk while waiting for her bus. Accompanying the images, a voiceover affirms that "Transantiago opened its doors and, as could be expected for such a big change, there were some difficulties … at the end a complicated day, people waiting for the bus for hours and lots of buses that were not in service. The situation was not nice."

The news story broadcast by Chilevisión Noticias is clearly constructed as a massive disruption, in which the failure of a determinate technical device (lack of enough buses) causes a negative effect on others (inhabitants of the city). By emphasizing this particular consequence of the failure (instead of talking, for example, about the economic costs of the situation), the news is presenting the story in what Boltanski (1999) calls a *politics of pity*. This particular kind of politics is characterized by two elements: a distinction between who is and who isn't suffering and an emphasis on the spectacle of suffering. Instead of focusing on the correction of the anomalous situation/s (as it would in a politics of justice, its alternative), it opts for the "observation of the *unfortunate* by those who do not share their suffering, who do not experience it directly and who, as such, may be regarded as fortunate or *lucky* people" (ibid., 3).

In order to function properly, the politics of pity must not only show visually the existence of sufferers to the lucky people, but do it in a way that is both general *and* particular. On the one hand, "as a *politics* it aspires to generality. Its role is to detach itself from the local and so from those necessarily local situations in which events provoking compassion may arise" (Boltanski 1999, 11). On the other hand, "in its reference to *pity* it cannot wholly free itself from the particular case. Pity is not inspired by generalities. ... To arouse pity, suffering and wretched bodies must be conveyed in such a way as to affect the sensibility of those more fortunate" (ibid.). In this sense the narrative and images described in box 4.1 are quite telling of the story being developed; you can sense the drama, but at the same time it is still too general. With the exception of the woman reading the newspaper there are no "singularities" that embody and personalize the drama being unfold and allow the politics of pity to work properly. This situation was rapidly corrected in the next segment of the story, reviewed in box 4.2.

This second clip starts by embodying the disruption described in the first one, through human devices in the form of images showing a rapid sequence of users clearly upset by the failures of the system. This situation is then confirmed by the voiceover that starts by simply saying "indignant," a word supposedly summarizing the state of mind of the users already shown, leaving no room for further explanations. This view is strengthened by further images of people trying to enter a completely packed bus through its back door, reproducing their angry comments. Finally in order to highlight the magnitude of the drama, the last section of the clip takes the audience to a different area showing a similar situation, with people trying to access buses that are much too crowded. Again several users are performed to embody the crisis in particular faces and words, ending with probably the most dramatic of them: an adult man on the verge of tears telling about how he had to run to avoid being robbed. Having succeeded in performing the crisis, the clip ends with the menacing information that this is just the beginning "because Transantiago is just starting."

Box 4.2
Chilevisión Noticias coverage of the start of Transantiago, February 10, 2007 (2).
Made by the author based on video transcript.

Sequence 1. The image of a packed bus passing. A caption informs us that we are in the borough of La Florida (southeast Santiago), adding that "low frequencies enraged neighbors." Then there are short sequences of users complaining:

User 1 (woman, adult, very angry): "I took a truck, in good Chilean [language], I took a truck, because if I start waiting for the bus I'll be at my work next year!"

User 2 (man, adult): "I come from Santa Raquel and Los Navios, there ... shhhh ... the people have been thrown out, everyone has been left [without buses]."

User 3 (woman, adult): "They said that there were going to be feeder buses, there are none in the neighborhoods, people have been abandoned."

User 4 (man, adult, very angry): "Since 6:30 in the morning I've been here, 6:30! What did I get for that? I have to go to my job now; I'm through with this thing!"

Sequence 2. Starts with the image of a bus stop full of people in Vicuña Mackenna Avenue, near the city center, and the voiceover affirms that users are enraged because "the buses simply did not pass and when one of them arrives this is what happened ... ," showing then a short sequence in which several dozen people try to enter through the back doors of a stopped bus while several others try to get off, all accompanied by multiple screams and whistles.

Sequence 3. It starts by showing different images of people trying to enter buses but failing because they are too crowded, another of a bus trying but failing to close its doors because there are too many passengers in the way. Then there are short sequences of users complaining:

User 5 (woman, adult): Since 5:30 in the morning we have been waiting for transport and we have to come walking.

User 6 (woman, adult): I entered the terminal at 5:30, at 6:00, ah? Imagine what time it is now; this should have been organized beforehand.

User 7 (man, adult): Since 5:15 we have been trying to reach our jobs, but we couldn't.

User 8 (man, young): There are no feeders [buses] anywhere!

User 9 (man, adult): The buses arrive here but you cannot go inside because they are blocked with people.

User 10 (woman, young): I've been waiting for the bus for two hours.

User 11 (man, adult, on the verge of tears): There are robbers there in Zapadores, there are no buses, nothing, because of the problem of this morning I had to leave earlier and I had to escape.

Finally the voiceover concludes, over more images of packed buses, that passengers "will have to be very patient because Transantiago is just starting."

From these extracts we can see clearly the performance of one particular kind of human device: the sufferer. Combining footage, captions, brief
pieces of interviews, and voiceover comments, Chilevisión Noticias constructed a narrative of chaos caused by the lack of buses on the streets of the
city. In the midst of it, users were performed in great pain and anger, even
desperation, given that by midmorning they were still unable to arrive at
their workplaces, even though some of them had left their homes at 5:00
in the morning.

Besides their evident suffering, these individuals are little else. They don't
even have names. This diffuse performance is not casual but constitutes a
key element in a politics of pity. Such a politics "is not just concerned with
one unfortunate and a particular situation. To be a politics it must convey
at the same time a plurality of situations of misfortune, to constitute a kind
of procession or imaginary *demonstration* of unfortunates brought together
on the basis of both their singularity and what they have in common"
(Boltanski 1999, 12). In order to function properly, the suffering users performed must manage to achieve this paradoxical state of being at the same
time carriers of credible experiences of suffering while remaining diffuse
enough to escape any particularization that would diminish their capacity
to engage larger audiences of lucky people. As Boltanski affirms, they must
be singular entities while at the same time exemplars of a widely experienced situation.

In the news clips this aim was met through the performance not of
recognizable human beings but of different "kinds of people" (Hacking
1996): a mature woman, a young adult, an adult woman, and finally an
adult man. To appear as credible spokespersons of the millions of different human beings interacting with Transantiago, they had to give up their
individuality and become exemplars. Against the highly varied and messy
experiences of each individual who used Transantiago to travel, Chilevisión
Noticias offered a limited stock of official users who embodied suffering in a
credible way but who also could be widely mobilized, allowing the politics
of pity to become the main force behind the story.

To the dismay of the actors in power, such performance of the sufferers
did not remain in Chilean media. International media outlets such as the
BBC or the *Economist* echoed it in the weeks and months after the system's
inauguration, generating their own versions of sufferers. Thus in the end
Transantiago did become a "worlding" project (Ong 2011), it did highlight

Santiago and its bold planners worldwide, but in a completely different way than expected, as "a model of how not to reform public transport" (Economist 2008). Instead of becoming a "world-class" system contributing to enact a "world-class" city/society, Transantiago rapidly become its complete opposite: a "world-class" mess.

Chileans

On the night of March 26, 2007, President Bachelet began a nationwide television broadcast to talk about the problems faced by Transantiago with the following:

Chileans, it is not common that a president stands in front of the nation and says: "Things have not been done well." But this is exactly what I would like to say tonight regarding Transantiago. ... It is unacceptable that a transport system made to better integrate the city has become a source of difficulties and discrimination. I'm not going to tolerate this anymore. I assume the state's responsibility in the deficiencies in the start of Transantiago, as well as in its design problems. ... I have always said that I am the president of all the Chileans. But let me say that in the first place I feel close to and moved by those who are suffering, by those in need. For this reason I have been deeply hurt by what has happened these last days, which has impacted strongly the poorest of our country and of Santiago, because no one deserves such miseries.

From the start, it should be noted, Bachelet is not only addressing public transportation users or the inhabitants of Santiago. She talks to "Chileans," enacting a certain national community as the ultimate addressee of her words, one that is supposedly experiencing distress and criticizing the government, demanding a strong corrective action.

As we have seen, the history of Transantiago was plagued with controversies. From the very origin of its brand to the determination of its starting date, its development can be seen as a concatenation of one controversy after another. Up to this point they had been seen largely as *technical* matters, remaining largely limited to struggles between different experts and devices. But the massive disruptions at the start of the system's operational phase changed this situation. They didn't only involve angry experts or untrusted models but human beings experiencing the failures directly. Transantiago had become a disrupted policy assemblage, causing the emergence of hundreds of thousands of discomforted bodies, like Santana's, and the very public sufferers broadcast over and over in the media, Chilean and international. With the televised image of a contrite Bachelet identifying

Chileans as her addressees, in her candid apologies, a fundamental change in the issue was taking place. It had become *political*.

Bachelet came to power in 2006 putting an emphasis on top-down technocratic policymaking as the best way to deal with the country's problems (Silva 2008), a common approach in Chile since the early twentieth century, as seen in chapter 1. Such an arrangement rested on a governmentality enacting subjects as passive citizen-consumers who accept being excluded from policymaking in exchange for experiencing improvements due to expertly designed policies. In accordance with most narratives, since the return of democracy such an arrangement had been able to deliver relatively successful policy assemblages, even some glaring successes that had contributed to the *worlding* of Chile as one of the most successful countries in the so-called developing world, an example to follow.

Nevertheless, becoming subjects of Transantiago did not translate into any kind of improvement or relief; on the contrary it led to distress and discomfort, even physical pain. More tellingly, such a situation did not arise because users were behaving as "bad subjects" (Nadesan 2008) or subjects unable to govern themselves in the way expected. Users were very much behaving in the way in-scripted during infrastructuration, at least in most aspects, but as a result they enacted not the happy citizen-consumer of a world-class society but its complete opposite. If discomforted bodies and sufferers were the only human devices emerging from this assemblage, Chilean state governmentality was clearly failing. Thus to act over the disruption caused by Transantiago was from the very beginning much more than repairing a failing public transport system; it was dealing with these masses of *Chileans*, restoring their confidence that the state and its cadres of experts could enact policy assemblages that effectively improve their lives.

5   Reactions

Patient Users

Given the massive disruptions caused by Transantiago, several actors in the government started wondering how the population of Santiago was going to react. After all, a whole set of long-established daily activities had been transformed in one way or another, starting with people's usual travel patterns, and the changes were not for the better. To make matters worse, such disruptions were expected to be long-lasting, given two related factors. First, the corrections of the technical failures of the system were probably going to take time. From remaking the contracts with bus providers to setting up an efficient fleet management system, several of the key changes that Transantiago needed would take several months to be operational, at the earliest. Second, these changes had to be made while millions of the city's inhabitants continued using the system in their daily mobility, given that there was no way to return to the former micros.[1] So a number of reactions on the part of users were seen as unavoidable, with consequences difficult to predict.

When asked about this issue, government actors overwhelmingly identified one kind of reaction that they were expecting: public demonstrations. Such a possibility had a quite recent example in the massive student protests that occurred in Santiago and the other main cities of the country during 2006,[2] which extended for months and ended up seriously damaging Bachelet's government. Given this antecedent, the disruptions caused by Transantiago appeared to be the perfect trigger for a new round of mass protest, with all the negative consequences for the government. This fear was especially intense because this time the protesters would potentially involve not only a particular group but the whole population of the city.

Given the impossibility of implementing fast solutions beyond some minor and mostly symbolic gestures, during the very first weeks of the system's functioning government actors were forced just to sit and wait for a new version of the student protests to happen. As one key member of the MTT confided to me, during this period they saw the system as being "sprayed with paraffin," needing only a single incident to ignite it and start a major social revolt.

This fear seemed to be confirmed with the emergence of the Committee of Transantiago Users (CdU in Spanish) in the days after the system's launch, aiming from the very beginning to become the main way to materialize citizen malaise over the plan. As could be expected, the CdU started by making a strong critique of the current state of public transport and demanding that the government fix it. In the next weeks its members started an ample program of actions involving both organizing users at the local level and carrying out demonstrations in the city center. Such actions proved to be effective during March and April, involving a growing number of people and gaining the recognition of authorities and the media. However, by mid-May the committee started to lose strength, with each further demonstration mobilizing fewer and fewer people and receiving decreased media and official attention. After this, the CdU tried to implement new actions to reignite the movement but with little success, and by midyear it was effectively finished.

Such an outcome was read in a particular way by the government, as can be extracted from the words of Eugenio Cardoso, an MTT engineer who was in charge of several critical tasks at the time:

The user of public transport could have made a giant revolution, like the student revolution in relation to public transport, but it has been patient, effectively it has been really patient, and the perceptions have been improving, the grades that they give us [in surveys]. In this sense we have to recognize the patience of users in respect to this.

In a perception that was shared by several other interviewees, the revolution that was so widely feared since the start of the disruptions had been luckily averted. The widespread malaise over Transantiago was not transferred into a general protest movement such as the one seen the year before. Such a conclusion rested on a performance of a human device in the form of a "patient" user: a passive entity that had given the government more time to implement the necessary changes instead of starting the feared revolution. To this patient user the government felt extremely grateful; it was the dream outcome, the only good news in the nightmarish weeks after the start of Transantiago.

However, an analysis of the material recollected during fieldwork shows us a different picture. Instead of a "patient" user who calmly waited for the system to improve, we found fairly active users who enacted different human devices in order to transform the system in accordance with their own dispositions. In this chapter I am going to explore two of the most usual materializations of these reactions: local demonstrations against devices of Transantiago and the emergence of massive fare evasion.

NIMBY Protesters

Although the much-feared massive social revolution did not happen, the first months of Transantiago were marked by dozens of local demonstrations throughout the city. In most cases such demonstrations were directed against particular aspects of Transantiago that were considered as harassing the local population, not against its existence as a whole, and occupied highly specific and emergent means, centrally among them human devices. In order to explore these issues in depth we will analyze one particular case, a demonstration carried out by residents of a neighborhood called Villa Pehuén against an informal parking lot of Transantiago's buses.[3]

Villa Pehuén is located in the borough of Maipú, at the very western border of Santiago. It is composed of a mixture of newly built social housing apartment blocks and small houses for lower-middle-class families. In comparison with Villa Chiloé, the situation of Villa Pehuén regarding public transport at the start of Transantiago was relatively good, with its inhabitants having close access to trunk bus lines 401 and 413 going directly to the city center. Also, as a consequence of both lines having their terminals in the area, they were able to board the buses when they were just starting their routes and so usually had the chance to travel seated, a complete luxury in the first months of Transantiago. However, the closeness of the bus terminal was also at the origin of a controversy. Given that the construction of the terminal buildings, located two kilometers from Villa Pehuén, was still in its early stages when Transantiago started operations, bus drivers opted to park their buses by the roadside on El Conquistador Avenue, almost at the corner of Nueva San Martín Street, the main road intersection of the area.

From the very first day, the fact that their streets had become an infor-mal bus parking lot became a nuisance for several people in Villa Pehuén. Among them were Laura Pascal and her husband Pedro Balboa, who have lived for several years in a house on El Conquistador Avenue. She remem-bers clearly the first days of the bus parking.

I was working and my husband calls me: "You know? Transantiago [buses] are in-stalled outside here." "How come?" and then some gentlemen arrived, they were 20 or 25 with plastic chairs, and they sat just outside our house, you know. My husband went out and left my daughter alone and the child couldn't go out to buy something in the corner shop because there were 30 men outside, at the door, then someone can push her and come in, because she's alone, I mean, you start going mental, the way things are nowadays, then we couldn't even work in peace, we were hysterical, our nerves were shot.

Thus the presence of the drivers seated in her front yard was first seen as a matter of concern regarding her daughter's safety, as she could have been assaulted by one of them. But rapidly her complaints included other issues, as she continues:

[We bought this house] in order to have tranquillity, in order to have clean air, not to have noise, and every day, every single hour, there was a bus outside, with the engine running, putting out fumes. Here everything looked [dirty] … you couldn't even eat, not even use the dining room, it pervaded everything, it was inside our house, the fumes were inside our house … from 7:30 in the morning, when my hus-band took our daughter to school, 7:30, and we had to ask the person in the bus to move [so we could take out the car] … every single day, at any given hour, one bus departs and another arrives.

Thus beside the drivers, Laura resented the fumes and the noise produced by bus engines continually running. This nuisance was more intense given that the noise and fumes, in contrast with the drivers, did not limit them-selves to the front yard but entered her house, pervading every space with noise and dirt. As seen in previous research in relation to noise (Ureta 2007), this situation was not only interpreted as environmental pollution but in a more basic sense as a violation of their private space, as a very specific and ubiquitous form of violence suffered by the members of her family.

This arrangement was also experienced as a nuisance by Sandra Navas, a preschool teacher working in a kindergarten located on El Conquistador Avenue.

What happened is that in March, when we started the [school] year, Transantiago [buses] were in front of the kindergarten and … well, the thing of Transantiago was modernity and all that story, and we couldn't go against it, so we took it with calm. ... As a kindergarten, as an institution, we had the problem that [the buses] were an obstacle to the children's arrival, I mean, how the school bus arrived at the kindergarten and how the parents arrived if they came by car, in case of an emergency; and how could I go out with the children? ... I spoke with this gentleman [the administrator of the bus terminal] and said that I needed a solution ... and we agreed on a solution, they passed me [traffic] cones, then I was going to delimit my sector ... so I said, "Let's see if this thing works."

Given her perception of Transantiago as a necessary modernization of public transport, Navas felt that it was not possible to make an immediate fuss about the issue of the parked buses, implicitly assuming that it was just a temporary situation. But when weeks passed and the situation was the same she was forced to change her attitude, starting by speaking directly to the drivers. They were receptive, agreeing to move their vehicles in order to clear the space in front of the kindergarten. But as soon as a new bus arrived, it again parked in front.

Given this situation Navas, Pascal, and Balboa decided in separate ways to step up their efforts to solve the situation. Their starting point was to make complaints through formal channels, from the local government to the central offices of Transantiago. But their efforts were only translated into a letter and telephones calls that did not solve the situation. Then they complained to the police, who came a couple of times and fined the bus drivers, but as soon as they departed the situation was more or less the same. As a consequence they became increasingly skeptical about the possibility of solving this problem through "the regular procedure," as Balboa concluded. In their words we can see how the stage was starting to be set for a new move in their efforts to remove the buses in front of their houses: direct demonstrations.

The trigger for such a change of strategy was a new human device performed by Navas: children being hurt by the situation.

We wanted to go out in the summer with the children to the public park, but the machines were there, with their engines running all day ... and I started to see things differently: "And the children? Where are the rights of the children?" ... I couldn't make any trip outside [with them], to the neighborhood, to the market, nothing, because for me it's a risk ... then I started to call the police every day, I called the police almost every single day and they fined them constantly, but they [buses] left just for a short time and then returned again. ... As I was enraged, I [decided to] celebrate Environment Day, so I put up all these posters and I said to all the kids' parents to bring something related to the environment, because this was truly ... what we were living and the children were being harmed, so this is what we had to fight for, for the children. ... The parents were against it [the parked buses], completely against it, they are ones who have supported us on all this ... they know that their children are here and came to give us support.

In place of her argument about the difficult access to the kindergarten as the main reason to ask for having the buses removed, she decided to "see the things beyond" and brought in a performance of the children as being affected by the situation, both in terms of their right to move freely and in relation to their inhaling of the carbon monoxide produced by the bus engines. By doing this she was able to effectively mobilize the children's parents in the controversy, who were willing to be involved in the fight for their children's rights.

The main materialization of such a new definition of the issue was her decision to celebrate an Environment Day using as her main topic the negative consequences to the children's health of the parked buses in terms of air and noise pollution. Along with the children and their parents, she made several posters and hung them the day before the celebration on the walls of the kindergarten facing the street, as can be seen in figures 5.1–5.3. Using slogans such as "Mr. Driver, turn off your engine, children studying, thanks!," "The noise that the buses make in front of my kindergarten

Figure 5.1–5.3
Posters attached to the kindergarten front on Environment Day. Images reproduced with permission from Wilson Muñoz.

annoys me," "We don't want more noise pollution," or "I want my lungs free from pollution," these posters performed these harmed children in a permanent and highly visible way. Also by speaking in the first person, even though they were written by Navas and the parents, she was able to give a certain degree of intimacy to the claims.

Along with the posters, on Environment Day she invited the neighbors and the parents of the children to demonstrate in front of the kindergarten, while at the same time calling a television station.

Then I made these [posters], and with these the neighbors were hooked, they were hooked and came to talk with me and they saw that all this was possible ... then I invited all the parents to participate in the demonstrations, I sent them an invitation saying that the ones who wanted to participate could do it ... and most parents agreed and on Friday the television came, they interviewed the children, the parents, and my colleague, and we were waiting for the tremors, the earthquakes.

As she recognized, this first demonstration was a success because she was able to make a highly public statement about their discontent and gather parents and neighbors. Besides, her telephone call to a TV station resulted in its mentioning their complaints in the news, transforming them into sufferers, as seen in the previous chapter. Finally the demonstration was seen as a success because it was able to start mobilizing or "hooking" neighbors who were unhappy with the situation. For this reason, as Navas said quite vividly, they "were waiting for the tremors, the earthquakes."

And the earthquakes came in rapid succession, as Balboa and Pascal recalled.

[Wilson Muñoz]   How did you get organized?

[Balboa]   Look, in reality we were the ones who started it, because my daughter couldn't sleep, because she sleeps in the front room, the engines, I couldn't sleep, then my wife for a long time was saying to me, "Pedro, let's make some posters and hang them outside," [and I said,] "No, the aesthetics, what are the neighbors going to say," seriously, because I like tranquillity, then finally one day I was enraged and I said, "No, my wife is right, I have to fight for my rights and the rights of my family."

[Pascal]   The kindergarten put up some posters, the kindergarten put some posters first and we [said,] "OK, if the kindergarten put them up, we can too," and this same day we hung similar posters.

[Balboa]   And this is how we got organized.

[Pascal]   We started to receive the support of our neighbors who had also made complaints similar to ours, telephone calls and things like that, and hadn't been heard, then we organized quite fast.

[Muñoz]   And they arrived because of the posters, or you knew them beforehand?

[Balboa]   First because of the posters, in order to give notice that something was happening, then we went to hang more posters with the neighbors who helped us, even the neighbors of the apartment blocks in front came, because they were affected by the dust that the buses produce, the stones, a lot of things, then we received their support because, hey, as I said they took care of their biological needs just there!

The posters in front of the kindergarten and the celebration of Environment Day started a chain reaction. First Balboa and Pascal hung their own posters complaining about the situation with the buses. These posters were not only about the problems caused by the buses ("No more engine noise," figure 5.4) but also about the lack of concrete solutions from the authorities ("The Ministry of Transport [and] the municipality allow the abuse," figure 5.5). The posters were only a starting point. As Pascal recalled, after they were hung several other neighbors who had been experiencing distress and were frustrated about the lack of results from their complaints came to visit them, and they rapidly got organized to hang more posters in other houses of the neighborhood.

What is interesting, as Balboa notes at the end, is that they didn't know most of these neighbors beforehand, so they couldn't be seen as members of a preexisting community, but just individual actors who got together because of an issue that was affecting them all. Such a situation seems to confirm Marres's (2007) point, derived from Dewey (1927), that the public of controversies mostly emerges not out of previous bonds but around issues that affect them all and move them together until the issue has been resolved.

With the constitution of this larger assemblage they were able to implement a more ambitious action: a large public demonstration on the morning of October 10, 2007, as recalled by Balboa on the evening of that day.

[Balboa]   Today in the morning we blocked the exits of the 401 and 413, we blocked their depot and we also blocked here, El Conquistador with Campanario [Street] ... we put cars across and barricades, the idea was to attract attention in order for the authorities to make themselves present here, because at that hour the micros were here already making noise, at that hour, at any hour, it was an incredible thing and thanks to this we succeed in attracting attention, because television arrived, they interviewed us, we showed the mayor as responsible, [he] sent representatives, all the television networks arrived, the radio arrived too, and you see that the thing is ... is not that it has been solved, but is much better ... I think 200 people participated, neighbors from here to there ... the press arrived, the police, because we were making

Figures 5.4–5.5
Posters attached to the fronts of houses in Villa Pehuén. Images reproduced with permission from Wilson Muñoz.

a peaceful demonstration, in no way aggressive, the television arrived, the representatives from the mayor arrived, and he's going to assume his role.

[Muñoz]   And what did they say?

[Balboa]   That tomorrow in the afternoon they are going to come and give us solutions in order to have a quieter life.

Through the coordinated action of more than 200 neighbors they were able to block the exit of buses from lines 401 and 413 using cars and barricades, completely paralyzing the service for a couple of hours. Given that those lines are the ones that connect the whole area of Maipú (with half a million inhabitants) with the city center, this blockage caused a massive transit disruption. Along the barriers stood the neighbors carrying posters with their demands and making noise with pots and pans (a traditional form of protest in Chile).

However, and beyond the involvement of the immediate neighbors, they were conscious that the blockage in itself would not have the effect that they wanted if it remained solely attached to their particular locality. They needed to mobilize it to other locations, transforming it into a much wider issue. To do so they opted to mediatize it by calling some television and radio networks the night before in order for them to be present on the scene.

One of the television networks present was Chilevisión, which recorded the demonstration for several minutes, interviewing the neighbors and some other actors. That night it became one of the main features on Chilevisión Noticias. The storytelling of the news story was quite similar to the one seen in the previous chapter. First, the news presenter introduced the story by giving general information about the unfolding drama, heightened with images of blocked streets and people loudly protesting. Then, and in accordance with the dictates of a politics of pity (Boltanski 1999), the protesters were performed as nameless "affected neighbors," sufferers who had been affected by this situation for a long time and were angry about the lack of response by the authorities to their complaints. Finally the story ended by performing more sufferers, this time because of the pollution caused by buses, with the threat that "the neighbors said they are going to continue with their mobilizations until the authorities give them a solution for their demands."

But there was no need for them to carry out their threats. The reactions to their mobilization were almost immediate. First some representatives of the mayor came to dialogue with the neighbors, convincing them to take down the blockage after promising to offer a permanent solution to their problem in a meeting next day. Even before this meeting, in the afternoon of the same day, all the buses were removed from El Conquistador Avenue and parked elsewhere in the borough. After eight months the issue has been solved, at least for the inhabitants of the houses on El Conquistador Avenue, and the assemblage of complaining neighbors was dismantled without further mobilizations.[4]

In all, their mobilization reveals a different kind of politicization of Santiago's inhabitants from the one expected by the actors from the government and the CdU. Its starting point was a group of individuals who had a very concrete claim against the system: the buses permanently parked in front of their houses and workplaces. But they didn't move from there to ask for general changes in the system or to form stable collectives. In this sense, they can be seen as performing NIMBY[5] protesters, actors who accept that buses have to be parked somewhere, just *not in their front yards*.[6] Given this, they started to act in multiple ways, first trying the formal complaint procedures and, when these didn't deliver results, organizing their own forms of demonstration. Afterward, and as soon as their issue of concern has been addressed, they dissolved rapidly as a collective, reaffirming Marres's (2005) assertion of "no issue, no public."

Even with the rapid dissolution of the collective, the waves caused by their "earthquake" did not remain solely *in their backyards*. The demonstrators of Villa Pehuén became one more component of an almost continual stream of protests occurring in different areas of the city broadcast by television and other media in the weeks and months following the start of Transantiago. In their differences and similarities these protests achieved what the members of the CdU only could dream about: to set up the sufferer as the ultimate user of Transantiago. With each further protest, each new inclusion in the news, this human device was reinforced, reenacting the politics of pity and stabilizing the *fact* of Transantiago as an ultimately failed system.

Wicked Evaders

The second case depicts a quite different form of reaction. It doesn't involve collectives or public demonstrations; it doesn't enact sufferers or the politics of pity. On the contrary, from the very beginning it was treated as a quite individual affair and, making a clear contrast with the sufferers' protests, it was massively censured by all responsible authorities. Concurrently, it has looped into a continual stream of disciplinary measures that are still trying to make it disappear (with little success). This second reaction was directly linked with Transantiago's Bip! card.

The Bip! card represented one of the most radical innovations proposed by Transantiago. Instead of paying the fare in cash directly to the driver, as was done in the former system, now the fare was going to be deducted automatically when users brought their smart card near a reader located at the entrance of buses and Metro stations. This device would force them to plan their trips in advance, at least in terms of topping up their cards with enough money to pay for the trip. Especially at the beginning, it would also require the trust of users with supposedly little or no experience in using smart cards that the system was not going to charge them a different amount than expected. After all, the system was completely new to the country, and any mistake in the first few days could mean that users were going to mistrust, even actively resist, the device.

This possibility did not seem remote to the actors involved in the infrastructuration of Transantiago. Actually the resistance that the Bip! card might face was their single most important fear concerning the system's users. About this issue Eugenio Cardoso recalled:

We were very fearful regarding the card, we had spent years at the Ministry [of Transport] trying to implement a system of payment with cash, a system of payment with tickets, we implemented the card in two months, we changed [the former payment system] completely … and we had an immense fear that it wasn't going to work and the people wouldn't get accustomed to it, that they wouldn't use it, that they wouldn't learn.

The fear was especially intense that the new payment system might cause a massive increase in the levels of fare dodging among passengers.

In the former bus system, fare dodging by passengers was relatively low. As the income of the micreros depended on the number of tickets sold, they were directly involved in forcing the passengers to pay their fare, even if that commonly involved using violent means. Another advantage of the old system for reducing evasion was its flexibility. It was quite usual for some users to ask the micrero to take them for a smaller amount than the fixed fare for a part of the route, to which he (because it was universally a "he") usually agreed but without giving them a ticket back. In strict terms this arrangement constituted another form of fare evasion on the part of the general system,[7] but in practice it was a central part of the micrero's monthly income and as such was usually tolerated by the bus owners.

Nevertheless, given that one of the main aims of Transantiago was to get rid of micreros, it was compulsory to separate the practice of driving from that of charging for tickets. This was done by introducing two separate entities: a professional bus driver who received a fixed salary for his work and whose only responsibility would be to drive the bus, and a technical system in charge of charging the users for their trips. This technical system was made up of several components, most visibly the Bip! card and an electronic card reader known as a "validador" (the device mounted on the pole in figure 5.6). In the call for tenders for the Financial Administration for Transantiago (AFT in Spanish) this device was defined as "electronic devices that are in charge of allowing or refusing each trip, based on the available amount in the access means [card] and/or the conditions established for its usage."

The delegation of former micreros' duties to the card reader is quite clear. From now on it was the reader, based on its software and the information that it read on each card, that decided whether or not to accept someone accessing the bus as a valid user. In fact the device is the one that gives "user" status to the human beings who want to use the system. As the AFT call for tenders clearly states, a user is a "person who accesses the transport services of the system through the payment of the corresponding fare, using the payment form defined in this contract." Conversely, the people who access the service without approval from the card reader have no such status. In carrying out this task the device was going to be completely inflexible, in clear difference from the micrero, so no passenger with less than the full fare amount in credit on her card could be considered a user, radically ending the traditional bargaining for the fare.

Figure 5.6
Card reader at the entrance of a Transantiago bus. Source: the author.

Once this system was selected, the question rose among the actors from CdT of how to force users to pay their fares, without having the micreros' recourse to violence. After studying several public transport systems around the world, one option they considered was using personnel to block the entrance and/or apply fines to users who didn't pay their fare. But in implementing this mechanism they faced an important obstacle: by law in Chile, the only actors who can take monetary fines are policemen. So if they wanted to implement this system they needed to change this law, and this would take several months to implement even if the government could get enough votes to pass such a regulation in the parliament.

After this, a dual solution to the issue was developed consisting of direct and indirect control mechanisms. The indirect mechanism was based on a technology known as an automatic passenger counter (APC). The APC uses infrared rays to count the number of people who enter and leave through each door of the bus. When this information is compared to the information provided by the card reader, the authorities are able to know in detail how many people are evading payment and where. The plan with Transantiago was to apply fines to the companies with high levels of evasion and reward the ones with low levels. Thus the AFT call for tenders stated that each bus of the system must carry an APC to determine the flow of passengers in and out, and the detailed amount of evasion.

For the direct control of evasion, the selection of the appropriate technical device was more controversial. The first option considered was turnstiles, such as the ones used in Metro stations, which would allow entry only to passengers who had passed their cards through the reader with a positive outcome. Several technical actors at CdT resisted this option, however. One of them was Vicente Ortiz, an engineer who had a central role in this area:

We studied the Metro, it has very low evasion, [but] the low evasion lasts until the security guy leaves, the turnstile is not something that averts evasion in itself, it averts evasion when there is a security guard by its side, because you can pass but you cannot fool the security guard. Then this is what I said: "If the turnstile is behind the driver, the card reader is behind, people are going to start passing below the turnstile." "No, man, this is not going to happen!" [they replied], then the discussion started, as I said it was subjective … so one guy said, "Let's see, wait, but this is nothing new, in Brazil's [public transport] turnstiles work." "Yes, man, but with a two-meter black guy standing right next to the turnstile! What stops the people is not the turnstile, it is the black guy … it is the security personnel standing by its side!"

Given the design of buses, the turnstile could only be located in the corridor between the front and the secondary doors, so the incoming passenger was going to face the card reader beside the turnstile unseen by the driver. For Ortiz this would make it quite easy to evade payment by passing below or jumping over it. In making this judgment, he is acknowledging that the technical device in itself is not strong enough to make human beings act in a certain way. In a contrary way to Latour's (1992) well-known example of the door-closer, here what is unreliable is the technology in itself. If turnstiles work at all in controlling evasion both in the Metro and in Brazil it is because they have a "two-meter black guy" by their side checking that users do not pass below or above them. If the security guard is absent, the turnstiles offer very little resistance to the evader, they become quite porous gatekeepers, giving access to several different sorts of human devices and not only to "users" who have paid the full fare for their journey.

Given this possibility, and after lengthy discussion, the turnstile was made only optional in the call for tenders[8] and another device was introduced to reduce the risk of fare evasion at the user level, this time involving both technical and human agency, as Ortiz continues:

We also defined certain layouts inside the buses, I mean, luckily with the layouts we were quite stubborn. ... If you look, the card readers are located at the driver's height, this is one of the things that we did for evasion, I always defended [the idea] that here in Chile public punishment is always stronger than any punishment or any punitive tool by the police; or something that resembles it, that has to do with social punishment. The card reader did not [originally] include this light that turns green when you validate ... [it] included the "tick" [sound] and a little square [screen]. We complained intensely, "Who's going to see if the guy has passed his card?" It's not going to be audible, no man, inside the bus you cannot hear anything, forget about it, a visible sign is needed, so when the guy passes [his card] and the thing is red, everyone sees that this guy didn't pay! ... I remember the fights, "Why do you need this traffic light? No man! Don't mess with me," "No man, we want all the world to see!" In fact I was of the opinion that we should put them [lights] further up the post, not so close to the reader, connected to LED panels [with messages such as] "This user did not pay!" or "The evader of the month!" I mean, whatever we can do, for me this was a much more effective tool than any other type of control. People in Chile are shameful, they're ashamed of not paying, they're ashamed of being caught when they are not doing what they should do; then let's expose them, it is the best way, you will never have the number of personnel necessary to be able to control the problem, only social punishment is permanent. This is the story of why the card reader has lights ... the original card reader had a light on its sides, like ears, but we changed it ... it wasn't so different from the others in some things, everything basic is on the inside; "OK with these changes, but you put the traffic light." I mean, with these silly "ticks" [sounds] nobody is going to understand anything, that way we would have a monstrous evasion today; who will know, if you are the only one who can see the little red light? "But the sound ..." "No man, the sound doesn't have any value, you can hear it, ok, but nobody cares if it goes 'pipipip' to one guy or just 'pip' to another."

Under the new arrangement the two card readers would be located in front of the bus driver, at either side of the doors (as seen in figure 5.6), at the same height as the driver's head, so the whole operation would be quite visible to her. Above the reader was located a white box, about ten centimeters in diameter, inside which a powerful light turned on after each validation indicating whether the operation was valid (green) or invalid (red), in a similar fashion to the typical traffic light. As Ortiz states, this external traffic light was not originally included with the reader, whose only devices to show the validity of the payment were different kinds of noise and a small LED screen in the middle of the card reader. But those devices were considered completely insufficient for launching the main strategy for the avoidance of fare evasion on buses: social control.

This strategy started with the performance of a particular human device in the form of a *shameful* Chilean: "People in Chile are shameful, they're ashamed of not paying, they're ashamed of being caught when they are not doing what they should do." Given this script, the main way to keep fare evasion under control appeared to be exposing potential evaders to the widest possible public exhibition, in front of both drivers and fellow passengers, so they would feel ashamed and gave up this practice. Given the extent of this "shamefulness" among the Chilean population, this public exposition as an evader would be more effective in controlling fare evasion than any other technical devices such as turnstiles or extra personnel to control the problem. Because these technical devices can fail or be absent, "only social punishment is permanent."

Following Foucault's (1979) classic studies on the prison, we can clearly see this arrangement as a technology of surveillance, "a mechanism that coerces by means of observation; an apparatus in which the techniques that make it possible to see induce effects of power, and in which, conversely, the means of coercion make those on whom they are applied clearly visible" (170–171). Therefore visibility is directly identified as the most valid way to discipline this shameful Chilean into paying. Rose (1999) has called this particular kind of rule "*government through the calculated administration of shame*" (73, emphasis in the original). Instead of applying direct control or violence (such as a security guard standing next to the turnstile) or completely autonomous self-government (such as leaving the turnstile by itself), this form of government uses shame based on visibility as the main disciplining mechanism. This shame is effective because it is supposed to "entail an anxiety over the exterior deportment of the self, linked to an injunction to care for oneself in the name of the public manifestation of moral character" (ibid., 74).

But in order for this strategy to work, the signals of the card reader, especially the negative ones, would have to be highly noticeable, not only to the driver but also to other passengers, so the visibility and its related social sanction/shame were extended to the whole trip of the evader. Sounds or little lights on the side of the card reader were not enough ("nobody cares if it goes 'pipipip' to one guy or just 'pip' to another"); there had to be something more manifest like the green and red lights. They also had the advantage of being easily associated with traffic lights, a widely used and respected technology of urban discipline. Then the highly visible red lights and the accompanying sound, the watching driver and other passengers, along with the shameful condition of the Chilean population, should produce a powerful mechanism for reducing fare evasion, much more potent than any technical device in itself like turnstiles.

As a consequence, the AFT call for tenders, in the part detailing the equipment that buses must have, stated that "Each card reader will identify by light and sound signals the validation of fares, indicating in different ways the use of special fares and optionally indicating in an audible and/or visual way when the remainder on the access mode [card] is not enough to make another journey in a trunk bus." Bright lights, sounds, visibility, and shame were going to be the main direct controlling devices for fare evasion in Transantiago.

As happened with several other components of Transantiago, the system developed to control fare evasion did not work as expected when the plan sent into operation, in either its indirect or its direct arrangements.

First, the indirect measures were never able to function properly. One of the main technical failures of Transantiago at the start was that the system for managing the bus fleet in a centralized way was not operational. Among other issues, this failure meant that it was impossible for the authorities to obtain any regular inputs from the equipment installed inside the buses of the system, among them the APC. As a result they were completely unable to establish where and how much fare evasion was happening. Then the system of distant control based on the delegation of responsibility from the authorities to each company never worked.[9] Given the lack of any quantification that would allow them to exert individual pressure on the companies, the issue remained a systemic problem and hence one for which the central authorities had most of the responsibility.

The controlling mechanism did not appear to work as expected at the level of direct measures either. On the one hand the design of the new bendy buses made it quite easy for users to enter the bus through either of the two back doors, thus making it unnecessary to face the card reader and its associated visibility/social sanction if they did not have enough credit, as can be seen in the field notes taken on August 13, 2007, at Las Rejas station, a quite busy node connecting the Metro with the buses going to the populous borough of Maipú.

It's 18:20 hrs. I go out of [the Metro] in Las Rejas station. ... A couple of meters away from the exit I find a bus stop of trunk lines 401 and 413 that go in the direction of Maipú. I cross the street and enter the bus stops, where there are quite a lot of people waiting now, there are at least 30 people waiting at the bus stop. After waiting five minutes a bus of route 401 arrives and most people throng in front of the bus's doors. A lot of young people go toward the back doors of the bus, waiting for them to open to go inside. However, the bus driver seems not to want to open the doors. Through the windows of the bus you can hear the users who want to get off the bus complaining, and the driver finally opens all doors. A couple of youngsters hang on the doors, to keep them from closing, while several others go inside the bus [without paying their fares]; even some adults join them. Even with this tactic it is very difficult to get inside the bus and most people, including me, remain at the bus stop waiting for the next bus. (Source: Wilson Muñoz)

On the other hand, even in the case of people entering through the front doors, the designed mechanism appeared not to be working as expected. Consider an extract from the field notes taken May 25, 2008, inside bus number 209e making the trip from Puente Alto, in the south of the city, to the city center via Santa Rosa Avenue.

I go inside bus number 209e, from Santa Rosa to the [city] center. It's 21:30 in the evening. I start the route alone. An adult man enters, stands on the stairs and does not pay the fare, he just stays there talking with the driver. ... Three other people go inside the bus. When one of them passes his card through the reader, the red light turns on. He passes it again and the light turns red again, he looks in the direction of the driver. The driver is still talking and doesn't look at the guy, so he moves on, surely taking the driver's omission as a yes or simply taking advantage of his lack of interest. ... At the next stop a young woman gets on, she passes her card and the red light turns on. She puts on a face like saying "Damn!" and looks in the direction of the driver. The driver is still speaking with the guy standing on the steps. Given his lack of answer and attention, the young woman continues. ... A woman with a little girl sleeping in her arms steps in. She stops for a second and looks at the driver. He's still talking and I cannot see if he made her a gesture or simply ignores her, but the woman passes without paying. ... A group of four men get on and the light turns red for one of them. After three or four failed attempts without looking at the driver he continues without paying. In the front the driver keeps talking. ... For the many times in which the alarm and the red light have sounded, it is hard to believe that the driver didn't take notice of the situation; on the contrary I think the driver noticed all the situations which happened but decided to ignore them and continue talking. (Source: Antonia Devoto)

As can be seen from both sets of notes, these users appear to be less shameful than expected. At least in relation to fellow passengers, such as the authors of the notes, the incoming individuals showed no detectable signs of embarrassment or guilt about entering the bus either through its back doors or even after the red light of the card reader indicated that they had not enough credit to pay, turning them into fare evaders. Only censure on the part of the bus driver in the second case seemed to be recognized as theoretically able to put into practice the control mechanism and its associated shame, as several users looked in his direction after the red light went on (but not all of them). But his open disinterest in exerting this role meant that the evaders could pass without further problems.

This last point, the issue of bus drivers who do not want to be involved as enforcers, was also mentioned in one of the interviews with Sergio Campos, a bus driver of the same trunk line in which the above field notes were taken:

[Ureta]   How does the Bip! card function?

[Campos]   The card has functioned well, I mean, when people want to pay the card functions well, the problem is that people don't want to pay ...

[Ureta]   And what do you do when that happens?

[Campos]   I cannot do anything because I can't put my physical integrity at risk for other people, I mean, I cannot clash with these people because, look, I would ruin my health, I would start having ... having more stress, you start to fail in your work and then, you start again to be angry and the things do not work out well, they stop functioning harmoniously. And then it does not correspond, why should you do something like this if it's not part of your primary function? This is the function of other people who are not doing it and I don't know, it worries me, the card is very simple, what happens is that people are wicked and don't want to pay, straightaway, I mean, it is not that they haven't got accustomed [to the payment system].

From the perspective of Campos, his resistance to playing the part of the censor of evaders had its roots in the same change in the driver's working conditions that Transantiago proposed from the start. Given this, to get directly involved in the matter of users who do not want to pay appeared to him like reperforming a micrero, with all the violence and the physical risks implied by incorporating this human device. Here Transantiago's "success" in turning micreros into bus drivers acted against the system's need to control fare evasion at the user level.

Given the refusal of bus drivers to censor the evaders, the whole system rested now on the shame that users themselves could feel from their fellow passengers, and, as seen above, this shame appeared not to be strong enough to stop them from doing it. Therefore in practice, instead of effectively controlling evasion, the devices simply ended up performing two kinds of human devices: the payer and the *wicked* evader.

From the very beginning the pervasiveness of this last human device caused great concern among the actors at the CdT and the government at large. As seen in chapter 4, and given the lack of a public subsidy and the performance of users as low-income *fare and time optimizers*, the financial stability of the system depended centrally on matching the cost of the system with its revenue. Under the modeling scenario finally adopted, this was done through an optimization of the former system, especially based on the reduction in the number of buses. But this scenario also estimated a fare evasion far lower than the level shown by the first data available after the start of operations. Given the levels of fare evasion initially found (estimations talked about 30% of the expected revenues), the model of financial sustainability out of which Transantiago had been built was not working and the government was forced to step in to provide the lacking revenues, an arrangement that was widely perceived as unsustainable in the long run. So fare evasion was not only a matter of users incorporating unforeseen kinds of human devices, but a critical menace to the government's capacity to finally enact the kind of ordering promised since the PTUS.

Strange Things

A usual ending to the interviews with former and current government actors on which this book is based was a reversal in the roles, with the interviewees asking me variations of a question that can be summarized thus: "You are a sociologist, right? Could you please explain to me why people behave like this?" Such a question, which I usually failed to answer comprehensively enough to end their apprehensions, revealed the degree to which they were baffled about the human devices incorporated by the users of Transantiago.

In this chapter we have seen two of them, but there were dozens of others. In each single area of the system we could find human beings incorporating completely unexpected human devices; not even behaving as "bad subjects" (Nadesan 2008), users who consciously act against their given scripts, but discarding them altogether and/or replacing them by completely unforeseen agencies that put the system under much strain. I have chosen to call such unexpected human devices, in all their multiplicity and messiness, *strange things*.

As seen in the introduction, strange things are human devices coproduced along with the overflowings that any ordering project generates, especially complex ones such as Transantiago. Beyond their differences, NIMBY protesters and wicked evaders represent unexpected outcomes of the system, actively challenging the governmentality it wished to enact. What is central is that strange things are not a permanent identity or stigma, contrary to classical understandings of the stranger, but a particular set of practices and devices that appear strange from a certain optic, usually the one of the actors in power. For example, probably no one accessing a bus without paying their fare was conscious of performing a particular kind of strange thing for actors such as Vicente Ortiz. They just wanted to save some money or defy a system that was functioning poorly, who knows? Only afterward was this practice perceived by someone to be challenging a preexisting script stating that Chilean users are governed by shame embedded in the original evasion control system.

This lack of self-consciousness is also reflected in their "social" status or the relations between different strange things. Contrary to traditional views on political mobilization and resistance that understand people mobilized as belonging to particular preexisting communities, strange things have very little previous knowledge (if any) of the existence of other strange things before performing one themselves. For this reason they do not necessarily perceive themselves as belonging to any kind of overarching social collective. In this sense, strange things as a collective should be seen, as Marres (2005) does, as forming a "public" that emerges around a particular issue or affair, a collective whose members don't have much previous knowledge of one another but that gets performed in relation to particular issues that concern them all. As we have seen, the neighbors of Villa Pehuén did not know each other before staging the protests and becoming strange things to the authorities of Transantiago. But in reaction to a practice of bus drivers and their machines, they reacted by performing NIMBY protesters, first individually and then as a collective, that mobilized to change this situation and swiftly disappeared afterward.

Therefore strange things do not get performed as a result of a personal identity or due to their belonging to particular preexisting communities. At least not necessarily. Above these elements, strange things should be seen as the unexpected by-products of ordering practices, especially of the deployment of scripts. In this sense, every single ordering exercise produces strange things as much as it produces *normal* subjects. This is especially so with massive ordering exercises such as Transantiago. As seen in the introduction, and following Callon (2007), we can see the development of such policy assemblages as "nothing but the long and interminable series of untimely overflowings, of sociotechnical *agencements* that have been caught out, unable to discipline and frame the entities that they assemble" (323).

Given their ubiquitous performance in highly contrasting forms, strange things represent in many cases the single most powerful entity acting against the infrastructural materialization of the new orderings proposed by policy assemblages. In doing so, strange things highlight how "infrastructural power" (Mann 1984), like any other kind of power, is never solely in the hands of a limited number of actors. Contrary to well-known readings of infrastructural oppression (such as Graham and Marvin 2001), strange things show us how the overflowings of infrastructural policies produce quite different kinds of powerful actors, even some who use components of the new infrastructure to challenge the very governmentality originally embedded in it. In a way we could say that strange things are so because they take infrastructural power into their own hands. For this reason they constitute one of the main challenges that any emerging policy assemblage faces, even threatening to deterritorialize it, and calling for the introduction of urgent measures to deal with them, as we will see in the next chapter.

6 Normalization

Crisis? What Crisis?

Given the massive performance of strange things, from sufferers in the media to users who were avoiding paying their fares, after just a few days Transantiago became one of the biggest public controversies any Chilean government had faced since the return of democracy in 1990. In this context, it was not surprising that in the weeks following February 10 multiple voices were raised arguing about the existence of a "crisis del Transantiago," or a particular crisis configuration caused by the disruptions being experienced by the users of the system. As usual with such a configuration, these claims were paired with calls to radically alter the system, such as by scrapping it altogether and returning to the former micros or by transforming several of its components, even its most basic rationale.

The opening of President Bachelet's television address of March 26, 2007, discussed in chapter 4, seemed to echo a crisis narrative in certain ways, talking about a system that was causing significant problems to users. However, the next section of her speech delivered a contrasting image:

I'm not here to lament. The people who elected me did so because they felt that I was going to work hard for progress to arrive at each home. This is my commitment and I'm not going to let them down. For this reason I take responsibility for the government's need to correct the deficiencies in the start and design of Transantiago. The people need solutions, solutions that are responsible and serious. This is why I took some time to find the answers and choose who should lead this new stage, in which no further mistakes will be accepted. Transantiago must improve the quality of life of the Santiaguinos, not damage it. Some have asked what the government has been doing in the last hours. The answer is that we have been talking less and working more, because the situation demands it. I have checked that the 23 [corrective] measures that I ordered are being implemented, but we need more speed, it is not enough. … The new minister of transport will make public an action plan and a new schedule [for the reforms].

Here we can see another narrative emerging. Leaving aside the repentance of the opening sections, a new version of Bachelet is enacted, one that shows her actively working for the improvement of the system on many fronts. In doing so, as she emphasizes, the solutions she was looking for were "responsible and serious." Leaving aside cries for scrapping the system or radical experiments, she argued for the need to "correct" the existing assemblage, not replace it. The tools for doing so were already there, in the multiple devices traditionally used to enact Chilean policy assemblages; they only needed to be put to work properly.

This strategy was especially evident in the selection of the person who was going to lead the process. A few hours before her statement, Bachelet asked for the resignation of Sergio Espejo, the minister of transport and telecommunications. A lawyer, Espejo was widely seen as a key guilty party in Transantiago's failures, given his lack of expertise in the area, mainly expressed in his blind pressure for the system to start as scheduled even though several key components were not yet ready. As his replacement Bachelet named René Cortázar. An economist with a PhD from MIT, Cortázar was widely perceived as the right man for the job. Even though he also didn't have any experience in the transport sector, successful past appointments as labor minister during the Aylwin administration, as head of the highly prestigious think tank CIEPLAN, and as director of the national broadcasting company TVN had lent him an aura of technical proficiency difficult to match by any other candidate for the job. Cortázar, we could say, was one of the most advantaged alumni of the kind of technocratic planning characteristic of Chilean governments since the 1930s. For these reasons, he was widely seen as capable of delivering the technical steering needed to put Transantiago to work as expected without doing any kind of risky experiment.

In the movement between Espejo's dismissal and Cortázar's appointment a key double operation was taking part. On the one hand, an intrinsically techno-political controversy such as the problems facing Transantiago was purified to a matter of *failed politics* and essentially presented as caused by politicians who did not behave correctly for some reason (mainly pure incompetence). On the other hand, through Cortázar *technical expertise* was restated as the most promising, even the only possible, way to fix such a mess. Turning a blind eye to its intimate participation in the development of the policy assemblage from its very beginnings, expertise such as that offered by Cortázar was reenacted as a new approach to the issue, the only one able to offer the "responsible and serious" solutions that the issue needed.

After taking some weeks to make a diagnosis of the situation, on May 19 Cortázar held a press conference to explain the new strategy for Transantiago, claiming:

Three months ago a plan of public transport started that has been—for many Chileans—an experience of sacrifice in their everyday lives. The government has worked intensely to give a solution to this problem. In the last 40 days we have made efforts so that every single actor that participates in Transantiago accomplishes its required compromises. We have made advances, but still without arriving at the definitive solutions that we need. Along with the above, the Ministry [of Transport] has designed a strategy that will allow the normalization of the system. For this reason I would like to give a schedule with the measures of different nature that will allow, before the end of the year, for the system of public transport to be normalized. ... There are some who say that the system of public transport of Santiago will not be able to recover from this crisis. I disagree; in accordance with our schedule certainly before the end of the year we will have a normalized public transport system.

Cortázar starts by acknowledging the existence of several technical failures constituting a particular "crisis." Labeling the disruptions caused by Transantiago as a crisis, however, opens the ground not to a massive revamping of the system but to a strategy he explicitly labels as "normalización" (normalization). The choice of this word is not meaningless.

As seen in the introduction, and derived from the work of Canguilhem and Foucault among others, the normal always lies in the tension of describing a supposedly average reality while performing a desirable state toward which the existing reality should evolve. Therefore, a normalization strategy usually consists of a double process. First, there is the identification of certain *abnormalities* based on a mismatch between the optimal model, usually taking the form of detailed scripts describing how the different components of the system should be ordered, and their actual behavior. After this a repair process is carried out (Graham and Thrift 2007; Henke 2007) consisting of the deployment of multiple "disciplinary devices," devices aiming to align abnormal components with their scripts. Disciplinary devices can take many forms: encoding the scripts in new ways so that the abnormal components start self-governing; materially enforcing their alignment (even using violent means); or, ultimately, removing components that are unwilling or unable to become normal.

In this case, the first stage of the process started with Cortázar (reversing the argument of Perrow, 1999) understanding the failures experienced by Transantiago as abnormal, a result of an erroneous implementation of the system's blueprint. In consequence, the normal was to be found in the correction of this situation, in a Transantiago that would work in accordance with its original script posited by the PTUS, as seen in chapter 1. Such a normal Transantiago would not only provide a "world-class" public transport service for the city, but also reaffirm the government's technocratic capacity to plan effectively. In summary, "progress and the normal state became inextricably linked" (Hacking 1990, 168).

Such a normalization strategy was materialized in terms of a series of quantitative standards (larger bus fleets, extended night bus routes, increased number of bus stop shelters, reshuffling of routes, etc.) that the system had to surpass within a temporal framework. With these standards in hand, several disciplinary devices were introduced to align the multiple actors related to Transantiago (government offices, entrepreneurs, technical devices, etc.) that were not behaving in accordance with the script. While some of them aligned themselves with the MTT through self-government, in other cases the MTT had to apply more direct disciplinary devices, even threatening the more rebellious components (such as the entrepreneurs running the bus network) with outright exclusion from the system. The subsequent weeks and months witnessed multiple transformations in the system's components, as they were progressively aligned with their original scripts: larger bus fleets, a relatively fluid payment structure, etc.

This normalization was not only aimed at repairing a series of failing technical devices, but also at the performance of "normal" human devices. No matter how well other failures were corrected, if human devices were not "normalized" Transantiago would never be fully repaired. Therefore, and in parallel with transforming technical components, a significant amount of effort was directed toward making "people repair" (Henke 2000, 65) or trying to finally materialize the user scripted in the original proposals: a subject that "move[s] with tranquility and in an expedited way between one place and the other, in comfortable and safe conditions" (MOPTT 2000, 48). Any other kind of users such as strange things were automatically deemed *abnormal*. For this reason important efforts were carried out to normalize the users of the system, while deterritorializing strange things. In the remainder of this chapter we will analyze two of the most salient ones.

Repair by Numbers

As seen in chapter 4, from the very start of the disruptions Chilean (and international) media outlets prominently carried pictures of and stories about suffering users, enacting a politics of pity. Such a situation caused actors from the MTT to recognize early on that their efforts to repair the system would be unsuccessful unless they were able to challenge this negative "public perception," as they called it. Therefore, from the very start, and besides repairing the technical components of the system, these actors engaged in *discursive repair* looking to "transform the frames around an ecology" (Henke 2008, 12). Such repair practices looked to align the public opinion versions of the "user of Transantiago" with the one that was rapidly gaining hold among MTT personnel, who had been reinvigorated by Cortázar's program: a user that was every day experiencing fewer and fewer problems and slowly starting to enjoy the benefits of the new system.

The starting point of the challenge was to develop a script of the current users as "traumatized" by the problems faced at the beginning of the implementation, as Matias Rojas, a high authority within the MTT, did when talking about ways to communicate the normalization program.

The perception of the people is quite fixed in the past. This was a very traumatic experience, very traumatic, very traumatic, and because of this the perception of the system is quite fixed in the past, even though if you look at the latest surveys it has started to improve. But there is a gap between perception and reality, very clear and very natural. I can prove this by the fact that in surveys users always have a better perception than nonusers. ... Nowadays Transantiago has become a villain, it is a generic word. As when people say that they're going to make a Xerox: it wasn't a brand, it was a synonym for a photocopy. Transantiago is a synonym of ... the trans-this, the trans-lousy, the trans ... it has become a synonym of a traumatic situation. It is quite difficult to fight against a generic name once it has been born, and therefore what we have to aspire to is to continue improving the system, to consolidate it, and know that these are social processes that have a periodicity, have a slow tempo and ... take time.

Rojas thus presented users as carriers of subjective perceptions that were expressed in opinions. Given the problems experienced when using Transantiago in its first weeks and months, users were traumatized, with the result that their perception about the system was quite negative no matter what; Transantiago became the epitome of something bad, as a "Xerox" became synonymous with a photocopy. Rojas presented the trauma as causing a *gap* between the reality of the system, which had objectively improved, and the opinions of users, which had remained more or less the same. From this perspective, and taking a quasi-mechanistic approach, the main way to normalize the system was to bring the realm of perceptions closer to the one of reality, so users would start perceiving the objective improvements in the system and change their perceptions about it.

As hinted at in the passage above, the main way to "prove" the existence of a trauma and challenge it was through a survey. As the literature on the subject has shown, quantifications have become a central technology of government, due to their capacity to bridge distances, both spatial and social (Porter 1995), allowing governments to "act at a distance" (Rose and Miller 1992). "Quantification offers a shared language and discipline that transcends other forms of differences that threaten collective or competing social projects" (Espeland and Stevens 2008, 419). Therefore, quantifications are central to normalizing powers in contemporary societies; they "create and can be compared with norms" (Porter 1995, 45) because they make behaviors and expectations uniform.

Given this, we can talk of the existence of *repair by numbers,* or a particular kind of repair that uses commensurations in general as disciplinary devices to align failing components of a system with a certain script. The effectiveness of repair by numbers is derived from the recognition that quantifications are never merely descriptive but also performative; they "not only *reflect* reality but, in a certain sense, *establish* it by providing the players with a language to put reality on stage and act upon it" (Desrosieres 2001, 352). When effective, repair by numbers creates a new commensurate reality in which the failing components work as expected, contributing actively to making "worlds embedded within wider social projects turning on authority and control" (Barnes and Hannah 2001, 379). Any component failing to align with the script proposed by the commensuration is immediately deemed abnormal, an object of further discipline or exclusion.

In this particular case, repair by numbers was based mainly on the regular production and diffusion through the media of quantitative indicators showing improvements in the system, especially at the user level. The MTT hired the Dirección de Investigaciones Científicas y Tecnológicas (Direction for Scientific and Technical Research) of the Universidad Católica (DICTUC in Spanish) to run this project. Belonging to one of the leading universities of the country, DICTUC was closely connected with the Transport Engineering Department which housed several highly respected actors in the field, endowing its measures with a double layer of prestige and technical proficiency. Starting from mid-2007, every two weeks DICTUC produced a series of indicators—for example, in terms of waiting and traveling times in different areas of the city. These numbers were not intended merely to show which areas required better attention but also, and centrally, to use the authority of objective data to repair the trauma the users had experienced. For this reason, from the very beginning both the MTT and DICTUC published these indicators, using them as the main displays of the increasingly satisfied users of the system they were hoping to mobilize in the media and public opinion, permanently replacing sufferers.

At first, this repair strategy did not seem to produce the expected results, as can be seen in this extract from Cortázar's statement of November 21, 2007, to a parliamentary committee investigating the problems faced by Transantiago.

In relation to restoring credibility to Transantiago, there is a wider issue that has to do with perceptions and reality. We know that when there is a crisis as acute as this one it is not enough to change reality for perceptions to adjust immediately; there is a process of adjustment, and in it everyone who has a certain degree of leadership in society has a function to accomplish. It is frustrating—I say this with all sincerity—when we are trying to change the system and the waiting times have decreased objectively that someone could say quietly that there are no improvements. How could there be no improvement if we just showed an independent study that shows that in June 20% of people waited for more than 10 minutes at each bus stop and now this indicator is 11%? How could it be no improvement? If we say to the population all day that the situation has not changed at all and that everything is the same, naturally the frustration is enormous. But we have objective improvements. Having 20% or 11% of people who wait more than ten minutes is not the same. With this I'm not saying that the problem has been solved or does not exist. I'm the uttermost critic of the system from the start in relation to the things that should be corrected and changed.

Here we have another demarcation between perception (abnormal) and reality (normal). On the one hand, in the realm of reality, Cortázar claimed that the quality of service had improved importantly. In order to ground this claim he showed a bar graph (figure 6.1) representing the reduction in proportion of people who wait for more than 10 minutes at a bus stop, from 21% in June to 11% in September. Above the graph it was affirmed that this

was "representative data for a work day," in order to leave no doubt about
the scientific value of the information. On the other hand, in the realm of
perception, there was the trauma, caused not only by the initial experiences
of users but also by actors with "a certain degree of leadership in society"
who "say to the population all day that the situation has not changed at all
and that everything is the same." Given this negative publicity, the population did not recognize improvements, with the result that "the frustration
is enormous." There were no numbers supporting negative perceptions,
and given that "commensuration is a prerequisite to rationality" (Espeland
and Stevens 1998, 324), the image of the user as still experiencing problems
should be discarded. In making this distinction Cortázar was heir to "a
peculiarly modern ontology, in which the real easily becomes coextensive
with what is measurable" (Espeland and Stevens 2008, 432). The *normal*

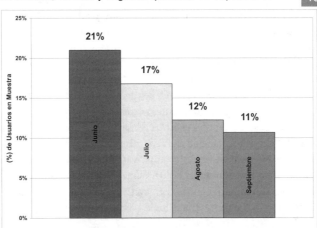

Figure 6.1
Percentage of people waiting for more than 10 minutes at the studied bus stops. Image reproduced with permission from the Directorate of Metropolitan Public Transport of Santiago (DTPM).

user of Transantiago, or so the numbers said, was the one experiencing continuous improvements in the service, nor the sufferer presented over and over again in the media.

At various points during 2008, DICTUC and actors at the MTT again referred to and/or displayed quantitative data showing further improvements in the quality of service. However, the shared perception was that none of these efforts were having enough impact on public opinion; the image of the sufferer proved to be much more resilient than expected, reappearing continually in the media. For this reason the MTT decided to hold a press conference on January 10, 2009, to publicize the fact that the system had finally reached "normality" in accordance with the standards set in May 2007.

The press conference started with a presentation by Juan Enrique Coeymans, a professor at the Transport Engineering Department of Universidad Católica and manager of DICTUC. Using a PowerPoint presentation containing several charts and tables, Coeymans showed how the waiting and travel times had decreased significantly in the previous year and a half. Figure 6.2 shows one example, in the form of a graph showing the decrease in both travel time (above) and waiting time (below) over the period from May 21, 2007, to November 21, 2008. He concluded that "these indicators show that we are fine at an international level and there is a clear tendency toward a decrease in waiting times because [bus] frequency has increased and there are more buses."

Cortázar followed Coeymans, presenting the plan for Transantiago in 2009 and commenting on the information provided by Coeymans:

I think the debate should be based on reality, and for this we must have objective indicators; and this thermometer, we believe, is a contribution to the debate, in order for public opinion to know the results of how the system has evolved regarding travel and wait times. ... Here is an independent academic institution, the Universidad Católica, that says that the system has drastically changed in terms of performance, and these numbers do not show a crisis any longer. This does not mean that there are no problems ... but the important thing is that we have to face them from the objective reality of the whole system. ... Here there is no message to anyone, nor is it part of a political controversy; what we gave today is a balance with the objective results of how the system is behaving, how it has evolved, and the actual levels. (Source: MTT)

Here again we can see repair by numbers in play. There is a world of debate that should be based on objective data, and out of which public

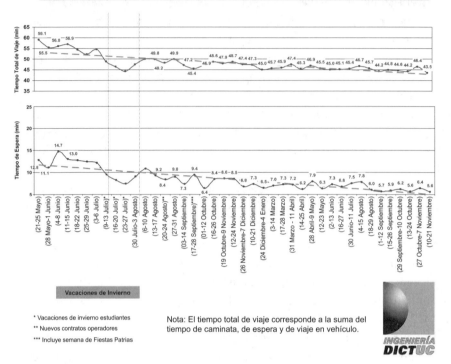

Figure 6.2
Overall evolution of total travel and waiting times, morning peak time. Image reproduced with permission from the Directorate of Metropolitan Public Transport of Santiago (DTPM).

opinion should be informed. The data is surrounded by an aura of scientific objectivity and speaks clearly: "these numbers do not show a crisis any longer." The system still has problems, but these problems have to be faced from a standpoint of normality.

Through numbers, Cortázar tried to depoliticize the discussion of Transantiago's failures, transforming it into a matter of certain quantitative standards. Given that the standards were surpassed, according to the data provided by DICTUC, he concluded that normalization had arrived and that any argument to the contrary, such as the insistence on the part of the media on enacting sufferers, was just part of a "political controversy" and should not be seriously considered.

Repair by Buffering

The second case to be analyzed relates to the fight to normalize the wicked evader through the introduction of a new disciplinary device: Zonas Pagas (prepay zones). In the weeks following the start of the plan, Zonas Pagas were constructed at the principal intersecting streets of Santiago. Each consisted of a fenced area around a bus stop, leaving only a couple of entrances. In order to catch buses in these locations users had to enter the Zona Paga, paying their fare while doing so. The main aim of creating these zones was to reduce the huge levels of fare evasion studied in the past chapter. This was done mainly by stationing an MTT employee at each entrance to a Zona Paga, resembling the "two-meter black guy" of former discussions on the issue, to check that each person entering paid for her trip by putting their card in front of a card reader.

Zonas Pagas also looked to increase the transfer speed of passengers between bus stops and buses, one of the most time-consuming operations of public transport systems. This was accomplished by allowing users within the Zona Paga to access arriving buses through all doors, since they had already paid their fares. As already seen, Transantiago was planned to operate without a public subsidy, so its revenues had to be at least equal to its costs. This mandate guided the design of the new buses for the system, with the consequence that the number of seats per bus was reduced substantially in comparison with the buses of the former system: more passengers could travel on each bus and so the system could require smaller fleets. Obviously, fewer seats and a higher number of passengers per bus meant that most users would travel standing and often in crowded conditions.

Such a loss of comfort, however, did not appear to be an issue for the system's designers because of the script of the user behind their models. As seen in chapter 3, the script of the user embedded in the engineering models of Transantiago enacted them as *fare and time optimizers*: rational consumers who when traveling value only low fares and reduced travel times. So the decline in the levels of comfort was compensated for by (1) reduced fares derived from the general optimization of the system and (2) an increase in traffic speed due in part to the smaller number of buses clogging the streets of the city. Thus introduction of Zonas Pagas not only looked to discipline wicked evaders but also to materialize this normal user as a *fare and time optimizer.* In so doing, the Zonas Pagas were to help increase the general satisfaction of the users with the system (a key issue, as seen above) and validate the transport and econometric models behind the planning of Transantiago.

Although relatively effective in reducing the levels of fare evasion,[1] the deployment of Zonas Pagas performed in parallel a new strange thing. Nicole Arias, an engineer working at the MTT at the time, talked about it in the following terms.

Zonas Pagas had two advantages. One, reducing evasion because people pay outside [the bus], ... and second to increase the speed of buses. ... So Zonas Pagas are very important, but the users have developed the habit of making queues ... because they want to travel seated on their return home and they are tired. [When] you try to get them [to enter the Zona Paga] they say, "No way, if I go inside I'll lose [my place in] the queue and if I lose [my place in] the queue I won't be able to travel seated and I want to travel seated and I don't care about people." ... As much as we have tried we haven't been able to convince them and ... the people wait [for their buses] outside [Zonas Pagas] because they want to travel seated. ... We said, "But if the bus arrives every two minutes you won't have to wait for a long time." "I don't care, I want to travel seated." ... So we can't reduce traveling times because people don't want to change their behavior.

Arias's argument shows a key problem in trying to mobilize the user as *fare and time optimizer* from Transantiago's models to the streets of the city. Such a script materialized more or less as expected during morning peak times. Given the need to arrive at their destinations on time, passengers accepted spending most of the trip standing in crowded buses, exchanging their comfort for (at least in theory) a general reduction in travel times. However, at other times of the day, especially during evening peak times, the situation was quite different. In the absence of pressure to arrive somewhere on time, users prioritized the comfort of traveling seated above savings in terms of travel time. They resisted being enrolled as *fare and time optimizers,* opting instead to enact a strange thing in the form of *comfort seekers*, a kind of users who highly value comfort in their travels, as happened with Lucía Santana in chapter 4. As Arias recognized, and this recognition is supported by the author's fieldwork, such users perceived the scripted mandate of entering the bus as fast as possible and through all its doors as openly impinging on the *fair* way of accessing the bus (and its scarce seats): based on users' order of arrival at bus stops. To diminish this risk, the users opted instead to make long queues materializing their order of arrival to the bus stop, as can be seen in figure 6.3, proceeding to board arriving buses following this sequence.

This human device greatly affected the performance of the Zona Paga in terms of its contribution to the overall speed of the system. First, given that the queues commonly were much longer than would fit in the area covered by the Zona Paga, all the temporal gains of people paying for their trips before the bus arrived were lost, because people occupying positions outside the Zona Paga had to pay for their trips when the bus arrived, as they would when taking a bus at an ordinary bus stop. Second, and more critical, people in the queues commonly refused to enter a waiting bus if all the seats were already taken, opting to wait until the next one arrived, greatly reducing the level of use of the fleet and making it necessary to have more buses to satisfy the same demand. In short, queuing all but nullified any advantage that Zonas Pagas could have had in terms of travel times, even further reducing the overall speed of the system.

Besides these immediate impacts, this human device openly defied the main script of the user behind Transantiago. From the bus design to the travel information system, most components of the system had been designed based on users as *fare and time optimizers*. For this reason, *comfort seekers* not only represented a problem in terms of the functioning of Zonas Pagas but challenged the *normal* governmentality that Transantiago planned to enact. As a result, urgent disciplinary devices were introduced to try to align these strange things with the original script.

Figure 6.3
Users queuing outside a Zona Paga in Plaza Italia. Source: the author.

At first such devices found little success, as Arias recalls:

The [authorities from the MTT] said, "We need help from the area of Transantiago Informa because we have immense queues and we want to break them down, so let's send instructors to teach the people not to make them." They [instructors] have received blows, have been fooled, policemen had to arrive, do you understand? It is always like ... we are not able to make them change this behavior. ... There are zones in which you just can't understand the logic of people to make it change. ... Obviously people only care about how they can ... travel seated, or be more comfortable, they don't care about the people that are by their side, who are tired or elderly, they don't matter, well and for this [they make the] queues, as the people don't care about this. People got used to doing this. They like the queue because it gives them ... it respects their place, I mean, the first to arrive is the first to leave; in contrast when there are no queues the strongest win.

Following the usual transport planning script of users as rational planners like the one seen in chapter 3, at first the queues were viewed as a matter of individuals behaving irrationally because of a lack of information. As soon as the relevant information was provided, or so this argument predicted, they would change their behavior and start acting as proper *fare and time optimizers*. Therefore, instead of carrying out repair through devices that physically discipline such abnormal behaviors, it was necessary only to produce a "technology of the self" through which these individuals would "act upon themselves, rendering themselves subjects of government" (Nadesan 2008, 9). Transantiago Informa[2] personnel were sent to the bus stops to provide arguments so that users would realize the irrationality of their behaviors and dissolve the queues. However, these attempts at "people repair" through self-government proved unsuccessful. Even after being informed, users resisted performing the *fare-and-time-optimizers* script in the afternoons, and the queues continued.

The failure of self-government efforts forced actors from the MTT to produce an alternative repair strategy. This was explained to me by Emilio Burgos, an engineer from the infrastructure area of CdT:

At the beginning we tried to break up the queues, having the buses open all their doors in the Zonas Pagas, because if off-bus payment was available it was as simple as just going inside, but no, [users] wanted order, and the order that they wanted was that a logic exists and the one who arrives first can travel seated. ... At the very end I think that they have won the battle because effectively nowadays what is consolidating in these points ... is that two groups are made, one for the users who want to travel seated and the other for the rest; in consequence our designs are mutating toward this arrangement.

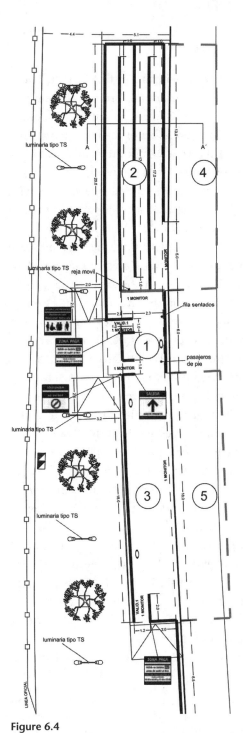

Figure 6.4

Design for the new Zona Paga at Manquehue Avenue. Image reproduced with permission from the Directorate of Metropolitan Public Transport of Santiago (DTPM).

As Burgos recognizes, *comfort seekers* "won the battle" in their efforts at comfort on their journeys home. Unable to transform all of them into proper *fare and time optimizers*, the MTT was forced to accept that regarding Zonas Pagas there was more than one version of the user, that strange things had a certain right to exist. This was a significant change, as we can see from one example mentioned by Burgos in an interview.

At the very beginning of Transantiago, and given the urgency to provide a solution to the huge levels of fare evasion, Zonas Pagas were makeshift pieces of infrastructure, little more than adjoined mobile fences surrounding the bus stops. However, with the passage of time the MTT provided more permanent designs for the most-used Zonas Pagas, among them the one located in front of the Clínica Alemana in the eastern borough of Vitacura. The use of this stop was more intense in the afternoons and evenings when people working in the surrounding areas take buses to return home. It was therefore a location where the queues were especially long.

In providing a new design for this Zona Paga, the recognition of two kinds of users was very much present. As can be seen in figure 6.4, the new design established that individuals enter the Zona Paga through the central area (1). After passing their card through a card reader, they have to decide which kind of user they want to perform (figure 6.5). If they want to perform *comfort seekers* they turn left and make a queue through the zigzag (2). If they want to perform *fare and time optimizers* they turn right and wait in an open area (3). When a bus arrives, it first stops in front of the *comfort seekers* section (4) and opens only its front door, through which queued users enter until all the seats are occupied. Then the bus continues and stops in front of the *fare and time optimizers* section (5), opening all its doors so these users fill all available standing space. Therefore, instead of insisting on forcing users into performing the "normal" *fare and time optimizers*, this design recognizes the existence of a dual version of the user, offering the people who want to use the system the option of choosing which one they want to perform at this particular moment.

Accepting such dual performance of users was not a trivial matter, as Burgos continues:

This is something that we would never have imagined. I mean, even more, if someone had said this to us before the start of the plan, we would have found it an aberration, an aberration, because effectively from the standpoint of the bus operation

Figure 6.5
Entrance to the Zona Paga at Clínica Alemana. Image reproduced with permission from Sylvia Dümmer.

the fact that it stops twice is like anti-nature. I mean, *the bus must stop once!* It is in the handbooks. The bus opens its doors and people rapidly get on and then pum!, it departs. [But] you cannot go against the habits of the people. People want to travel seated and you have to answer with a design in accordance with this. ... Thus we are developing a design that is utterly "made in Chile" that can solve this phenomenon. At the very end engineering, architecture, must be in the service ... of the phenomenon and not the other way round. We tried, we tried to get people to get used to this other way, but no ... people value a lot, a lot, the fact of traveling seated, and this is something that they are not willing to lose.

This new design was not repair as usual. There was nothing in the handbooks of transport planning from which the plans for the new design could be taken; there was no restoration to any pregiven blueprint or state. On the contrary, it was an "aberration," as Burgos called it, from the original script of how Zonas Pagas should be designed. The improvised design was "utterly made in Chile" because it recognized the existence of certain "virtual infrastructures of habits" (Bissell 2015) that made users perform strange things when they were asked to perform solely *fare and time optimizers*. Only by introducing this aberration at this particular location was the MTT able to produce a design for the new bus stop that was able to house both human devices, while also increasing the overall speed of the system.

However, from the perspective of the whole infrastructure this aberration looks quite different. First, the fieldwork on which this paper is based revealed that only a handful of Transantiago's devices used the *comfort seeker* as a valid script of the user. As seen in other chapters, all the major components—new buses, information devices, smartcards, etc.—were designed mainly to enact solely the *fare and time optimizer*. Given this, the Zonas Pagas' new design should not be seen as a radical departure from the normalizing project of Cortázar and the MTT but as a particular kind of disciplinary device: a buffer.

A *buffer*, its definition tells us, is a device that "separates potentially antagonistic entities, as an area between two rival powers that serves to lessen the danger of conflict" (Collins 2000). The new design is a buffering device mediating between, on the one hand, people with multiple motivations to use public transport and, on the other, a system that mostly enacts them as *fare and time optimizers*. Instead of the single normalization offered by the earlier design, this buffer offers people two options to become users. In doing so it makes a key dual operation: (1) it eases the tension for users that resulted from being considered only as *fare and time optimizers*, and (2) it provides much-needed fare-paying users for the system. Therefore buffering devices should be seen above all as technologies of transition, of interchange, between the external and the internal components of a policy assemblage, continually helping to deal with the strange things arising from the limited number of scripts embedded in each of its components.

Repair by buffering, however, is still normalization. The bus stop only gives two options for the prospective users to take, not whatever they choose. No doubt there are other (potential) strange things still not considered by the new design. In addition, and more importantly, once inside the bus the situation was mostly business as usual. Beyond the fact of traveling seated (typically for only a short while, given the need to transfer to another bus or the Metro to complete most trips), the comfort seekers were treated as *fare and time optimizers* all along their trip. There were no special entrances at the Metro, nor more breathing space inside the next crowded bus to be taken. Therefore from the perspective of the whole system, this device was ultimately disciplinary, easing the entrance of the two kinds of users into the system and then normalizing by force *comfort seekers* into *fare and time optimizers*. Using again the categorization developed by Henke (2007), we can see this as a case of a transformative repair (for actors such as Burgos and his team) turned into mere maintenance repair when moving from the local case to its place in a complex system.

Transantiago Prevails

On the occasion of Transantiago's fifth anniversary in February of 2012, Andrés Chadwick, the government's spokesman, called it "the worst public policy ever implemented in our country." Besides the curious fact of speaking in such a critical way about a policy that the government he represented was managing,[3] what was striking about his declaration was that no one really disagreed or found it an exaggeration. Since February 2007, Transantiago has erupted every few months in new controversies regarding an ample variety of problems: users who protest about the poor quality of service, bus companies on the verge of going bankrupt, bus drivers who strike for higher wages, Metro breakdowns that have almost paralyzed the city, etc. In STS terms we could say that Transantiago has never become fully black-boxed, has never reached anything resembling closure, but that its characteristics (and even its own existence) have been a matter of continual debate and critique with each new failure. As a consequence, Transantiago can be easily seen as a "permanently failing organization" (Meyer and Sucker 1989), or an infrastructure "which continues to exist yet fails to achieve … [its] avowed objectives over long periods of time" (Hood 2000, 44). Millions of people still travel every day throughout the city using it, but the original promise of a "world-class" public transport system is still far from being delivered, especially at the user level. For this reason the original script of the user of Transantiago has never materialized, the happy member of the world-class society, being replaced by individuals who reluctantly agreed to be partially governed to use public transport and/or perform strange things that continually destabilize the system. In this sense we can conclude that Transantiago is still very much *under repair,* it has never become fully normalized in accordance with the script set out in 2000.

Given this, it is interesting to end this chapter by asking why such a situation happened. Why, even taking into consideration how little successful were the attempts to normalize the system, a more radical solution was not considered. This "transformative" repair (Henke 2008) would probably have required changing several key elements of the system, from the trunk-feeder scheme to the payment system. It would have involved an important number of risks, but at the same time it promised to end up performing different human devices, ones that could not automatically be associated with the adjective "strange." But this option was not taken. Actually, apart from some individual claims, it was never seriously considered.

One way to explain why this happened would be to say, following Hommels (2005), that Transantiago has acquired a degree of obduracy that, even taking into consideration all the problems involved in its implementation, made it very difficult to change it radically. The most straightforward line of argumentation for such obduracy would invoke reasons financial ("it's too expensive to change") or social ("the social 'trauma' is too recent, people will resist a new change"). But neither of these is enough to explain completely why Transantiago did stay almost untouched. After all, as commonly happens, in this case "maintaining the structure of an ecology may take just as much effort or as many resources as transforming it" (Henke 2007, 138).

The authorities' insistence on normalizing Transantiago could be explained in other terms, as looking to achieve other ends. Even though the normalization program has not been able to deliver the promised world-class public transport system and its world-class society, it has been much more effective regarding another major aim of repair practices. As noted in the STS literature, infrastructures such as Transantiago are usually invisible when functioning correctly, exerting power in a seemingly natural way. Failures make them visible (Star and Ruhleder 1996), however, opening the black box of infrastructural power to possible questionings and/or transformations by actors who might feel alienated from it. Thus dealing effectively with the system's problems, especially in an unnoticed and routine way, is key for the involved actors' ability to maintain power. As a result, "repair is not at the margins of order, waiting to be deployed if something goes wrong. Instead, it is a practice at the center of social order: repair work makes ... [an infrastructure] normal" (Henke 2000, 57). It is through continual repair work that complex systems are able to *normalize* their existence and, by doing so, give a certain naturalness to a particular kind of power.

In this last sense the normalization configuration was quite effective. With the exception of some scattered comments in the very first weeks, the Chilean traditional "rule of experts" (Mitchell 2002) was never thoroughly questioned after the Transantiago fiasco. Despite how deeply involved different kinds of experts, institutions, and devices were in the planning and running of it, from highly prestigious academics to up-to-date transport models, no major criticisms were made about the particular kind of power they have in Chilean policymaking. On the contrary, as the arrival of Cortázar showed, the problems experienced by Transantiago were dealt with by reinforcing this kind of rule.[4] Even though the system is still under repair almost a decade after its start, the faith that it is going someday to be fully functional in the terms set up originally in the PTUS remains largely intact.[5]

Such an option was taken not only because of a blind adherence to transport planning and its prestigious practitioners. In parallel it was forced by the implicit assumption that there was no alternative; that beyond transport planning there was no body of knowledge or actors, whether experts or not, that could provide answers to the issues raised by Transantiago. In this perception we could see operating again the "boundary configuration" (Van Egmond and Bal 2011) that characterized the infrastructuration of the policy assemblage. As seen in chapter 3, such a configuration was quite useful for the actors involved in modeling the system to exclude any dissonant voice, making the process advance quite fast. However, such a boundary did not only work to limit the entrance of *outside* actors with different knowledge into the planning process. In parallel, it worked as a boundary to the actors located *inside*, blinding them to anything valuable beyond the limits set by the existing boundary, marking it as a complete wasteland.

The emergence of the normalization configuration allowed them to avoid stepping into these wilds. In the confusion that followed the messy start of the system, the program offered a clear way out; it promised that if some neat steps were taken, in due course everything would be back to "normal." Not only in terms of the public transport system (everyone knew that this was going to take a long time) but mainly in relation to the "normal" kind of rule exerted by Chilean governments. And most of the actors involved followed suit. After all, as Foucault (2008, 17) has recognized, "the greatest evil of government, what makes it a bad government, is not that the prince is wicked, but that he is ignorant." The government must know what to do about a failing infrastructure, especially a government in which expertise occupies such a high place, and this was what the normalization program offered. Even though it did not properly repair Transantiago, it repaired Bachelet's government, transforming it from the confused entity of the first weeks back to a business-as-usual technocratic machine that delivered results of reasonable quality. And this was more than enough.

Conclusions

Te dimos un diamante y lo trataste como un pedazo de carbón, ¡huevón!
[We gave you a diamond and you treated it like a lump of coal, stupid!]
Pablo Azócar

In the run-up to Chile's presidential election in December of 2009 Sebastián Piñera and his team faced a tough challenge. He was the candidate of the Coalición por el Cambio, the latest incarnation of a coalition of major right-wing parties that had not been able to win a presidential election since 1958. Besides, and probably more tellingly, his opponent, the former president Eduardo Frei, was the candidate of the Concertación, the most successful political coalition in Chile's history. Attaining power right after the dictatorship of General Augusto Pinochet, the Frei campaign argued, Concertación governments had been able to reduce significantly the levels of poverty while at the same time maintaining relatively high levels of economic growth, to consolidate democratic rule (dealing as well with the dark legacy of the dictatorship in terms of violation of human rights), to massively build infrastructure and social housing, etc. Although several aspects of this line of argument could be contested, the available narratives of the period, even the ones made by commentators from the opposition, were quite positive.

Implicitly recognizing this position of strength, Piñera's presidential campaign was not focused on an outright critique of the Concertación period. Instead it opted to make an argument about the wear and tear of twenty years in power and the need for new leadership to reinvigorate the country's development process. This is clear in the following extracts from Piñera's program of government:

The Concertación of today is not yesterday's. The Concertación of yesterday had a mission, had ideals, principles, projects, and unity. It was a valid option and without a doubt it played an important role. However, 20 years in power have wrinkled its face and soul. ... They promised us a modern system of public transport and they gave us Transantiago. (Piñera 2009, 4)

The governments of the Concertación have not modernized the state in order to equip it for the requirements of the twenty-first century ... the reforms have been slow and insufficient. ... This attitude has produced disasters in the management of the state, as in the case of Transantiago, with a misguided design and an even worse implementation. (ibid., 32)

The Concertación of today, according to this argument, had lost the strength and ideals that characterized its first years. As a consequence it had not been able to keep its promises and modernize the state in accordance with "the requirements of the twenty-first century." In order to ground such claims, both extracts locate one example in the most prominent space: Transantiago. Before anything else, Transantiago was presented as the seemingly most obvious embodiment of everything that was wrong with the governing coalition. Transantiago was "the Concertación of today"; Transantiago was a "disaster in the management of the state." This narrative was repeated over and over again until the runoff election in January of 2010 when Piñera was declared winner, ending twenty years of Concertación governments.

What was remarkable in this use of Transantiago as the ultimate exemplar of failed policymaking is that it didn't restrict itself to attacks against the Concertación. During Piñera's (2010–2014) and now the second Bachelet (2014–2018) government, every single major policy controversy, such as the ones involved with problems in the sampling process for the national census of 2012 or during the current contentious discussion of a comprehensive reform of the country's education system, was rapidly nicknamed as "El Transantiago de ..." ("The Transantiago of ...") or "the new Transantiago." Thus instead of territorializing a world-class public transport system and its happy users, the implementation of Transantiago has remained a world-class mess, the ultimate materialization of a failed policy assemblage.

This last territorialization of the assemblage shows us how the effects of the controversies seen in this book have extended well beyond the issue of a public transport system functioning poorly. Besides the part it played in ending the Concertación period, Transantiago seriously damaged the Chilean state's perceived capacity to plan effectively. Nowadays every failure of a policy assemblage, sometimes even a minor misstep, automatically triggers comparisons with Transantiago, forcing the actors in the government to defend themselves by arguing why *these issues* could not remotely be compared to *those ones*. In parallel, at the user level, the multiple experiences of disorientation and discomfort caused by the start of the plan (and continuing until today in several cases) motivated an extended discourse about a state that did not really care about its citizens, especially low-income ones, and whose projects were only carried out to benefit a small technical and/ or economic elite.

In all, and quite paradoxically, although the case did not really hinder the Chilean "rule of experts," it did seriously damage the idea of an active state. In governmentality terms, the ultimate version of the Chilean state that emerged from Transantiago was certainly not the benevolent entity that controlled at a distance active citizen-consumers living in a world-class society promised by the PTUS. On the contrary, the state appears as an entity unable to design and implement large and complex policy assemblages in a competent way, ending up producing human devices that accept being governed only reluctantly, do not really enjoy any substantive benefit from it, and usually overflow in the form of different strange things.

Given this outcome, it seems expectable that questions about alternatives would be posed. Or, more precisely, about possible ways in which some of the blunders of Transantiago could have been avoided or at least minimized. Were there other ways to enact Transantiago, and its related human devices, that could have produced better results? That could have enacted configurations different from disruptions and normalizations? That could have reduced the chances of causing pain to its users and/or weakening the very notion of an active state?

Among the several answers that such questions received in the months and years after the start of Transantiago's disruptions, there was one argument that usually occupied the most central position: a demand to increase public participation in policymaking. Such an argument emerged from a view on Transantiago as a policy assemblage that not only had several faulty components but was designed and implemented with a complete absence of lay participation. Silva states this argument in the following way:

> This episode has revealed the urgent need for the governmental technocracy to be more receptive to how the people and the sectors involved will be affected at the moment of designing public policies. This would make it possible not only to prevent

planning mistakes, but also to generate a stronger commitment among the people to the new policies and their successful implementation. In this way, public policies would no longer be exclusively "top down" initiatives, as has been the rule ever since the return to democracy in 1990, and would, in a certain sense, become everybody's. (Silva 2008, 233–234)

Then the best way to avoid the pitfalls experienced by Transantiago, and produce policy assemblages that not only would function properly but also would reinforce state power, was to sum up the views and actions of lay people regarding the different configurations of the plan, especially during infrastructuration. With their involvement, so this argument goes, it would be possible to produce policy assemblages that not only materialize utopian schemes developed by experts but also solve the *real* needs of the population.

In this conclusion I am not going to follow this path. This is why I am using as epigraph an extract from one of my interviews with Pablo Azócar:[1] "We gave you a diamond and you treated it like a lump of coal, stupid!" Transantiago was undoubtedly a diamond of a case study from which to make an argument such as the one outlined above. Almost every single aspect of previous analyses of the problems of technocratic/top-down governmental planning (Escobar 1995; Ferguson 1994; Scott 1998) can be found here, amplified to the highest level. It provides the perfect material for a critique of technocracy, for an argument for the relevance of local knowledge, for a democratization of planning as a necessary step toward the improvement of public action in contemporary societies. That would have been to make full use of this diamond, to put it on highly visible display, to show the world its undeniable beauty.

But, from this perspective, I'm going to treat it as a lump of carbon, making myself a deserved object of Azócar's rage. The reason this conclusion will not be an argument about the relevance of democracy and lay knowledge in planning is quite simple: because democracy and the valuation of local knowledge in themselves are not enough answer to the issues raised by Transantiago.

In affirming this I fully agree with one of the opening paragraphs of Cruikshank's (1999) book *The Will to Empower*:

Although I am deeply sympathetic to the project of radical or participatory democracy, I am skeptical that such a project presents an answer to the questions of power, inequality and political participation. Like any mode of government, democracy both enables and constrains the possibilities of political action. Democratic modes of governance are not *necessarily* more or less dangerous, free, or idealistic than others. Even democratic self-government is still a mode of exercising power—in this case, over oneself. Like government more generally, self-government can swing between the poles of tyranny and absolute liberty. One can govern one's *or* others' lives well or badly. (1–2, emphasis in the original)

Democratic forms of government, and their associated human devices, as Cruikshank affirms, are not necessarily the remedy for technocracy and top-down application of power. As Foucault has shown, power in society is never a zero-sum equation, in which the increase in the power of certain actors necessarily means the diminishing of somebody else's. In this sense the deployment of participatory human devices might well be included in a major technocratic project, with the only result that power would not be exerted by an external entity but by the citizens in themselves in the form of self-government, as the analyses of Cruikshank and several others in the governmentality tradition have shown.

In a similar vein, although I am sympathetic to proposals for the revaluation of lay and local knowledge in planning such as the one proposed by Scott at the end of his book *Seeing Like a State* (1998), again I am mindful that such proposals are commonly oblivious to their own politics. After all, "practices and arrangements of participation are both enabling and restricting at the same time" (Braun and Schultz 2010, 404). Even a "small is beautiful" approach in policy assemblages, based on highly localized actions embedded in the knowledge of communities, involves the deployment of human devices that are not automatically or necessarily "liberating" or conducive of better results than the ones of top-down technocratic action.

To identify a single and well-defined remedy (whether increased democracy or something else) as the main component that will finally allow us to avoid/alleviate the kinds of disruptions raised by Transantiago appears to oversimplify not a little. As seen throughout this book, policy assemblages are complex and multifaceted entities that resist being understood, and explained, in terms of neat arguments such as the need to increase democratization to avoid technocratic excesses. For this reason, in the remainder of this conclusion I am not going to offer a step-by-step solution or a grand narrative that could be used to avoid some of the configurations seen in this book. Instead, and with a much humbler attitude, I would like to return to some of the points raised in these pages in order to highlight promising paths, possible contributions toward alternative configurations of policy assemblages and their human devices.

My starting point is that to advance toward alternative configurations we need to take seriously the affirmation set out in the introduction, that policies are assemblages. Such an attitude starts by accepting that *there is no single rational or optimal way of ordering* things in the world. Understanding policies as assemblages forces us to accept that "ordering is partial, incomplete, always more or less local, more or less implicit, and therefore more or less disconcerting" (Law 2009a, 11). As a large tradition in both STS and poststructural theory has shown, in practice entities are never clearly demarcated or ultimately defined but are always in a process of becoming, performing themselves in ways that are never exactly the same. Thus all forms of ordering are always emergent and fleeting, existing in one particular performance in a certain temporo-spatiality and disappearing in the next one. Also orderings are always heterogeneous; several human and nonhuman entities participate, each with its own agency. Nothing is completely demarcated and fixed forever, but it must be achieved in constant and recurrent practices. As a consequence, ordering practices, quite paradoxically, always end up producing more or less messy entanglements composed of a large variety of entities that usually behave in ways quite different from the ones expected at the outset.

Taking this approach will necessarily imply assuming that any assemblage at the same time *territorializes and deterritorializes* entities, that each time we enact a new ordering we are also vanishing other/s. This second point is seldom considered in the analysis and/or design of policy assemblages, which are almost always focused on what is enacted into being, on the new and shiny. Such a perspective turns a blind eye to what is left aside, to the orderings and entities that are displaced, even destroyed, in the process of territorializing a new scheme. And when they are considered, they are valued exclusively from the standpoint of what it is to be territorialized, appearing as remnants of the past, something to be reconfigured and/or removed usually in the name of concepts such as "modernization," "improvement," "development," and the like.

This attitude was recognized by Patricio Fierro when I asked him in our last interview to reflect on his responsibility regarding the disruptions caused by the start of Transantiago:

We self-convinced that the existing rage toward micros was so huge that anything would be better, it didn't matter what. So there wasn't much need to evaluate and say "Is this really better?" because we were so convinced that ... "Hey, they should count themselves lucky, we are going to change the worst of disgraces!" And looked at from the outside, the truth is that it wasn't the worst of disgraces, it had elements needing correction, like any other system, but not at any cost, not at any cost. ... I mean, to design a system that says that you will have to get on and off a bus twice each time you make a trip sounds very nice on paper, but at six in the morning doesn't sound that nice, especially if there are no enough buses so you will have to wait [to catch the next one]. ... We undervalued how these things weighted; this is more or less the story.

An equal emphasis on deterritorialized orderings would lead us to develop a reflective stance toward what is being left out and why, and to explore ways to integrate some entities whose current space seems prominent or which promise to further enrich configurations of the assemblage. Such a move would not necessarily imply discarding configurations such as that of crisis, but it would force actors such as Fierro to take seriously the possibility that the ordering they are deterritorializing forms an important part of the entities involved, even being the subject of affections and strong attachments.

To consider policies as assemblages would also mean taking seriously the politics of human devices. As seen in the introduction, this politics lies in the continual tensions between particular ways of governing human beings and the overflowings they undeniably cause, between scripts/subjects and strange things. Such a recognition should start by *not delimiting from the outset the kinds and number of human devices* to be accepted as valid during the different configurations of a policy assemblage. As seen in this book, to close these possibilities off usually leads to the deployment of normalizing strategies in which unexpected human devices emerging along the way are rendered either normal or strange things, matters to be disciplined or excluded. On the contrary, the development of a policy assemblage should be open to continually including new kinds of human devices, mainly through three interrelated processes: heterogeneous testing, continual porosity, and modes of coordination.

The relevance of *heterogeneous testing* derives from the recognition of policy assemblages as experiments in which some entities are expected to be produced through particular procedures, but whose results are never secure from the start. This experimental character means necessarily that "some actors might be invisible when the experiment starts and might become visible later on; others are engendered—rendered explicit—by the experiment itself and the trials it organizes" (Muniesa and Callon 2007, 178). For this reason, while assembling a policy, especially in its early configurations, it becomes central to develop different kinds of tests through which these invisible actors might come to light, so they can be taken into account while deploying the assemblage. However, we should be wary of expecting to extract final resolutions from such tests. As the literature on the issue has revealed, testing practices are always "messy, contingent processes in which the management of ambiguity, rather than clear-cut relationships of similarity or dissimilarity, is the norm" (Sims 1999, 512). For this reason it is rarely the case that a test provides us with neat answers about the usability of the devices being tested. More frequently tests provide the actors involved with multiple traces, more or less ambiguous results that must be interpreted and usually open the ground for further testing.

The need to carry out continual tests is especially relevant in relation to human devices, given how humans tend to continually overflow the scripts provided to them. Thus tests in policy assemblages must be "construed to be as much about testing the user as they are about testing the machine" (Pinch 1993, 36). Such tests must be heterogeneous in the sense of making all efforts to include an ample variety of human devices, especially reaching out beyond the frames established by the existing boundary configurations. This will imply constituting spaces in between (and even beyond) demarcated disciplines, mixing a large variety of actors and knowledges. Testing human devices should be seen as similar to performing a reduced version of democracy, a space in which the affordances and restrictions involved in becoming subjects of the assemblage are embodied, dissected, and debated. As in any other parliament, probably no unanimous positions will be achieved, and resolutions will emerge out of precarious alliances, reluctant partnerships that could easily dissolve in the next round of tests.

Such constant testing is fueled by a second key demand: the need for the assemblage to remain porous. *Continual porosity* means keeping the assemblage open to considering the multiple strange things appearing along the way, both via predesigned tests and from the overflows caused by the deployment of the policy. Recognizing the unavoidable noncoherence of assemblages from the start, policy assemblages should opt not to fight to keep such messy entities *out*, but to bring them *inside* the policy assemblage or, even better, to accept their *liminality*, the way they are never going to be clearly either inside or outside but always standing in between, thus show-ing us where the limits stand. Only through this acceptance will they be able to produce orderings better fitted to deal with the found complexity. From this stance, strange things would appear to be an opportunity for the system to adapt and to correct devices, an informal and highly distributed testing from which new knowledge could be obtained. Obviously this pro-cess would not mean taking into account all the different strange things arising from the deployment of the system, because such a task would be endless, but at least it would force the actors involved to deal with the most recurrent and ubiquitous ones, like the comfort seekers creating queues in the Zonas Pagas that we saw in chapter 6.

Both in tests and through porosity the actors involved should be suspi-cious if they are too comfortable with the human devices performed within their policy assemblages, especially in early configurations. After all, "good experiments are those where surprise occurs" (Gomart and Hajer 2003, 40). If there is no surprise, if a configuration of the assemblage does not pro-duce any unexpected human device, there is more reason to worry than to celebrate. In this sense, to use an analogy, rather than unconditional allies of our projects we should better see human devices as spies entangled in a continual game of espionage and counterespionage. They are on our side, providing valuable information, but at the same time they could be working for the enemy and just deceiving us with unusable snippets. Or, as Gladwell nicely described it, "the proper function of spies is to remind those who rely on spies that the kinds of things found out by spies can't be trusted" (Gladwell 2010, 78).

The consideration of these contrasting human devices will demand, in due course, the development of highly specific *modes of coordination* between devices claiming to represent the same entity (for example the "user of pub-lic transport"). This coordination, as Mol noted, "doesn't depend on the possibility to refer to a preexisting object" (Mol 2002, 70), but refers to very specific sociotechnical mechanisms through which "the various realities of … [an entity] are balanced, added up, subtracted. That, in one way or another, they are fused into a composite whole" (ibid.). Then in the emer-gence of policy assemblages there is always the pressing need to develop effective coordination mechanisms between the multiple human devices appearing, especially when they are mobilized to different localities. The risk of not doing so from the very beginning is the "simultaneous existence of different objects that are said to be the same" (Law 2004, 158–159), as happened in the case of the user of Transantiago after February 10, 2007.

What is important to keep in mind, and going beyond the usual naive claims about the benefits of "diversity" or "participation," is that a policy understood as an assemblage will assume from the beginning that this increased heterogeneity does not translate naturally into consensus or equality but more probably into increased levels of struggle between the different entities included. This struggle will make the whole coordination process more demanding, cumbersome, and slow, but it will also heighten the chances of establishing relatively stable alliances between human devices emerging on the multiple locations in which the policy assemblage extends.

Finally, to take seriously the politics of human devices should force the human actors involved, from government officials and expert consultants to the media and daily users, to take into consideration their own *ontological politics* on the issue. This concept, coined by Mol and Law (Mol 1999; Law and Mol 2002; Law 2004), starts from the realization that "reality does not precede the mundane practices in which we interact with it, but is rather shaped within these practices" (Mol 1999, 75). Thus any knowledge practice is never a mere representation of what exists but is also (and in this sense is included in the term "politics") "[a]n interference in the conditions of possibility for the kinds of things that might exist in the world" (Law 2002, 198). Then, and following Foucault, any kind of knowledge is not innocent or merely descriptive but always an expression of power; it always creates a new kind of ordering out of the messiness of the world.

The recognition of the ontological politics inherent in any policy assemblage involves the need to adopt a key maxim as a guideline: *we must take full responsibility for the entities we perform.* The entities performed are not just simply "there" in an independent reality that methods help to represent; they must be performed into being, and this means transforming them into something, slightly or manifestly, different from what they were before our intervention. Then the implementation of policy assemblages must be always a reflexive endeavor in which the involved actors consider their own politics on the issues under study: Why are we doing this? What entities are we hoping to perform? How are we going to coordinate them?

This exercise is especially relevant in relation to human devices. As Hacking wrote, "making up people changes the space of possibilities for personhood" (2002, 107). Human devices encourage or repress, celebrate or forbid, some ways of being human rather than others, greatly affecting the populations who enter into contact with the policy assemblages in which they are embedded. So the actors involved must take full responsibility for the human devices they are creating, even if (or especially so) they are making them for the best reasons. Thus to replace top-down subjects with "participatory" ones is not enough at all, because they are both performed as the result of the application of certain human devices and they could have been otherwise; so we should always ask ourselves why they are this way and not otherwise.

In particular it is compulsory to take full responsibility for the violence embedded in large and complex infrastructural policy assemblages such as Transantiago. Pushing human beings from micros into buses, from long routes into feeder-trunk schemes, from coins into contactless smartcards was not trivial. It caused several unwanted effects on the inhabitants of the city, from a sense of disorientation to physical pain. Then radical (re-) orderings must go hand in hand with heightened responsibility, with an increasingly sophisticated ontological politics that postulates and gives some valid answers to questions about the need for such changes, the best ways to deal with their overflowings, and, crucially, who is going to pay if the bet ends up being misplaced. And to be effective such a politics cannot be concentrated in one particular moment but must accompany each new configuration of the assemblage, changing along the way as new entities are incorporated and/or discarded.

To summarize, taking seriously the conception of policies as assemblages and the politics of human devices implies seeing policies as experiments involving multiple and messy elements and erasing traditional disciplinary demarcations in order to position themselves as platforms of struggle and accords. Many of these struggles are derived from these experiments' continual *territorializing* and *deterritorializing* of orderings, always creating and destroying arrangements and entities as they move from configuration to configuration. In such constant transformation the capacity of the involved human devices to *surprise* us through tests and overflowing should always occupy a central place, the absence of surprises be taken as an indication that we are not looking hard enough. In parallel, significant effort should be invested in *coordination* in order to be able to establish alliances between the emerging human devices. Finally, in the development of these assemblages the actors involved are not located in some overhead position but form a deeply active and involved part in the process. Derived from this key element is their *political ontology*, or the constant reflexivity about how their own agency and ends relate to the kind of human devices being performed.

Taking into consideration my own ontological politics, I should end by saying that the elements included in my particular version of Transantiago should not be seen as an official history of the plan or any other kind of *ultimate* analysis. It is a partial story, leaving more things out than in.[2] In the conceptual scheme developed here, this book should better be seen as a further configuration of the policy assemblage known as Transantiago. A humble configuration, no doubt about it, that enacts versions of some of its elements in order to develop a narrative about the relevance of human devices in policy assemblages.

The elements presented in this conclusion should be taken in similar ways. They are suggestions, pieces of the jigsaw from which alternative ways of enacting policy assemblages and their human devices could emerge. These human devices would probably be much less compliant and agreeable, more demanding and critical, malleable, noisy, and active than the ones scripted in the Transantiago case. It is going to be much tougher to work with them, to understand their multiple and dissonant voices, to truly satisfy their demands for involvement, to provide services and goods that they find satisfying. But the challenge, I believe, is worth it. Because in their voices and actions, in their struggles and victories, lies a rich matrix out of which contemporary policy assemblages, in Chile and elsewhere, could be transformed toward increased levels of plurality, reflexivity, and responsibility.

Appendix: Methods

As stated in the introduction, this book is a genealogy of some of the human devices emerging from the different configurations of a policy assemblage known as Transantiago. The selection of the term *genealogy* to describe the methodological approach of the book is not casual. A genealogy, Foucault tell us, is "a form of history which can account for the constitution of knowledges, discourses, domains of objects, etc., without having to make reference to a subject which is either transcendental in relation to the field of events or runs in its empty sameness throughout the course of history" (Foucault 1984, 59). Thus in choosing to do a genealogy I understand human devices neither as transcendental ontologies (as "real" human beings or objects) nor as stable entities, but as the precarious and constantly evolving result of particular practices whose results are never known from the outset and in which several entities participate.

Following this, the approach taken in this book since the start of fieldwork in mid-2007 was to conduct a genealogy of the human devices performed in the process of developing and implementing Transantiago, from its origins in 2000 through its official start in 2007 and until early 2009. Such fieldwork was mainly focused on trying to "grasp the interactions (and disjunctions) between different sites or levels in policy processes … even where actors in different sites do not know each other or share a moral universe" (Shore and Wright 1997, 11). More particularly, and in accordance with the different configurations of policy assemblages identified above, I opted to take a dual approach.

In order to deal with human devices as performed during the first two configurations of Transantiago (crisis and infrastructuration), the strategy taken was to collect and analyze several highly different entities (research reports, material devices, images, media campaigns, etc.) through which the most recurrent human devices of Transantiago were performed into being. Among them a key position was occupied by the different policy documents produced, understanding them as "classificatory devices, as narratives that serve to justify or condemn the present, or as rhetorical devices and discursive formations that function to empower some and silence others" (Shore and Wright 1997, 11–12). In order to understand the practices through which these devices were developed, more than eighty in-depth interviews were conducted with different actors involved in the different stages of the development of Transantiago. Most of these interviews consisted of speaking about the different human devices with which each actor was involved, trying to reconstruct the genealogy of their development and their practical usage.

In parallel with the above, and in order to study the incorporations of human devices during the disruption and normalization configurations, several sessions of participant observation of daily use of the system were carried out, involving both following complete trips of single users and particular observations of the use of specific devices. In-depth interviews were also carried out with some of the participants in the observations, in order to reconstruct the argumentations developed to engage in such practices. Finally several in-depth interviews were carried out with actors in charge of the daily functioning of Transantiago during this period in order to see how they were reacting to these transformations, especially in relation to the development of new human devices to modify/govern them. All this material was later used in constructing the narratives presented in each chapter.

Finally I would like to add a brief note on anonymity. As could be expected, since the start of Transantiago's disruption on February 2007 the policy rapidly became one of the most intensely fought-over controversies in Chile in the last few decades. For this reason, and respecting an explicit demand made by some of my sources, I have changed all the names of the human actors participating in the fieldwork, also blurring their ranks and positions inside institutions as much as possible in the case of current and former government officials. The reason for the change is well explained by Richard Rottenburg's account of why he chose to make a similar move in his book.

Identifying real actors would only encourage readers to latch onto questions of individual responsibility. The fictionalization of my account was intended to counter this. I wanted to direct attention away from the strengths and weaknesses of specific real actors and toward the significance of general structural principles and the contingencies of the mundane practices. (Rottenburg 2009, xviii)

Probably for some Chilean readers, or anyone relatively familiar with the case, it will not be difficult to guess who several of my main characters are, but I hope this will not distract from the idea that what is important here is not who said or did what, but how particular human devices came into being or disappeared and what the consequences of such a process were for Transantiago and the population of Santiago.

Notes

Introduction

1. A point derived from the performative character of human devices is that no radical separation is possible between a particular subject and the human devices through which it is performed into being. Contrary to the usual distinction between "productive" and "end" technologies, a performative approach will consider the practices and techniques through which a particular subject is produced as irreducible parts of it. This is due to the fact that in performance everything is relationally involved and cannot be easily demarcated into "stages" of a process without transforming it into a completely different entity. Then in this book when speaking about human devices I will always be referring both to the technical devices that perform subjects and the result/s of such performances.

2. This is especially so because human beings are rarely faced with just one single human device that they have to perform. On the contrary, any single human being commonly has to perform a multiplicity of human devices during a normal day. In each of them they "are addressed as different sorts of human being, presupposed to be different sorts of human being, acted upon as if they were different sorts of human being" (Rose 1996, 35). Then reactions are not only related to a resistance, but also to the coordination between the new human devices and all the preexisting ones.

3. The concept of "strange thing" was originally taken from Noortje Marres's (2005, 58–59) understanding of publics as a "community of strange things." I identify this element as one of the key components of my own version of the concept, but I also add several elements that were not included in the relatively brief use of the term by Marres, so our two concepts cannot be seen as equal.

4. In this sense my own conceptualization of strange things is different from the "human kinds" as defined by Hacking (1995; 1996; 2002). For Hacking one of the key elements that differentiate human kinds from natural kinds is that the former are interactive in the sense that "the classification and the individual classified may

interact, the way in which the actors may become self-aware as being of a kind ... and so experiencing themselves in that way" (Hacking 1999, 104). In the case of strange things, this interactivity is not a precondition for performance.

5. Such rationality, which could be defined as "a logical way to determine the optimal available means to accomplish a given goal" (Alexander 2000, 245), rests on a realistic framing that assumes that the "data and observations that form the input of [policies'] analytic techniques are non-problematical" (Hajer and Wagenaar 2003, 16). As a consequence concrete policies are seen as merely "the principles that govern action directed towards given ends" (Titmuss 1974, 23). If such principles are rightly applied, then the policy will be successful.

6. Hajer and Wagenaar (2003) outline the three main components of such an approach as follows. First, there is an emphasis on policy analysis as an interpretive endeavor. By this they mean that the ultimate meaning of any policy practice can only be understood "by reconstructing, on line, during their interactions with others, what it is that the actors want to convey" (17–18). Second, there is a strong emphasis on policy as practice-based. In contrast with the former approach which emphasizes the concepts and ideas guiding policies, the focus now is on the concrete practices through which policies are implemented. This is a sphere of uncertainty, conflict, and serendipity, but usually constitutes the main arena where the ultimate essence of the intervention is defined. Finally, there is a view of policy as a deliberative process. By this they mean that policy practice is always a space of discussion and dissent, a space of multiple (and often conflicting) argumentations and actions. In all, this approach looks to shift policy analysis from its emphasis on the rationality of actors and plans to the very processes through which policy is done, with all its complexity, ambiguity, and contradictions.

7. A mode of ordering, according to Law (1994), is a complex involving multiple elements such as "the character of agency, the nature of organizational relations, how it is that interorganizational relations should be properly ordered, and how machines should be" (20).

8. It is important to note that in adopting this definition I am adhering to a more traditional sense of crisis as a moment of rupture rather than to its more contemporary versions, as noted by Roitman (2013), as a "protracted historical and experiential condition" (2) that is "mobilized as the defining characteristic of historical situations, past and present" (3).

9. It could be argued that this position can also be occupied by other entities, such as the market in neoliberal regimes. However, even in these cases some version of the state must be enacted (usually assigning it the role of the arbiter of the good functioning and/or correcting the externalities of these markets).

10. See the appendix for a detailed description of the methods and fieldwork on which this book is based.

Chapter 1

1. La Concertación was a center-left political coalition formed by the Partido Democrata Cristiano (PDC), the Partido por la Democracia (PPD), the Partido Socialista (PS), and other minor left-wing parties. Since the return of democracy in 1990 it managed to win four consecutive presidential elections and kept power until 2010, becoming the most successful political coalition in Chile's history.

2. All the names of the actors involved have been replaced by pseudonyms. See the appendix for a justification of this move.

3. However, such reorganization was never carried out due to the coup d'état of September 11, 1973.

4. Originating in the US and the UK in the aftermath of World War II (Lay 2005), origin-destination surveys had the main aim of describing in detail the patterns of daily mobility of a certain population through the use of a questionnaire about trips on a given day to a random sample of people. The data produced was then used not only to describe the existing daily mobility patterns but also to produce estimates about future demand through the use of mathematical models mixing the data from the surveys with projections about land use, infrastructures to be built, etc.

5. At least until 1982 when a huge economic crisis, caused both by the radicalism of the neoliberal transformations in the economy and by external factors, forced them to return to a more protectionist economic policy. In 1985, when the economic situation was stable again, the neoliberal reform program was resumed.

6. As has been widely explored by social studies of the economy and markets (Callon 1998b; MacKenzie 2007), and contrary to the neoliberal discourse, to enact markets was not as simple as reducing and/or eliminating state intervention. In most areas the "free" market was very much a state project, carried out through the development of infrastructures different but not less complex and totalizing than the ones created before 1973.

7. Aylwin was the candidate of La Concertación (see note 1 above).

8. The Aylwin administration was marked by several citywide strikes carried out by the micreros as a form of protest against the new regulations, which were successful in almost paralyzing the whole city. The micreros also developed several sophisticated ways to avoid the new regulations, importantly minimizing their practical effect.

9. 7 being the best possible grade in the school grading scale used in Chile.

10. As an example of the pervasiveness of this performance of the user, in one of my 2008 interviews with Pedro Suárez, a key actor in the development of the business model of Transantiago (and who only started working on the project on 2003),

when I asked him about the source of the idea that users negatively evaluated the former public transport system, he answered that "it wasn't an idea, I mean, we had evaluations that classified all the public services, and the public transport system was classified as worse than the systems of telephony, water, energy, it had a 3.5 in a scale of 1 to 7 ... then effectively it was a badly evaluated system."

11. A not-for-profit organization formed by the Chilean market research companies Adimark and Praxis and Adolfo Ibañez University in 2000.

12. As an example, in 1998 an acid and quite public controversy started among some key members and intellectuals of the Concertación based on the hypothesis of the existence of a certain *malestar* (malaise) in Chilean society of the time (Silva 2008, 191–193). For its proponents, this *malestar* was caused by the uncritical adoption by the Concertación governments of public policy devices developed under the dictatorship, mostly based on top-down market-based measures, generating an important weakness in civil society's representation in the design and implementation of public policies.

13. One leading figure of the transport engineering academic community, for example, claimed in a magazine article that the PTUS "contains most of the proposals of SOCHITRAN" (Martínez 2000).

14. The Asian crisis hit the Chilean economy quite hard, as it did other Latin American countries, especially in terms of a significant increase in unemployment.

Chapter 2

1. In the process of becoming a proper policy of the government, the original PTUS proposal was stripped down to just its first component, the reform of the surface public transport system, leaving aside all the other measures, mainly regarding urban planning in general.

2. During the Allende administration (1970–1973) Azócar was involved in running the *promoción popular* (popular enhancement) program, one of the first policies in Chile's history directly designed to foster public participation.

3. Such an ambiguity about the exact meaning of an active citizen is shared by the literature on public understanding of science. Although several definitions have been given, in practice they tend to leave too much "room for variable interpretation, because the public may be *involved* (in policy formation, etc.) in a number of different ways or at a number of *levels*" (Rowe and Frewer 2005, 254). While in some cases public participation is nothing more than the open diffusion of information regarding the policy, in others it involves more comprehensive exercises and even participatory decision making and implementation. To some degree such multiplicity seems understandable, but in the end such an entity is noncoherent. The prob-

lem, usually forgotten in practice, is one of taking citizen involvement as something solid and self-evident when it is not.

4. The Acceso Universal de Garantías Explícitas (Plan of explicit warrants for universal access, AUGE) was a plan started in 2005 with the aim of securing the access of the whole Chilean population to treatment regarding a number of highly complex diseases.

5. In this respect they argued that "to accept that the government can spend ... to disseminate plans that it intends to develop in the future ... would imply understanding that the authorities are allowed to make disbursements for advertising about any matter without any limitations" (CGR 2003).

6. This consisted mostly of Azócar and members of his team visiting most of the boroughs of the city, explaining to the authorities the details of the plan and inviting them (especially the transit directors) to form a permanent committee in order to provide the CGTS with local information and field-test the feasibility of measures designed at the central level. It was expected that each local representative would connect directly with neighborhood associations and individuals to ask for their opinions on each particular matter and allow them to participate without the hassle of a massive direct mechanism, replicating the delegative approach to citizen participation.

7. The attributes were that (1) "the proposal must be for Santiago, have a local character," (2) it had to emphasize that "the success of the Transport Plan for Santiago depends on a **change of conduct by people**[;] it is important that they feel proud about public transport, that this is a patrimony of the city," and (3) "the graphic element must be simple, easy to remember, and versatile, offering the possibility of being applied in many forms, with a diversity of interpretations" (CGTS 2002b; emphasis in the original).

8. Along with the name, the selection of the slogan "Súbete" also shows what a different human device this new brand was. As seen above, the slogan "Un transporte como la gente" had the explicit objective of performing users as active citizens who would be directly responsible for the final results of the plan. In contrast, "Súbete" is, above all, an order. It asks the future users of the plan to step into the plan, but without stating any role for them beyond being users. Then the invitation carried out by "Súbete" is much more ambiguous. It could be an invitation to get involved in the whole planning process (as the model of the active consumer-citizen proposes), but it could be also an order to be subjected by the plan, to be enrolled in a technological system whose characteristics were defined elsewhere.

9. For example, there was a huge divergence of opinion regarding a proposal to build a completely alternative system of public transport in the city (known as Plan SACYR for the Spanish company supporting it), there was an organizational problem inside the DTS regarding decision-making processes, there were differences

about whether the future bus operators should be paid per number of kilometers traveled or number of passengers transported, there was no clarity about how the Metro was going to be integrated with the whole system, there were power struggles among the members of the DTS about who was going to receive credit for the future success of the plan, and so on (for a detailed account see Quijada et al. 2007).

10. The only exception to this trend was a campaign to inform public transport users carried out in late 2005, consisting of presentation at schools and workplaces and, mainly, television ads in which a famous Chilean football player invited the public to "subirse" to Transantiago, then described the multiple ways in which the system was going to improve everyday life in the city.

11. They might have become coordinated, for example, had instances been carried out in which the actors involved could clarify what each of them understood as an active citizen and how they might put their different definitions to work in a common direction.

Chapter 3

1. For example in 1995 the then president of the Chilean Society of Transport Engineering (SOCHITRAN), in his opening address to the VII national congress, stated that "the level of development both in the creation and transmission of knowledge in this area in Chile is extraordinarily high, using objective measurements" (Jara-Diaz 1995, 3).

2. One of the first working papers of the recently established department of transport engineering at Universidad Católica de Chile (Fernández and Willumsen 1974) gives the following verdict: "Right now, the urban transport system of our cities is a system in crisis; it is no longer possible to think in terms of solutions that contemplate the system already in existence. It long ago reached the limit of its possibilities, and it is no use to keep increasing its size; the only real solution is to modify the system" (3). Such a modification was going to be "a combination between a rationalization of the current organization of the system and the change and technological adaptation of its elements" (ibid.).

3. This culminated with the publication of an academic paper explaining the methodology of the model in one of the world-leading research journals of the field authored by the two main consultants and the head of SECTRA at the time.

4. In making the objective reducing the social costs of the system, they were adhering to one of the most usual, albeit controversial, assumption behind econometric models: "that there exists such a thing as a benefit (singular) to society. This relies on a notion of society as essentially homogenous, sharing both circumstances and aspirations" (Goulden and Dingwall 2012, 5).

5. For example, several of the values used to calculate the function of waiting times (*pwait*) were produced in previous consultancy work for SECTRA by FDC (1997, 228) based on the use of microsimulation methods on data from the 1991 EOD survey.

6. Actually this *fact* about users of public transport proved to be one of the most pervasive found while conducting fieldwork for this project. At least half a dozen interviewees, several of them not related at all to the modeling process, mentioned it as a reality while talking about such different things as the architectural design of bus stop shelters or the marketing campaign for the plan.

7. As the CGTS was known after the approval of the Transantiago brand.

8. Also in providing the inputs to this scenario, the projected growth in public transport demand between 2001 and 2005 fell from the 12% used in scenario 6-200R to only 7%.

Chapter 4

1. The Ministry of Transport and Telecommunications (MTT) was separated again from the Ministry of Public Works (MOP) at the beginning of Michele Bachelet's government (2006–2010).

2. Using Perrow's (1999) conceptualization, we can hypothesize that what prevented the start of Transantiago from becoming a full disaster was that the parts of the system, although complexly interactive, were not "tightly coupled," so a failure of one of them cascaded relatively slowly into the others, allowing the system to continue functioning (albeit poorly) despite numerous failures of single components.

3. The only new device that received mostly positive evaluation was the Bip! card, especially given that it allowed users not to be forced to carry money and be subject to assaults for that. Curiously, as we will see in the next chapter, this was the same device that the actors of the government had singled out as having the highest risk of being rejected by users.

4. This point was fairly evident on October 22, 2005, when president Lagos "officially" inaugurated Transantiago, showing it as one of the key achievements of his soon-to-be-finished government. Given that the system was not yet ready, the inauguration consisted solely of replacing micros with the new bendy buses of Transantiago on a number of routes, explicitly presenting this replacement as a the first materialization of the "world-class" city/society that was about to emerge out of Transantiago.

5. In the published decree 122 there is no acknowledgment of the directive 2001/85/EC as the origin of the image.

6. Such a lack of testing was evident in 2006 when several underpasses in the city center had to be deepened in a hurry so the bendy buses could pass through them.

7. According to an official survey from 2004 (MINSAL 2004) the average height in Chile is 1.69 meters for males and 1.55 meters for females.

Chapter 5

1. One of the biggest ironies of Transantiago was that although the actors involved failed in territorializing the users in-scripted during infrastructuration, they were quite successful in deterritorializing the system's opposite: the feared micreros and their micros. Even though it seemed an almost herculean task beforehand, the first light of February 10 showed that the micreros had disappeared almost completely, leaving the place to professional drivers and new buses. Through a mixture of new concessions and regulatory schemes, they were effectively removed from the system, forever. The problem with such effectiveness was that there was no option to return to the former system, either temporarily or for good, once the massive problems of Transantiago were evident. Micreros, both as bus drivers and as entrepreneurs, were a thing of the past from day one.

2. Starting in April 2006, just one month after Bachelet took office, and lasting until June, the secondary students of the country mobilized to ask for improvements in public education, hijacking schools and carrying out massive strikes in which more than 600,000 students from all over Chile participated, constituting the biggest public demonstration since the return of democracy in 1990.

3. Several of the empirical materials (interview transcripts and pictures) used to write this section were adapted from the account of this controversy presented in the thesis entitled "Proceso de traducción entre Transantiago y usuarios de estratos socioeconómicos medios-bajos y bajos" [Translation processes between Transantiago and middle- to low-income users] submitted in December 2007 by Wilson Muñoz and Juan José Richter under the supervision of the author in fulfillment of the requirements for the degree of BA in sociology at the Instituto de Sociología, Pontificia Universidad Católica de Chile. Such research was funded by a Fondecyt grant (project number 11060348) awarded to the author on 2006.

4. At the time, Balboa talked about bringing a lawsuit against Transantiago for the problems experienced during the eight months of the informal parking lot, but this action, to my current knowledge, did not prosper in the end.

5. NIMBY (acronym for "not in my back yard"), a concept widely used in urban studies, refers to "the protectionist attitudes of and oppositional tactics adopted by community groups facing an unwelcome development in their neighborhood. ... Residents usually concede that these 'noxious' facilities are necessary, but not near their homes, hence the term 'not in my back yard'" (Dear 1992, 288).

6. Actually, and as a clear example of the perspective, they were quite happy with the solution of moving the buses to the new location in Nueva San Martín Avenue,

even though their presence there was probably going to annoy people living there in ways no different from them.

7. As was noted in the PTUS when criticizing the high levels of fare evasion of the former system: see chapter 1.

8. In practice only one bus company chose to install them.

9. This situation was worsened by the fact that bus companies had no proper incentives to reduce fare evasion. Given the characteristics of the contract signed with the authority, as seen in the case of the business model, which secured in some cases almost 90% of the companies' revenue regardless of the number of passengers carried, bus companies initially really did not care about fare evasion, because they were not the ones who were paying for it. And even if they had cared, because of the lack of the designed technology they were not able to say for sure how much fare evasion they had and where it was located.

Chapter 6

1. At least in the few points in the city in which they were built. In all the other bus stops of Santiago the situation regarding evasion remained unchanged.

2. Transantiago Informa was the office in charge of communications to and education of Transantiago's users.

3. A move that could be explained by noting that Chadwick was part of Sebastián Piñera's administration (2010–2014). As he represented a coalition that was in the opposition during Bachelet's time, the harshness of his words could be seen mainly as a critique to the former administration. This is why he uses the term "implemented" and not managed, making an implicit difference between the work they were doing and the work of the Bachelet period.

4. For example, several key academics on transport engineering who have been involved in designing components of Transantiago (such as the models seen in chapter 3) formed part of the "expert commission" set up by the government late in 2007 to propose solutions to the problems faced by the system (Allard et al. 2008), a commission that included only one member who was not a transport engineer/planner.

5. This is evident from an analysis of the section on Transantiago in Piñera's government program. Even though it starts by making a dramatic statement ("Transantiago has signified a dramatic deterioration in the quality of life of Santiaguinos and a bleeding in financial terms"), the detailed proposals are quite similar to the ones included in the program of the Concertación's candidate Eduardo Frei. Beyond the issue of implementing an effective user information system, there are no substantive differences between the two programs. Thus even though it holds Transantiago to

be a "disaster in the management of the state," Piñera's program did not opt for a transformative repair (Henke 2007), as actors disfranchised from power usually do. In most senses his program can be seen as a continuation of the "maintenance" strategy of repair started by Bachelet's government actors after February 2007.

Conclusions

1. He is not referring to me, thankfully, but to a certain high authority of the MOPTT who didn't take advantage of the many strong "selling points" of the original PTUS project to publicize it more widely when it was launched.

2. For example, several elements that occupied key positions on the disruptions caused by Transantiago (such as the lack of a bus fleet management system) are only briefly mentioned.

References

AD-Aditiva. 2004. *Análisis de medidas del Plan de Transporte Urbano de Santiago (PTUS) para favorecer a las personas con discapacidad*. Santiago: Asesorias para el Desarrollo y Aditiva.

Akrich, M. 1992. The De-Scription of Technical Objects. In *Shaping Technology/Building Society: Studies in Sociotechnical Change*, ed. W. E. Bijker and J. Law, 205–224. Cambridge, MA: MIT Press.

Akrich, M. 1993. Essay of Technosociology: A Gasogene in Costa Rica. In *Technological Choices: Transformation in Material Culture since the Neolithic*, 289–337. London: Routledge.

Alexander, E. 2000. Rationality Revisited: Planning Paradigms in a Postmodernist Perspective. *Journal of Planning Education and Research* 19: 242–256.

Allard, P., L. Basso, J. E. Coeymans, A. L. Covarrubias, J. de Cea, L. de Grange, J. E. Doña, et al. 2008. *Diagnóstico, análisis y recomendaciones sobre el desarrollo del transporte público en Santiago—informe final*. Santiago: Ministerio de Transporte y Telecomunicaciones.

Allen, J. 2011. Powerful Assemblages? *Area* 43 (2): 154–157.

Baden-Fuller, C., and M. Morgan. 2010. Business Models as Models. *Long Range Planning* 43 (2–3): 156–171.

Baillie, C., E. Dunn, and Yi Zheng. 2004. *Travelling Facts: The Social Construction, Distribution and Accumulation of Knowledge*. Frankfurt: Campus Verlag.

Baistow, K. 2000. Problems of Powerlessness: Psychological Explanations of Social Inequality and Civil Unrest in Post-War America. *History of the Human Sciences* 13 (3): 95–116.

Barnes, T., and M. Hannah. 2001. The Place of Numbers: Histories, Geographies, and Theories of Quantification. *Environment and Planning D, Society and Space* 19 (4): 379–383.

Barry, A. 2001. *Political Machines: Governing a Technological Society*. London: Athlone Press.

Bauman, Z. 1990. Modernity and Ambivalence. In *Global Culture: Nationalism, Globalization, and Modernity*, ed. M. Featherstone. London: Sage.

Becker, G. 1997. *Disrupted Lives: How People Create Meaning in a Chaotic World*. Berkeley: University of California Press.

Bijker, W., T. P. Hughes, and T. Pinch. 1989. *The Social Construction of Technological Systems: New Directions in the Sociology and History of Technology*. Cambridge, MA: MIT Press.

Bissell, D. 2008. Comfortable Bodies: Sedentary Affects. *Environment and Planning A* 40: 1697–1712.

Bissell, D. 2015. Virtual Infrastructures of Habit: The Changing Intensities of Habit through Gracefulness, Restlessness and Clumsiness. *Cultural Geographies* 22 (1): 127–146.

Boeninger, E. 1997. *Democracia en Chile: Lecciones para la gobernabilidad*. Santiago: Editorial Andrés Bello.

Boltanski, L. 1999. *Distant Suffering, Morality, Media and Politics*. Cambridge: Cambridge University Press.

Boumans, M. 1999. Built-In Justification. In *Models as Mediators: Perspectives on Natural and Social Science*, ed. M. S. Morgan and M. Morrison. Cambridge: Cambridge University Press.

Braun, K., and S. Schultz. 2010. "... A Certain Amount of Engineering Involved": Constructing the Public in Participatory Governance Arrangements. *Public Understanding of Science* (Bristol, England) 19 (4): 403–419.

Breslau, D., and Y. Yonay. 1999. Beyond Metaphor: Mathematical Models in Economics as Empirical Research. *Science in Context* 12 (2): 317–332.

Cáceres, G. 1995. Modernización autoritaria y renovación del espacio urbano: Santiago de Chile, 1927–1931. *EURE. Revista Latinoamericana de Estudios Urbano Regionales* 21 (62): 99–108.

Callon, M. 1998a. An Essay on Framing and Overflowing: Economic Externalities Revisited by Sociology. In *The Laws of the Markets*, ed. M. Callon. London: Blackwell.

Callon, M., ed. 1998b. *The Laws of the Markets*. Oxford: Blackwell.

Callon, M. 1999. The Role of Lay People in the Production and Dissemination of Scientific Knowledge. *Science, Technology and Society* 4 (1): 81–94.

Callon, M. 2007. What Does It Mean to Say That Economics Is Performative? In *Do Economists Make Markets? On the Performativity of Economics*, ed. D. MacKenzie, F. Muniesa, and L. Siu. Princeton: Princeton University Press.

Canguilhem, G. 1978. *On the Normal and the Pathological*. London: D. Reidel.

Carroll, P. 2006. *Science, Culture, and Modern State Formation*. Los Angeles: University of California Press.

CdT. 2003. MODELO DE NEGOCIO (Versión 6.0). Coordinación de Transantiago, Gobierno de Chile, Santiago.

CGR. 2002. Dictamen No 47.311 del 19-11-2002. Contraloría General de la República, Gobierno de Chile, Santiago.

CGR. 2003. Dictamen No 25.406 del 18-06-2003. Contraloría General de la República, Gobierno de Chile, Santiago.

CGTS. 2002a. Participación ciudadana y comunicaciones. Coordinación General de Transporte de Santiago, Gobierno de Chile, Santiago.

CGTS. 2002b. Resultados del concurso "Creación de un Isotipo, un Nombre y un Eslogan para el Plan de Transporte de Santiago." Coordinación General de Transporte, Gobierno de Chile, Santiago.

CGTS. 2002c. Sistematización del taller, 19 de diciembre de 2002. Coordinación General de Transportes de Santiago, Gobierno de Chile, Santiago.

Colebatch, H. 2006. What Work Makes Policy? *Policy Sciences* 39: 309–321.

Collins. 2000. *Collins English Dictionary and Thesaurus*. London: HarperCollins and Times Books.

Coutard, O. 1999. *The Governance of Large Technical Systems*. London: Routledge.

Cruikshank, B. 1999. *The Will to Empower: Democratic Citizens and Other Subjects*. Ithaca: Cornell University Press.

Dear, M. 1992. Understanding and Overcoming the NIMBY Syndrome. *Journal of the American Planning Association* 58 (3): 288–300.

De Laet, M. 2000. Patents, Travel, Space: Ethnographic Encounters with Objects in Transit. *Environment and Planning D, Society and Space* 18: 149–168.

DeLanda, M. 2006. *A New Philosophy of Society: Assemblage Theory and Social Complexity*. London: Continuum.

Deleuze, G., and F. Guattari. 1988. *A Thousand Plateaus: Capitalism and Schizophrenia*. London: Athlone Press.

Desrosieres, A. 2001. How Real Are Statistics? Four Possible Attitudes. *Social Research* 68 (2): 339–355.

Dewey, J. 1927. *The Public and Its Problems*. Oxford: Holt.

Dewsbury, J.-D. 2011. The Deleuze-Guattarian Assemblage: Plastic Habits. *Area* 43 (2): 148–153.

Diaz, G., A. Gómez-Lobo, and A. Velasco. 2004. Micros en Santiago: De enemigo público a servicio público. *Estudios Públicos* 96 (Spring): 5–48.

Doganova, L., and M. Eyquem-Renault. 2009. What Do Business Models Do? Innovation Devices in Technology Entrepreneurship. *Research Policy* 38 (10): 1559–1570.

EC. 2001. White Paper: European Transport Policy for 2010: Time to Decide. Office for Official Publications of the European Communities, Luxembourg.

Economist. 2008. The Slow Lane: Fallout from a Botched Transport Reform. *Economist*, February 7.

Engel, E., R. Fischer, and A. Galetovic. 2000. El programa chileno de concesiones de infraestructura: Evaluación, experiencias y perspectivas. In *La transformación económica de Chile*, ed. F. Larraín B. and R. Vergara M. Santiago: Centro de Estudios Públicos.

Errázuriz, T. 2010. La experiencia del tránsito: Motorización y vida cotidiana en el Santiago metropolitano, 1900–1931. Doctoral thesis, Facultad de Arquitectura, Diseño y Estudios Urbanos, Universidad Católica de Chile, Santiago.

Escobar, A. 1995. *Encountering Development: The Making and Unmaking of the Third World*. Princeton: Princeton University Press.

Espeland, W., and M. Stevens. 1998. Commensuration as a Social Process. *Annual Review of Sociology* 24: 313–343.

Espeland, W., and M. Stevens. 2008. A Sociology of Quantification. *European Journal of Sociology* 49:401–436.

FDC. 1997. Análisis y calibración de modelos de asignación de transporte público con restricción de capacidad. SECTRA, Santiago.

FDC. 2004. Nota técnica escenario 11. Fernández & de Cea Ingenieros Ltda, Santiago.

FDC and CIS. 2003. Análisis modernización transporte público, V etapa. Consorcio Fernández & de Cea Ingenieros Ltda.—CIS Asociados Consultores en Transporte S.A., Santiago.

Ferguson, J. 1994. *The Anti-Politics Machine: "Development," Depoliticization, and Bureaucratic Power in Lesotho*. Minneapolis: University of Minnesota Press.

Fernández, J. E., J. de Cea, and H. Malbrán. 2008. Demand Responsive Urban Public Transport System Design: Methodology and Application. *Transportation Research Part A, Policy and Practice* 42: 951–972.

Fernández, J. E., and L. Willumsen. 1974. Perspectivas tecnológicas para el transporte urbano. Documento de Trabajo—Departamento de Transporte, Universidad Católica de Chile 3.

Figueroa, O. 1990. La desregulación del transporte colectivo en Santiago: Balance de diez años. *EURE. Revista Latinoamericana de Estudios Urbano Regionales* 16 (49): 23–32.

Foucault, M. 1979. *Discipline and Punishment: The Birth of the Prison.* Harmondsworth: Penguin.

Foucault, M. 1980. *Power/Knowledge: Selected Interviews and Other Writings 1972–1977.* New York: Pantheon Books.

Foucault, M. 1982. The Subject and Power. In H. L. Dreyfus and P. Rabinow, *Michel Foucault: Beyond Structuralism and Hermeneutics.* Chicago: University of Chicago Press.

Foucault, M. 1984. *The Foucault Reader.* New York: Pantheon Books.

Foucault, M. 1993. About the Beginning of the Hermeneutics of the Self; Two Lectures at Dartmouth. *Political Theory* 21 (2): 198–227.

Foucault, M. 2006. Governmentality. In *The Anthropology of the State: A Reader,* ed. A. Sharma and A. Gupta. Oxford: Blackwell.

Foucault, M. 2007. *Security, Territory, Population: Lectures at the Collège de France, 1977–1978.* Basingstoke: Palgrave Macmillan.

Foucault, M. 2008. *The Birth of Biopolitics: Lectures at the Collège de France 1978–79.* Basingstoke: Palgrave Macmillan.

Gieryn, T. 1983. Boundary-Work and the Demarcation of Science from Non-Science: Strains and Interests in Professional Ideologies of Scientists. *American Sociological Review* 48 (6): 781–795.

Gladwell, M. 2010. Pandora's Briefcase. *New Yorker* (May 10).

Godfrey-Smith, P. 2006. The Strategy of Model-Based Science. *Biology and Philosophy* 21: 725–740.

Goffman, E. 1990. *The Presentation of Self in Everyday Life.* London: Penguin Books.

Gomart, E., and M. Hajer. 2003. Is That Politics? For an Inquiry into Forms in Contemporary Politics. In *Social Studies of Science and Technology: Looking Back, Ahead,* ed. B. Joerges and H. Nowotny. Dordrecht: Kluwer.

Goulden, M., and R. Dingwall. 2012. Managing the Future? Models, Scenarios and the Control of Uncertainty. In *Transport and Climate Change,* ed. T. Ryley and L. Chapman. London: Emerald Group.

Graham, S., ed. 2010. *Disrupted Cities: When Infrastructure Fails.* London: Routledge.

Graham, S., and S. Marvin. 2001. *Splintering Urbanism: Networked Infrastructures, Technological Mobilities and the Urban Condition*. London: Routledge.

Graham, S., and N. Thrift. 2007. Out of Order: Understanding Repair and Maintenance. *Theory, Culture and Society* 24 (3): 1–25.

Greenhalgh, S. 2008. *Just One Child: Science and Policy in Deng's China*. Berkeley: University of California Press.

Gross, P. 1991. Santiago de Chile (1925–1990): Planificación urbana y modelos políticos. *EURE. Revista Latinoamericana de Estudios Urbano Regionales* 17 (52–53): 27–52.

Grosz, E. 2013. Habit Today: Ravaisson, Bergson, Deleuze and Us. *Body and Society* 19 (2–3): 217–239.

Hacking, I. 1990. *The Taming of Chance*. Cambridge: Cambridge University Press.

Hacking, I. 1995. The Looping Effects of Human Kinds. In *Causal Cognition: A Multidisciplinary Debate*, ed. D. Sperber, D. Premack, and A. J. Premack. Oxford: Oxford University Press.

Hacking, I. 1996. Normal People. In *Modes of Thought: Explorations in Culture and Cognition*, ed. D. R. Olson and N. Torrance. Cambridge: Cambridge University Press.

Hacking, I. 1999. *The Social Construction of What?* Cambridge, MA: Harvard University Press.

Hacking, I. 2002. *Historical Ontology*. Cambridge, MA: Harvard University Press.

Hacking, I. 2004. Between Michel Foucault and Erving Goffman: Between Discourse in the Abstract and Face-to-Face Interaction. *Economy and Society* 33 (3): 277–302.

Hacking, I. 2007. Kinds of People: Moving Targets. *Proceedings of the British Academy* 151: 285–318.

Hajer, M. A., and H. Wagenaar. 2003. *Deliberative Policy Analysis: Understanding Governance in the Network Society*. Cambridge: Cambridge University Press.

Hay, C. 1999. Crisis and the Structural Transformation of the State: Interrogating the Process of Change. *British Journal of Politics and International Relations* 1 (3): 317–344.

Hayles, N. K. 1999. *How We Became Posthuman: Virtual Bodies in Cybernetics, Literature, and Informatics*. Chicago: University of Chicago Press.

Henke, C. 2000. The Mechanics of Workplace Order: Toward a Sociology of Repair. *Berkeley Journal of Sociology* 44: 55–81.

Henke, C. 2007. Situation Normal? Repairing a Risky Ecology. *Social Studies of Science* 37 (1): 135–142.

Henke, C. 2008. *Cultivating Science, Harvesting Power: Science and Industrial Agriculture in California*. Cambridge, MA: MIT Press.

Hidalgo, D., and P. Grafiteaux. 2007. *Planning and Implementation Issues of a Large Scale Transit Modernization Plan: The Case of Transantiago, Chile*. Washington, DC: World Resources Institute.

Hohmann, C. 1993. La encrucijada del transporte en Santiago. *EURE. Revista Latinoamericana de Estudios Urbano Regionales* 16 (50): 9–27.

Hommels, A. 2005. *Unbuilding Cities: Obduracy in Urban Sociotechnical Change*. Cambridge, MA: MIT Press.

Hood, C. 2000. *The Art of the State: Culture, Rhetoric and Public Management*. Oxford: Oxford University Press.

Howlett, P., and M. Morgan. 2010. *How Well Do Facts Travel?* Cambridge: Cambridge University Press.

Hughes, T. P. 1983. *Networks of Power: Electrification in Western Society 1880–1930*. Baltimore: Johns Hopkins University Press.

Jackson, S. J., P. Edwards, G. Bowker, and C. Knobel. 2007. Understanding Infrastructure: History, Heuristics and Cyberinfrastructure Policy. *First Monday* 12 (6).

Jara-Diaz, S. 1995. Discurso inaugural. VII Congreso Chileno de Ingeniería de Transporte. Pakata, Santiago.

Jasanoff, S. 2004a. Ordering Knowledge, Ordering Society. In *States of Knowledge: The Co-production of Science and Social Order*, ed. S. Jasanoff. London: Routledge.

Jasanoff, S. 2004b. Science and Citizenship: A New Synergy. *Science and Public Policy* 31 (2): 90–94.

Knorr-Cetina, K. 1982. Scientific Communities or Transepistemic Arenas of Research? A Critique of Quasi-Economic Models of Science. *Social Studies of Science* 12 (1): 101–130.

Koselleck, R. 2006. Crisis. *Journal of the History of Ideas* 67 (2): 357–400.

Latour, B. 1983. Give Me a Laboratory and I Will Raise the World. In *Science Observed: Perspectives on the Social Study of Science*, ed. K. D. Knorr-Cetina and M. Mulkay, 141–170. London: Sage.

Latour, B. 1991. Technology Is Society Made Durable. In *A Sociology of Monsters: Essays in Power, Technology and Domination*, ed. J. Law. London: Routledge.

Latour, B. 1992. Where Are the Missing Masses? The Sociology of a Few Mundane Artifacts. In *Shaping Technology/Building Society: Studies in Sociotechnical Change*, ed. W. E. Bijker and J. Law. Cambridge, MA: MIT Press.

Latour, B. 1993. *We Have Never Been Modern.* Cambridge, MA: Harvard University Press.

Latour, B., and S. Woolgar. 1986. *Laboratory Life: The Construction of Scientific Facts.* Princeton: Princeton University Press.

Law, J. 1994. *Organizing Modernity.* Oxford: Blackwell.

Law, J. 2002. *Aircraft Stories: Decentering the Object in Technoscience.* Durham: Duke University Press.

Law, J. 2004. *After Method: Mess in Social Science Research.* London: Sage.

Law, J. 2009a. The Greer-Bush Test: On Politics in STS. Version of 23 December 2009. Available at http://www.heterogeneities.net/publications/Law2009TheGreer-BushTest.pdf

Law, J. 2009b. Seeing Like a Survey. *Cultural Sociology* 3 (2): 239–256.

Law, J., G. Afdal, K. Asdal, W. Lin, I. Moser, and V. Singleton. 2013. Modes of Syncretism: Notes on Non-Coherence. CRESC Working Paper Series 19: 1–17.

Law, J., and A. Mol. 2002. *Complexities: Social Studies of Knowledge Practices.* Durham: Duke University Press.

Law, J., and J. Urry. 2004. Enacting the Social. *Economy and Society* 33 (3): 390–410.

Lay, M. 2005. The History of Transport Planning. In *Handbook of Transport Strategy, Policy and Institutions*, ed. D. Hensher and K. J. Button. St. Louis: Elsevier.

Lee, N., and S. Brown. 1994. Otherness and the Actor Network: The Undiscovered Continent. *American Behavioral Scientist* 37 (6): 772–790.

Mackay, H., C. Carne, P. Beynon-Davies, and D. Tudhope. 2000. Reconfiguring the User: Using Rapid Application Development. *Social Studies of Science* 30 (5): 737–757.

MacKenzie, D. 2006. *An Engine, Not a Camera: How Financial Models Shape Markets.* Cambridge, MA: MIT Press.

MacKenzie, D. 2007. *Do Economists Make Markets? On the Performativity of Economics.* Princeton: Princeton University Press.

Mann, M. 1984. The Autonomous Power of the State: Its Origins, Mechanisms and Results. *European Journal of Sociology. Archives Européennes de Sociologie. Europäisches Archiv für Soziologie* 25 (02): 185–213.

Marante, A., M. Guggenheim, P. Gisler, and C. Pohl. 2003. The Reality of Experts and the Imagined Lay Person. *Acta Sociologica* 46 (2): 150–165.

Marres, N. 2005. *No Issue, No Public: Democratic Deficits after the Displacement of Politics.* Amsterdam: University of Amsterdam.

Marres, N. 2007. The Issues Deserve More Credit: Pragmatist Contributions to the Study of Public Involvement in Controversy. *Social Studies of Science* 37 (5): 759–780.

Martínez, N. 2000. Noviembre 2000, el mes del transporte urbano. *Revista Tranvía* 5. http://www.cec.uchile.cl/~tranvivo/tranvia/tv5/index.html.

Meyer, M., and L. Sucker. 1989. *Permanently Failing Organizations*. Newbury Park: SAGE.

Middleton, J. 2011. "I'm on Autopilot, I Just Follow the Route": Exploring the Habits, Routines, and Decision-Making Practices of Everyday Urban Mobilities. *Environment and Planning A* 43: 2857–2877.

MIDEPLAN. 2001. Bases de licitación del estudio "Análisis de modernización de transporte público, V etapa." Secretaría de Transporte, Ministerio de Planificación, Santiago.

Miller, P., and N. Rose. 1990. Governing Economic Life. *Economy and Society* 19: 1–31.

MINSAL. 2004. *Encuesta nacional de salud (ENS)*. Santiago: Ministerio de Salud, Gobierno de Chile.

Mitchell, D. 1995. Governing the Unemployed Self in an Active Society. *Economy and Society* 24 (4): 559–583.

Mitchell, T. 2002. *Rule of Experts: Egypt, Techno-Politics, Modernity*. Berkeley: University of California Press.

Mol, A. 1999. Ontological Politics: A Word and Some Questions. In *Actor Network Theory and After*, ed. J. Law and J. Hassard. Oxford: Blackwell.

Mol, A. 2002. *The Body Multiple: Ontology in Medical Practice*. Durham: Duke University Press.

Mol, A. 2009. Good Taste: The Embodied Normativity of the Consumer-Citizen. *Journal of Cultural Economics* 2 (3): 269–283.

MOP. 1966. Encuesta de origen y destina del movimiento de personas en el Gran Santiago. Primera parte. Ministerio de Obras Públicas, Santiago.

MOPT. 1969. Plan regulador de transporte metropolitano—Santiago-Chile. Santiago: Ministerio de Obras Públicas y Transportes.

MOPTT. 2000. Plan de Transporte Urbano de Santiago 2000–2010. Ministerio de Obras Públicas, Transporte y Telecomunicaciones, Santiago.

MOPTT. 2004. Transantiago subete—Plan de transporte urbano de Santiago, Chile. Ministerio de Obras Públicas, Transportes y Telecomunicaciones, Santiago.

Morin, E. 1993. For a Crisiology. *Organization and Environment* 7 (5): 5–21.

Morrison, M., and M. S. Morgan. 1999. Introduction. In *Models as Mediators: Perspectives on Natural and Social Science*, ed. M. S. Morgan and M. Morrison. Cambridge: Cambridge University Press.

Moser, I., and J. Law. 1999. Good Passages, Bad Passages. In *Actor Network Theory and After*, ed. J. Law and J. Hassard. London: Blackwell.

Moss, T. 2000. Unhearting Water Flows, Uncovering Social Relations: Introducing New Waste Water Technologies in Berlin. *Journal of Urban Technology* 7 (1): 63–84.

MTT. 1996. Política de transporte urbano—Versión aprobada en reunión de ministros del 27.06.96. Gobierno de Chile, Santiago.

MTT. 2004. Modifica decreto n° 122, de 1991. Fija requisitos dimensionales y funcionales a vehículos que presten servicios de locomoción colectiva urbana que indica. Diario Oficial de La República de Chile, Jueves 8 de Enero de 2004.

Muniesa, F., and M. Callon. 2007. Economic Experiments and the Construction of Markets. In *Do Economist Make Markets? On the Performativity of Economics*, ed. D. MacKenzie, F. Muniesa, and L. Siu. Princeton: Princeton University Press.

Muniesa, F., Y. Millo, and M. Callon. 2007. An Introduction to Market Devices. *Sociological Review* 55: 1–12.

Muñoz, J. C., and A. Gschwender. 2008. Transantiago: A Tale of Two Cities. *Research in Transportation Economics* 22: 45–53.

Myantz, R. E., and T. P. Hughes. 1988. *The Development of Large Technical Systems.* Boulder, CO: Westview Press.

Nadesan, M. H. 2008. *Governmentality, Biopower, and Everyday Life.* London: Routledge.

Ong, A. 2011. Introduction: Worlding Cities, or the Art of Being Global. In *Worlding Cities: Asian Experiments and the Art of Being Global*, ed. A. Roy and A. Ong. London: Wiley-Blackwell.

Oudshoorn, N., and T. Pinch. 2003. *How Users Matters: The Co-Construction of Users and Technologies.* Cambridge, MA: MIT Press.

Paley, J. 2001. *Marketing Democracy: Power and Social Movements in Post-Dictatorship Chile.* Berkeley: University of California Press.

Paley, J. 2004. Accountable Democracy: Citizens' Impact on Public Decision Making in Postdictatorship Chile. *American Ethnologist* 31 (4): 497–513.

Pavez, M. I. 2006. *Vialidad y transporte en la metrópolis de Santiago 1950–1979: Concepto y estrategia de ordenación del territorio en el marco de la planificación urbana y regional por el estado de Chile.* Madrid: Universidad Politécnica de Madrid.

Pérez, F., and J. Rosas. 2002. Cities within the City: Urban and Architectural Transfers in Santiago de Chile, 1840–1940. In *Planning Latin Americas Capital Cities, 1850–1950*, ed. A. Almandoz. London: Routledge.

Perrow, C. 1999. *Normal Accidents: Living with High-Risk Technologies*. Princeton: Princeton University Press.

Pinch, T. 1993. "Testing—One, Two, Three … Testing!": Toward a Sociology of Testing. *Science, Technology, and Human Values* 18 (1): 25–41.

Piñera, S. 2009. *Programa de gobierno para el cambio, el futuro y la esperanza, Chile 2010–2014*. Santiago de Chile: Coalición por el Cambio.

Porter, T. 1995. *Trust in Numbers: The Pursuit of Objectivity in Science and Public Life*. Princeton: Princeton University Press.

Quijada, R., A. Tirachini, R. Henriquez, and R. Hurtubia. 2007. Investigación al Transantiago: Sistematización de declaraciones hechas ante la Comisión Investigadora, resumen de contenidos de los principales informes técnicos, información de documentos públicos adicionales y comentarios críticos. Santiago. http://ciperchile .cl/wp-content/uploads/Reporte_Transantiago.pdf.

Roitman, J. 2013. *Anti-Crisis*. Durham: Duke University Press.

Rose, N. 1996. *Inventing Ourselves: Psychology, Power and Personhood*. Cambridge: Cambridge University Press.

Rose, N. 1999. *Powers of Freedom: Reframing Political Thought*. Cambridge: Cambridge University Press.

Rose, N., and P. Miller. 1992. Political Power beyond the State: Problematics of Government. *British Journal of Sociology* 43 (2): 173–205.

Rottenburg, R. 2009. *Far-Fetched Facts: A Parable of Development Aid*. Cambridge, MA: MIT Press.

Rowe, G., and L. Frewer. 2005. A Typology of Public Engagement Mechanisms. *Science, Technology and Human Values* 30 (2): 251–290.

Schiefelbusch, M. 2005. "Citizens" Involvement and the Representation of Passenger Interests in Public Transport: Dimensions of a Long-Neglected Area of Transport Planning and Policy with Case Studies from Germany. *Transport Reviews* 25 (3): 261–282.

Schiefelbusch, M. 2010. Rational Planning for Emotional Mobility? The Case of Public Transport Development. *Planning Theory* 9 (3): 200–222.

Schild, V. 2000. Neo-Liberalism's New Market Citizens: The Civilizing Dimension of Social Programs in Chile. *Citizenship Studies* 4 (3): 275–305.

Scott, J. C. 1998. *Seeing Like a State: How Certain Schemes to Improve the Human Condition Have Failed*. New Haven: Yale University Press.

SECTRA. 1990. ESTRAUS: Estudio de evaluación y desarrollo del sistema de transporte urbano de la Ciudad de Santiago. Comisión de Transporte Urbano, Santiago.

SECTRA. 1991. Encuesta origen y destino de viajes, Santiago 1991. Subsecretaría Interministerial de Transportes, Gobierno de Chile, Santiago.

SECTRA. 2000. Resumen ejecutivo del plan de transporte urbano de Santiago, 2000–2006. Subsecretaría Interministerial de Transportes, Gobierno de Chile, Santiago.

Shapin, S. 1992. Why the Public Ought to Understand Science-in-the-Making. *Public Understanding of Science* (Bristol, England) 1 (1): 27–30.

Shapin, S. 1995. Here and Everywhere: Sociology of Scientific Knowledge. *Annual Review of Sociology* 21: 289–321.

Shore, C., and S. Wright. 1997. Policy: A New Field of Anthropology. In *Anthropology of Policy: Critical Perspectives on Governance and Power*, ed. C. Shore and S. Wright. London: Routledge.

Shore, C., and S. Wright. 2011. Conceptualising Policy: Technologies of Governance and the Politics of Visibility. In *Policy Worlds: Anthropology and the Analysis of Contemporary Power*, ed. C. Shore, S. Wright, and D. Però. London: Berghahn Books.

Shove, E., and A. Rip. 2000. Users and Unicorns: A Discussion of Mythical Beasts in Interactive Science. *Science and Public Policy* 27 (3): 175–182.

Silva, P. 2008. *In the Name of Reason: Technocrats and Politics in Chile*. University Park: Pennsylvania State University Press.

Simmel, G. 1908 [1964]. The Stranger. In *The Sociology of Georg Simmel*, trans. and ed. K. H. Wolff. New York: Free Press.

Sims, B. 1999. Concrete Practices: Testing in an Earthquake-Engineering Laboratory. *Social Studies of Science* 29 (4): 483–518.

Sims, B., and C. Henke. 2012. Repairing Credibility: Repositioning Nuclear Weapons Knowledge after the Cold War. *Social Studies of Science* 42 (3): 324–347.

Sismondo, S. 1999. Models, Simulations, and Their Objects. *Science in Context* 12 (2): 247–260.

Sismondo, S. 2000. Island Biogeography and the Multiple Domains of Models. *Biology and Philosophy* 15: 239–258.

Smart, B. 1985. *Michel Foucault*. London: Routledge.

Star, S. L., and G. Bowker. 2006. How to Infrastructure. In *Handbook of New Media: Social Shaping and Social Consequences of ICTs*, ed. L. Lievrouw and S. Livingstone. London: Sage.

Star, S. L., and K. Ruhleder. 1996. Steps toward an Ecology of Infrastructure: Design and Access for Large Information Spaces. *Information Systems Research* 7 (1): 111–134.

Summerton, J. 1994. *Changing Large Technical Systems*. Boulder, CO: Westview Press.

Taylor, M. 2006. *From Pinochet to the "Third Way": Neoliberalism and Social Transformation in Chile*. Ann Arbor, MI: Pluto Press.

TEC. 2003. Análisis de las características de vehículos para el transporte público y de carga—Informe ejectivo. Consultores en Ingeniería de Transporte, TEC Ltda, Santiago.

Titmuss, R. 1974. *Social Policy*. London: Allen and Unwin.

Tomic, P., and R. Trumpen. 2005. Powerful Drivers and Meek Passengers: On the Buses in Santiago. *Race and Class* 47 (1): 49–63.

Ureta, S. 2007. Noise and the Battles for Space: Mediated Noise and Everyday Life in a Social Housing Estate in Santiago, Chile. *Journal of Urban Technology* 14 (3): 103–130.

Ureta, S. 2013. Waiting for the Barbarians: Disciplinary Devices on Metro de Santiago. *Organization* 20 (4): 596–614.

Valderrama, A. 2009. How Do We Co-produce Urban Transport Systems and the City? The Case of Transmilenio and Bogota. In *Urban Assemblages: How Actor-Network Theory Changes Urban Studies*, ed. I. Farías and T. Bender. London: Routledge.

Valdés, J. G. 1995. *Pinochet's Economists: The Chicago School in Chile*. Cambridge: Cambridge University Press.

Van der Ree, G. 2007. *Contesting Modernities: Projects of Modernisation in Chile, 1964–2006*. Amsterdam: Dutch University Press.

Van Egmond, S., and R. Bal. 2011. Boundary Configurations in Science Policy: Modeling Practices in Health Care. *Science, Technology and Human Values* 36 (1): 108–130.

Van Fraasen, B. 1980. *The Scientific Image*. Oxford: Oxford University Press.

Wilkie, A., and M. Michael. 2009. Expectation and Mobilisation: Enacting Future Users. *Science, Technology and Human Values* 34 (4): 502–522.

Wise, J. M. 2005. Assemblage. In *Gilles Deleuze: Key Concepts*, ed. C. Stivale. Montreal: McGill-Queen's University Press.

Wynne, B. 1995. Public Understanding of Science. In *Handbook of Science and Technology Studies*, ed. S. Jasanoff, G. Markle, J. Petersen, and T. Pinch, 361–388. London: Sage.

Index

Aberration, 152–153

Active citizens, 19–20, 21, 37, 47–52, 53, 56–57, 61, 64–66

Administrador Financiero de Transantiago (AFT), 83–84, 126, 128, 131

Assemblages, 11–13, 14, 16, 21–22, 90, 111, 160, 164–165, 166, 169

Azócar, Pablo (pseud.), 23–25, 30, 43, 47, 49–50, 52, 54–55, 57, 60–65, 68, 85, 159, 162

Bachelet, Michele, 110–111, 113, 137–138, 157, 160

Bad subjects, 111, 135

BIP! Card, 95, 96, 125–126, 133

Boundary configuration, 70, 71, 75, 87, 89, 157, 166

Boundary work, 41

Branding, 57–63

Buffering, 21, 154

Bus design, 38, 88, 128, 131–132, 147

Bus handgrips, 98–99, 101, 103–104

Bus seats, 88, 97–104, 147, 148, 149, 152

Bus stop, 132, 143, 144

Calculative agency, 68, 72, 74, 90

Callon, Michel, 10, 49, 51, 57, 68, 136

Card reader, 126–133, 147, 152

Citizen-consumers, 29, 45, 111, 161

Citizens' representative, 55–57

Comfort seekers, 148–149, 152, 154, 167

Comisión Bicentenario, 43, 45

Comité de Usuarios de Transantiago (CdU), 114, 124

Commensuration, 21, 67, 71, 74, 78–79, 88, 142–144. *See also* Quantification

Communications brief, 60–61

Concertación, 23, 42, 43, 159–160

Configurations, 13–18, 19, 21, 25, 31, 32, 36, 45, 90, 137, 156, 157, 161–167, 169–170

Consumers, 4, 5, 6, 19, 20, 21, 28, 29, 31, 33–36, 39, 41, 45, 48, 65, 69, 79, 81, 83, 90, 147

Coordinación de Transantiago (CdT), 80, 82, 86, 87, 103, 104, 127, 128, 134, 150

Coordinación General de Transporte de Santiago (CGTS), 47, 50–52, 54–59, 63–65

Coordination, 47, 51, 64, 69, 90, 103, 167–169

Cortázar, René, 138–140, 141, 143–146, 154, 156

Crisis, 14–15, 18, 19, 21, 25–26, 28, 30, 31, 33, 36, 37, 43–44, 45, 67, 69, 99, 105, 107, 137, 139, 143, 146, 165, 171

Democratization, 19, 21, 42, 161–163

Demonstrations, 109, 113–115, 117, 120, 121–125

Devices, 6–7
Dirección de Investigaciones Científicas y Tecnológicas de la Pontificia Universidad Católica de Chile (DICTUC), 142–143, 145–146
Directorio de Transporte de Santiago (DTS), 47, 52, 56, 59–60, 61, 63–65, 67, 68, 71, 80, 82, 87
Disciplinary devices, 18, 21, 59, 125, 130, 139–140, 142, 147, 149, 154
Discomfort, 88, 95, 97–99, 104, 110, 111, 161
Disorientation, 17, 95, 97, 161, 169
Disruption, 16–17, 20–21, 94, 99, 105, 106–107, 110, 111, 113, 114, 137, 139, 141, 161, 163, 172

Empowering, 20, 21, 172
EOD-Buses (survey), 71, 72, 76, 84, 89
Experiment, 7, 93, 138, 165–166, 167, 169
Experts, 5, 19, 25–27, 30, 42, 44, 49, 50, 51, 55, 58, 61, 66, 71, 78, 110, 111, 138–139, 156, 157, 161, 162, 168

Failure, 3, 21, 74, 94, 95, 96, 106, 107, 110–111, 112, 125, 130, 131–133, 138–140, 142, 146, 150, 156, 157, 160
Fares, 19, 20, 23, 38, 39, 40, 44, 45, 77, 81–84, 86, 90, 91, 97, 125–127, 129, 131, 147
Fare and time optimizers, 20, 69, 90–91, 95, 96, 104, 134, 147–150, 152–154
Fare evasion, 39, 40, 115, 126, 128–131, 134–135, 147, 148, 152
Fare-paying user, 34, 42, 48, 66, 154
Fierro, Patricio (pseud.), 81, 86, 164–165
Foucault, Michel, 8–9, 17–18, 41, 50, 130, 139, 157, 163, 168, 171

Governmentality, 8–9, 11, 12–13, 19, 27, 28, 29, 31, 51, 52, 66, 91, 111, 135, 136, 149, 161, 163

Grosz, Elizabeth, 40
Growth with equity, 29, 30, 37, 44, 55, 80, 81

Habits, 17, 20, 32, 36, 40–41, 50, 52, 54, 84–86, 88, 90–91, 96, 148, 153
Hacking, Ian, 4, 5, 6, 11, 12, 109, 140, 168
Human devices, 4–11, 13, 17, 18–21, 25, 27, 29, 31–33, 36, 41, 43, 48, 50–52, 56, 64–65, 69–70, 77, 84, 89, 90, 95, 103–106, 109, 111, 114, 124, 129, 134–135, 140, 149, 161, 163–170, 171–173
Human kinds, 5

Incorporation, 11, 17–18, 20, 40, 96, 97, 99, 104, 134–135, 169, 172
Infrastructural policies and projects, 3, 4, 5, 22, 43, 80, 136, 169
Infrastructuration, 15–16, 19, 41, 47–48, 51, 54, 56–58, 64, 67, 68, 95–96, 103, 111, 125, 157, 162, 171
In-vivo experiment, 93
Issues, 14–15, 20, 23, 26, 28, 43, 56, 64, 111, 121, 123, 124, 131, 135, 139, 160, 161

Lagos, Ricardo, 23, 24, 43, 44, 45, 48, 60, 70, 81
Latour, Bruno, 4, 6, 9, 36, 78, 128–129
Law, John, 5, 12, 36, 99, 164, 168
Looping effects, 11, 18, 125

Marketing, 50, 52, 53, 58, 60–61
Markets, 8, 9, 28–30, 31, 33, 37, 39, 40, 42, 43, 45, 48, 62
Media, 24, 25, 53, 62, 95, 105–106, 109, 110, 114, 123–124, 137, 141, 142, 143, 145, 146, 168
Metrological realism, 71, 75, 89
Micreros, 23–24, 28, 30–31, 34, 39, 43, 45, 80, 90, 96–97, 99, 126, 133–134
Micros, 2, 25, 38, 99, 113, 137, 165

Ministerio de Obras Públicas (MOP), 27, 38, 80
Ministerio de Obras Públicas, Transportes y Telecomunicaciones (MOPTT), 23, 24, 25, 39, 42, 47, 63, 71, 79, 87, 100, 140
Ministerio de Transportes y Telecomunicaciones (MTT), 24, 30, 70, 93, 101, 114, 125, 140, 141–143, 145, 147–148, 150, 152, 153, 154
Model, 20, 27, 63, 68–69, 89, 90
  business, 63, 64, 79–84, 86, 89–90, 134, 148
  engineering, 69–71, 74–79, 84, 87, 88, 104, 134, 139, 147, 156
Mol, Annemarie, 5, 8, 64, 167, 168

Neoliberalism, 24, 27–29, 33, 38, 80
NIMBY protesters, 124, 135, 136
Normal, 10, 17, 40, 94, 136, 139, 144, 146, 147, 149, 152, 157
Normalization, 13, 17–18, 21, 75, 139–141, 142, 146, 147, 154–157, 161, 165, 172

Obduracy, 86, 156
Orderings, 8, 10, 11, 12, 13, 15, 16, 18, 21, 25, 31, 36–38, 42, 45, 68, 79, 85, 91, 134–136, 164–165, 167–169
Origin-destination scripts (ODS), 32, 40, 42, 45, 48, 65, 66, 69, 72, 74, 84, 85, 88, 90
Origin-destination surveys, 27, 32, 71, 73. See also EOD-Buses
Overflowings, 8, 10–11, 17, 18, 28, 30, 40, 94, 95, 135, 136, 161, 165, 166, 169

Pain, 99, 109, 111, 161, 169
Patience, 114–115
Permanently failing organization, 21, 155
Plan de Transporte Urbano de Santiago (PTUS), 19, 20, 25, 27, 31, 32–45,

47, 48, 51, 52–57, 59–62, 64, 66, 67, 75, 80, 81, 91, 97, 99, 105, 134, 140, 157, 161
Policy assemblages, 10–14, 16, 18, 21, 25, 27, 37, 42, 48, 53, 54, 57, 60, 90, 110, 111, 136, 138, 139, 154, 157, 160–171
Political ontology, 170
Politics of pity, 106–107, 109, 123–125, 141
Power
  infrastructural, 27, 28, 30, 37, 38, 40, 42, 136, 156
  political, 4, 8–10, 13, 17, 24, 27–30, 45, 52, 56, 63, 66, 89, 130, 136, 156, 162–163, 168
Public debate model, 49
Public participation, 35, 39, 41, 42, 49, 51, 53–58, 63, 65, 68, 161–163, 168
Public perception, 72, 78, 79, 114, 141–145

Quantification, 27, 28, 31–33, 35, 42, 67–69, 76, 78, 85, 86, 131, 140, 142–146. See also Commensuration

Repair, 18, 21, 111, 139–140, 155–157
  by buffering, 147–154
  by numbers, 141–146
  people repair, 18, 140, 150

Scripts, 9, 11, 13, 16–20, 40–41, 44, 48, 52, 55, 64, 68, 69, 76, 85, 90, 95, 96, 103–104, 111, 130, 135, 136, 139–142, 147–150, 153, 155, 165, 166
Secretaria de Planificación de Transporte (SECTRA), 25, 30, 32, 34, 42, 47, 63, 69, 70, 71, 73, 75, 78, 87, 89
Shame, 129–131, 133, 134, 135
State, 9, 12, 15, 18, 19, 21, 25, 27–31, 37, 39, 40, 42, 45, 54, 64, 67, 82, 110, 111, 160, 161
Strange things, 10–11, 17, 18, 21, 30, 134–136, 137, 140, 141, 148, 149, 152, 153, 155, 161, 165, 166, 167

Subjects, 8, 9, 10, 11, 13, 18, 21, 37, 48,
    49, 50, 111, 136, 140, 150, 165, 166,
    169, 171
Subsidies, 19, 40, 68, 80, 81, 86, 90, 91,
    134, 147
Sufferers, 20, 21, 105–111, 116, 120,
    123–124, 125, 137, 143, 145, 146
Surprise, 22, 167, 169

Techniques of the self, 9, 14, 29, 41, 45,
    50, 51, 52, 59, 130, 139, 140, 150,
    163
Technocracy, 42, 64, 81, 111, 138, 140,
    157, 161, 162–163
Technologies of surveillance, 130
Technoscience, 3, 4, 5, 6–9, 14
Territorizalization/deterritorialization,
    11, 12–15, 16, 25, 30, 31, 36, 37, 42,
    43, 44, 45, 51, 52, 55, 59, 64, 65, 67,
    90, 91, 99, 136, 141, 160, 164–165,
    169
Transantiago standard, 100, 103, 104
Transport engineers, 30, 42, 50, 69, 70,
    71, 74, 143, 145
Transport planning, 30, 40–42, 49, 50,
    51, 54, 66, 70, 85, 89, 150, 153, 157
Trauma, 141–144, 156

Violence, 11, 13, 24, 104, 116, 126, 127,
    130, 134, 140, 169

Wickedness, 133–135, 147, 157
World-class city, 44, 45, 60
World-class mess, 110, 160
World-class public transport, 91, 100,
    110, 140, 155, 160
World-class society, 45, 52, 91, 110, 111,
    155, 156, 161
Worlding, 44, 60, 62, 109, 111

Zonas Pagas, 147–154, 167